How Buildings Work

How Buildings Work

THE NATURAL ORDER
OF ARCHITECTURE
Third Edition

EDWARD ALLEN

Drawings by David Swoboda and Edward Allen

OXFORD

UNIVERSITY PRESS

2005

OXFORD
UNIVERSITY PRESS

Oxford University Press, Inc., publishes works that further
Oxford University's objective of excellence
in research, scholarship, and education.

Oxford New York
Auckland Cape Town Dar es Salaam Hong Kong Karachi
Kuala Lumpur Madrid Melbourne Mexico City Nairobi
New Delhi Shanghai Taipei Toronto

With offices in
Argentina Austria Brazil Chile Czech Republic France Greece
Guatemala Hungary Italy Japan Poland Portugal Singapore
South Korea Switzerland Thailand Turkey Ukraine Vietnam

Published by Oxford University Press, Inc.
198 Madison Avenue, New York, New York 10016
www.oup.com

Library of Congress Cataloging-in-Publication Data
Allen, Edward.
How buildings work : the natural order of architecture / Edward Allen. — 3rd ed.
    p. cm.
Includes bibliographical references and index.
Cover title: Natural order of architecture.
ISBN-13: 978-0-19-516198-4
ISBN-10: 0-19-516198-X
1. Buildings — Environmental engineering.
I. Title: Natural order of architecture.   II. Title.

TH6021.A44 2004
721 — dc22   2004021414

9 8 7 6 5 4 3 2
Printed in the United States of America
on acid-free paper

With thanks to the people
who helped make it happen:

JOYCE BERRY

NOEL CARR

ALBERT G. H. DIETZ

ELLEN R. FUCHS

N. J. HABRAKEN

CATHERINE HUMPHRIES

FRANK JONES

DONLYN LYNDON

DOUGLAS MAHONE

JAMES RAIMES

ELDA ROTOR

J. N. TARN

CYBELE TOM

WACLAW ZALEWSKI

and especially
MARY M. ALLEN

Preface
to the Third Edition

Over the past quarter century, the practice of building has undergone significant changes in several areas, notably mechanical, electrical, and communications systems. Researchers have added to our knowledge of building function. New areas of social concern have emerged, especially for buildings that are accessible by all, and for building in a sustainable manner. This third edition, in the tradition of its predecessors, sticks to the basics, but includes hundreds of changes both large and small that reflect the current state of the art and science of building. I have retained the basic organization of the original volume, along with its look and feel, all of which have worn well. The mission and premise of the book remain unchanged.

South Natick, Massachusetts   E. A.
January 2005

Contents

Prologue: Sustainable Building

Buildings represent a huge investment, not only of money and time, but also of the world's resources. In constructing and occupying buildings, we consume vast quantities of materials and generate a major portion of the world's environmental pollution. According to the Worldwatch Institute, buildings consume more than 40 percent of the energy utilized in the world each year and, in so doing, release into the atmosphere one-third of the carbon dioxide and two-fifths of the compounds that cause acid rain. In the United States, our buildings use about one-sixth of the fresh water consumed each year and a quarter of harvested wood. Our buildings release about half of the fluorocarbons that escape into the upper atmosphere and destroy the ozone layer that shelters us from the sun's ultraviolet rays. About 40 percent of our landfill material comes from construction projects. We see in these statistics that buildings are responsible for many forms of environmental degradation. They place a heavy burden on the earth's resources, most of which are nonrenewable and finite, and they jeopardize the health and welfare of humanity. Thus it is increasingly urgent that we learn to build and operate buildings in a sustainable manner.

Sustainability may be defined as *meeting the needs of the current generation without compromising the ability of future generations to meet their needs*. When we burn fossil fuels, we consume a portion of a finite, nonrenewable resource so that it will not be available a generation or two in the future. We also generate greenhouse gases that promote global warming. This will confront a near-future generation with the problem of a world in which glaciers and ice caps are shrinking, seas are rising to perilous levels, and weather is violent and unpredictable. When we build sprawling residential subdivisions on fertile land once used for growing food crops, we reduce the stock of agricultural land that will be available to future generations. When we use wood from forests that are not replanted with trees, we make it more likely that our children and grandchildren will find wood to be a scarce, expensive commodity.

We have it in our power to change this situation. We can reduce substantially the energy needed by our buildings. We can meet much of this need with solar and wind energy, both of which are renewable, nonpolluting, and available on the site itself. In many instances, we can build on land that has been recovered from abusive practices of the past such as contaminated industrial sites, demolished tenement apartment buildings, and land on which poor agricultural practices have led to extensive soil erosion. We can build with wood from certified forests, ones that are harvested and replanted in such a way that they will produce wood forever. We can build with wood recovered from old buildings that have been taken down. In each of these examples, we are building in such a way as to pass on to future generations the means to build in a similar fashion.

A number of organizations and manufacturers are working diligently toward sustainable construction practices (also referred to as *"green" building*). Some relate to particular resources such as forests. Some have to do with recycling materials such as scraps of gypsum wallboard or worn-out tires into new building materials: gypsum wallboard, roofing slates. Some are promoting renewable energy sources such as solar, wind, and photovoltaic technologies. Some concentrate on improving the energy performance of buildings through better thermal insulation, more airtight construction, and more efficient heating and cooling machinery. And some focus on educating architects and engineers, the designers of buildings, who by siting and orienting buildings intelligently, configuring them appropriately, selecting materials knowingly, and detailing the construction properly, can greatly reduce their impact on the earth and its resources.

Several organizations are working to educate architects and engineers in how to build sustainably. Prominent among these is the United States Green Building Council, which sponsors the LEED system for evaluating the sustainability of a building. LEED stands for Leadership in Energy and Environmental Design. The evaluation process is summarized by a checklist that is used in evaluating the degree of sustainability that is attained in a building. It is instructive to look at the categories on this checklist. The first broad category, "Sustainable Sites," includes, among other factors

- whether a building will improve its site or degrade it;
- whether the users of the building will be able to come and go by foot, on bicycles, or by public transportation so as to save fuel and reduce air pollution;

- the extent to which the site is disturbed by the new construction; and
- how storm water is managed (is it stored for use on-site, used to recharge the aquifer in the area, or dumped into a storm sewer?).

The second category, "Water Efficiency," includes

- use of stored storm water or "gray" wastewater (discarded wash water that does not contain human wastes) for irrigation;
- innovative wastewater treatment; and
- use of fixtures that reduce water consumption.

Category 3, "Energy & Atmosphere," relates to

- efficiency of the building's heating and cooling devices and systems;
- use of renewable energy resources on the site; and
- the potential of the building to contribute to ozone depletion.

Category 4 is "Materials & Resources." It includes

- recycling of building materials and building wastes;
- waste management on the construction site;
- recycled content in building materials used;
- use of local and regional materials, which consume less fuel in transportation, rather than materials that must be transported long distances;
- rapidly renewable materials; and
- wood from certified forests.

"Indoor Environmental Quality," the title of the fifth category, covers

- indoor air quality;
- elimination of tobacco smoke;
- ventilation effectiveness;
- air quality during construction;
- use of materials that do not give off toxic gases;
- control of chemicals used in the building;
- thermal comfort; and
- use of daylighting.

The sixth and last category is titled "Innovation & Design Process." It is an open category that awards credits for original design ideas that lead to more sustainable buildings. It also awards credits if an architect or engineer who has been accredited as a LEED expert is involved in the design of the project.

Although this list is still evolving, it is already serving as the basis for certifying the degree to which a building is sustainable. Additionally, it is a powerful vehicle for raising the environmental awareness of architects, engineers, and builders.

Throughout the pages that follow, you will find information relating to sustainability in the design, construction, and operation of buildings. Every chapter tells how to build in such a way that resources are used wisely, energy is conserved, waste products are reduced, and buildings are made comfortable, durable, and healthy with the minimum possible cost to the environment. Many of these practices are old and well-known. Some are new and innovative. In either case, architects and engineers must become familiar with them and use them more consistently if we are to pass on to our children and grandchildren a world as lovely, hospitable, healthy, and resource-rich as the world into which we were born.

What Buildings Do

1
The Outdoor Environment

The Earth and the Sun

Earth is unique among the planets of our solar system in offering all the basic necessities of life. But human life is far from easy on most parts of the globe. A planet-sized atmospheric engine, fueled by radiation from the sun and cooled by the radiation of heat back into the emptiness of space, moves air, moisture, and thermal energy across its surface in restless patterns that create an outdoor environment of varied and often extreme conditions.

The sun is the single most important factor in the lives of people and their buildings. The oxygen we breathe, the food we eat, and the fuels we burn are created by the action of sunlight on green plants. The water we drink is purified in an atmospheric distillation process powered by heat from the sun. Sunlight warms our bodies and buildings by direct radiation or through warming the air around us, sometimes enhancing our comfort and other times making us uncomfortable. Sunlight illuminates the outdoors, disinfects the surfaces it touches, creates vitamin D in our skin, and has an uplifting effect on our dispositions. Sunlight also disintegrates the materials with which we build, burns our skin, and promotes skin cancer. The sun is both the giver of life and its destroyer.

Sunlight includes electromagnetic radiation of varying wavelengths. Fewer than 1 percent of the sun's rays that reach sea level on earth are too short in wavelength to be visible. These ultraviolet rays range between about 160 and 400 nanometers (nm) in wavelength. The visible solar wavelengths, ranging between 400 and 780 nm, contain about half the energy of sunlight. The other half of the energy lies in the infrared part of the spectrum, the invisible wavelengths between 780 and 1500 nm. (A nanometer is one-billionth of a meter. A dime is about one million nanometers thick.)

3

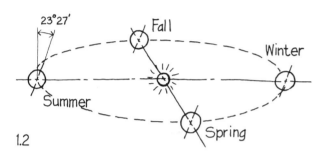

1.1

1.2

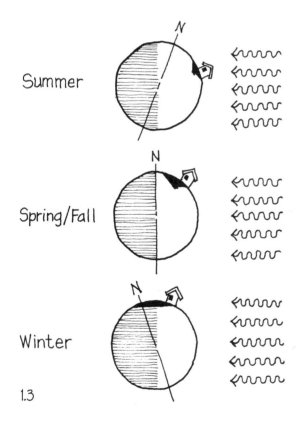

Summer

Spring/Fall

Winter

1.3

The earth loops around the sun in a slightly elliptical orbit with a mean radius of 92.9 million miles (149.5 million kilometers). It rotates about its own axis once each day and completes an orbit every 365¼ days. The half of the globe that is oriented away from the sun at any moment is in darkness, and the other half is sunlit (1.1). The earth's orbit is out of round by about 3 percent. Thus the distance between the earth and the sun changes enough to cause a variation of about 7 percent in the intensity of solar radiation on the earth over a six-month period. However, this variation is not the creator of the earth's seasons. In fact, the earth is closest to the sun in winter, so the orbital eccentricity helps slightly to moderate the seasons. The seasons are created, instead, by the tilt of 23°27′ between the axis of the earth's rotation and a perpendicular to the plane of its orbit (1.2).

The Summer Solstice

At the position in the earth's orbit where the North Pole is tilted closest to the sun, the sun's rays in the Northern Hemisphere pass through the atmosphere and strike the earth's surface at a steep angle (1.3). The path of the rays through the atmosphere is short, so that the air absorbs and scatters relatively little sunlight before the radiation reaches the ground. Because the sun is so high with respect to the surface of the land in the northern hemisphere, solar radiation is received in a maximum concentration per unit area of soil. The sun's rays are at their hottest at this orbital position, known as the *summer solstice*, which occurs about June 21 of each year. The total solar heat gathered by the Northern Hemisphere on June 21 is further increased by another important factor: the sun is seen for a longer period of time on this day than on any other day of the year. The sun rises to the north of east before six o'clock in the morning and sets to the north of west after six o'clock in the evening. How long before and after six o'clock sunrise and sunset occur is wholly dependent on latitude. On the equator, the day from sunrise to sunset is always 12 hours long regardless of the time of year. Moving northward to the Tropic of Cancer, June 21 is only slightly longer than 12 hours, and the sun at noon appears directly overhead at an altitude of exactly 90°. (The Tropic of Cancer is at 23°27′ north latitude, the same angle as the inclination of the earth's axis.) As we move farther and farther to the north, we find that June 21 has longer and longer hours of sunlight, with the sun rising and setting farther and farther toward the north, until at the Arctic Circle the sun never sets at all but merely skims the horizon at midnight, giving 24 hours of sunlight. Simultaneously, however, the noontime sun's altitude decreases as one moves northward, from 90° at the Tropic of Cancer, to 70° at the latitude of New York City, to 47° at the Arctic Circle, and to 23°27′ at the North Pole. This reduces the heating effect of the sun on the earth's surface so that, in general, the farther north one goes, the cooler the climate will be.

Not surprisingly, the summer solstice occurs during the warm season of the year. On the average, however, the hottest weather of the year comes four to six weeks later than the summer solstice, in late July and early August. This delay occurs because the land and water absorb and hold considerable solar heat during the warmer days of the year. By late in the summer, however, the earth gives back this stored energy to the cooler air, thus moderating the effect of the lower solar flux in that season.

In the opposite orbital position, which occurs about December 21, the *winter solstice* in the Northern Hemisphere, the North Pole is tilted directly away from the sun. The sun's rays arrive at a low angle to the surface of the earth after losing much of their energy in a long, flat passage through the atmosphere, and their heating effect on the ground is correspondingly weak. This day has the fewest hours of sunlight of any day of the year, with the sun rising late and to the south of east, climbing to a low noontime, and setting early and to the south of west. Above the Arctic Circle, the sun never rises at all but appears as a faint glow in the southern sky at midday. The land and seas are still giving off stored heat from the warmer autumn days, however, so that the coldest part of the winter does not come until late January or early February.

The Equinoxes

On or about March 21 and September 21, known respectively as the *vernal equinox* and the *autumnal equinox*, the North and South Poles are equidistant from the sun. Everywhere on earth, the sun rises exactly in the east and sets exactly in the west 12 hours later, except at the extreme poles, where the sun travels just along the horizon for 24 hours.

The Annual Cycle

It is useful to keep in mind that the seasonal variations in length of day and the maximum daily sun altitude are least pronounced in the tropics and most exaggerated in the polar regions. In the tropics, the length of day is always close to 12 hours but, except on the equator itself, is slightly longer in summer and slightly shorter in winter. The sun always rises in the vicinity of due east, a bit to the north in summer and a bit to the south in winter, and sets in the vicinity of due west, traveling very nearly directly overhead at noon. The sun always

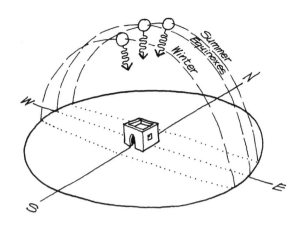

Equatorial Zone
1.4

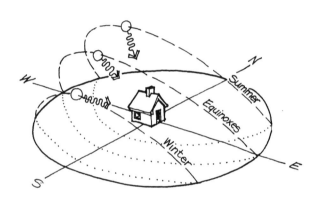

Temperate Zone
1.5

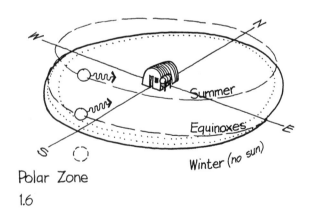

Polar Zone
1.6

intercepts the horizon in the mornings and evenings at a steep angle, producing very brief sunrises and sunsets (1.4).

As one moves northward in latitude, seasonal variations increase gradually. Summer days are longer than they are in the tropics, and winter days are shorter. Noontime sun altitudes are lower, giving a lower solar flux per unit of ground area. The directions of sunrise and sunset show a more marked seasonal swing, and sunrises and sunsets are more prolonged (1.5). In the Northern Hemisphere the limiting case is the North Pole, where day and night each are six months long: the sun rises on March 21, climbs to a low "noon" on June 21, and sets on September 21 (1.6). Over the course of a year, every point on the globe is exposed to direct sunlight exactly half the time. At the poles, the half portion of sunlight comes in one continuous six-month period. At the equator, each day of the year is evenly divided between sunlight and darkness. At intermediate latitudes, longer days in summer compensate for shorter ones in winter.

In the Southern Hemisphere, the sun resides in the northern half of the sky, and the seasons are reversed from those in the Northern Hemisphere, with longer days and higher solar fluxes occurring while the days are short and the sunlight is weak in the Northern Hemisphere. The progression of seasonal effects from the equator to the pole is the same as for the Northern Hemisphere.

Effects of Solar Radiation on the Earth

A number of factors affect the amount of solar radiation that reaches a particular surface. As we have already seen, these include the length of day, the angle of incidence of sunlight on the ground at each time of day, and the amount of atmosphere traversed by the radiation at each time of day. Of these three, atmospheric interference is the most difficult factor to evaluate. Solar intensity just outside the earth's atmosphere is about 130 watts per square foot (1,400 watts/m^2). At an altitude of about 15 miles, a stratum of ozone and nascent oxygen absorbs most of the ultraviolet portion of the solar waves. In the lower reaches of the atmosphere, carbon dioxide, water vapor, clouds, dust, and pollutants work in various ways to reflect, scatter, absorb, and reradiate different parts of the spectrum. The shorter wavelengths of sunlight, which are the most affected, produce the blue appearance of the daytime sky. A considerable portion of the sunlight's energy is stripped away by the "clear" atmosphere—nearly half, on the average, worldwide. Most of this energy is then reradiated from the atmosphere into space, but a significant amount is reradiated from the atmosphere to the earth as diffuse sky radiation, thus slightly increasing the total amount of solar

6

energy available at the earth's surface. Clouds, which cover roughly half the earth's surface at any given time, block much of the sun's direct radiation but still pass a considerable quantity in diffuse form.

Taking all these factors into account, a square foot of land at 45° latitude, in a location with a 50 percent incidence of cloud cover, receives about 75 kilowatt-hours of direct solar radiation each year, plus roughly another 20 kilowatt-hours of diffuse sky radiation, for a total of nearly 100 kilowatt-hours annually. A square meter of land receives almost 11 times these quantities.

The sun imparts little heat directly to the earth's atmosphere. Instead, the ground and objects on it are warmed by solar radiation, and they in turn pass some of their heat to the air. The rate at which a patch of ground is warmed depends on several factors, beginning with the amount of solar energy that arrives at the surface. Assuming equal atmospheric conditions, a patch of ground nearer the equator receives more solar heat than one farther from the equator because of the higher angle of incidence of the sun's rays on the ground. For much the same reason, a south-facing hillside receives a higher intensity of sunlight than a flat field, and a steeply north-facing slope may receive none at all.

A second factor affecting the rate at which ground is warmed is the portion of solar radiation that the ground reflects. This is typically about 20 percent, leaving 80 percent to be absorbed. Of this 80 percent, a portion may go to warm the soil and thus is stored temporarily. Some is expended in evaporating moisture from the soil. Some is radiated at long infrared wavelengths from the soil back to the sky and to cooler terrestrial objects that the patch of ground can "see": treetops, fences, buildings, and so forth. The remainder of the 80 percent warms the air above the patch of ground.

Night Sky Radiation

So far we have been considering the tremendous influx of solar radiation on the earth in the daytime. At night, the flow is reversed, with the dark side of the earth radiating energy into space at infrared wavelengths ranging from 4,000 to 80,000 nm, considerably longer than the sun's infrared rays. On cloudy, humid nights, water vapor in the atmosphere, which is particularly absorptive of this long-wave infrared radiation, serves to block much of the outflow of energy, but on clear, dry nights, a very powerful cooling effect is exerted by rapid radiation from the warm earth to the cold blackness of the sky. Dew frequently condenses from the air onto radiationally cooled surfaces of the ground and the roof surfaces of automobiles and buildings. These cold surfaces cool the adjacent air. A stagnant layer of cold air may form near the ground in a stable atmospheric configuration known as an *inversion*. Ground fog may form as moisture condenses in this cold layer, and frost may occur along the ground even when thermometers at eye level are reading temperatures well above freezing. A nighttime wind tends to mix earth-cooled air with warmer air, making dew, frost, and ground fog less likely to form. Over bodies of water, the large heat capacity and convective mixing of the water generally result in a less pronounced nocturnal cooling of the air than over land.

Weather

If atmospheric conditions are the same in all parts of the world, nighttime heat loss by radiation occurs at an equal rate regardless of latitude. But daytime heat gain, as we have seen, is not equal in all locations. On any day of the year, the tropics and the hemisphere that is experiencing its warm season receive much more solar radiation than do the polar regions and the colder hemisphere. Averaged over the course of the year, the tropics and latitudes up to about 40° receive more total heat than they lose by radiation. Latitudes above 40° receive less total heat than they lose by radiation. This inequality produces the necessary conditions for the operation of a huge, global-scale engine that takes on heat in the tropics and gives it off in the polar regions. Its working fluid is the atmosphere, especially the moisture it contains. Air is heated over the warm earth of the tropics, expands, rises, and flows away both northward and southward at high altitudes, cooling as it goes. It descends and flows toward the equator again from more northerly and southerly latitudes. Meanwhile, the earth's eastward rotation deflects these currents westward along the earth's surface to form the trade winds. Farther toward the poles, similar but weaker cells of air convection are set in motion, resulting in a generally eastward flow of air (1.7).

The heat of the sun evaporates water continuously from the seas and land into the air. The warm, moist air thus produced eventually rises, either because of convection or because the air is contained in winds that blow up the slopes of rising landmasses. As the air rises, it expands because of decreasing atmospheric pressure. As it expands, it undergoes adiabatic cooling until it reaches the temperature at which its moisture begins to condense. The condensing moisture evolves latent heat into the air, offsetting some of the cooling effect of expansion. But a slower rate of cooling continues as the air continues to rise; moisture continues to condense; and clouds of water droplets and ice crystals are formed. Considerable quantities of water are often involved; a single large cumulus cloud is estimated to weigh 100,000 tons (10^8 kg).

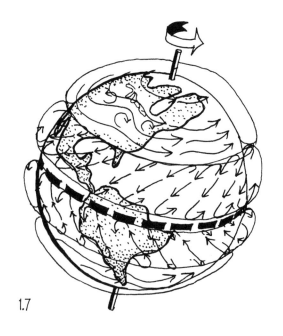

1.7

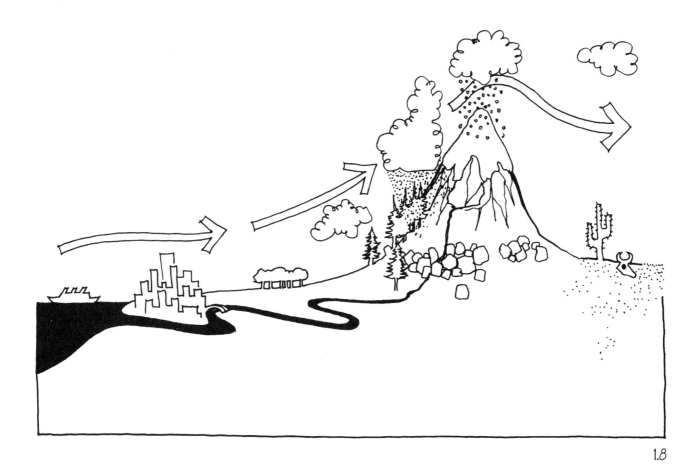

1.8

Precipitation

The exact mechanism by which a cloud releases its moisture is not well understood, but it generally involves both further cooling and the presence in the cloud of microscopic particles of dust around which the tiny cloud droplets can aggregate to form raindrops or ice crystals. Precipitation tends to be heavier over mountain ranges because of the rapid cooling of the rising winds and is usually sparse to the leeward side of mountains, where the descending winds have already been wrung dry of excess water (1.8). Rainwater and snow melt are gathered by the earth's surface into streams and rivers and eventually flow to the seas, evaporating moisture into the air along the way to start the cycle again.

In the temperate latitudes, large masses of warm, moist air from more tropical climates advance northward to meet masses of cooler, drier air from the polar regions. The warm front, characterized by low barometric pressure, and the higher-pressure cold front collide and swirl about each other, increasing local wind velocities and releasing precipitation where the warm air is suddenly cooled by contact with the cold air (1.9). Weather patterns in the temperate

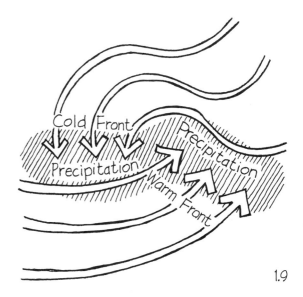

1.9

latitudes are predominantly the result of such frontal systems. They are less stable and predictable than tropical weather, which is dominated by the general sun-induced circulation of the atmosphere.

Wind serves an important function in the earth's weather, distributing both water and heat more equitably about the globe. Wind flow at high altitudes is generally rapid and fairly smooth. In the vicinity of the earth's surface, however, the wind is subjected to interference from hills, mountains, trees, buildings, and various convective flows of air. The average wind speed is progressively reduced by these obstacles nearer the ground, and the wind flow becomes more turbulent, fluctuating rapidly in both velocity and direction.

The atmospheric engine converts vast quantities of energy from sunlight to wind and from sunlight to falling precipitation. Despite its being only about 3 percent efficient in transforming radiation into motion, the engine operates at a level that would be measured in trillions of horsepower (multiples of 10^{12} watts). But this immense flow of energy is difficult to tap for direct human use: wind is diffuse, and it is difficult to harness at the high altitudes and polar latitudes where it is strongest. Only a minute percentage of all precipitation falls in mountain valleys that may be dammed for power generation; the rest lands on the oceans or on watersheds that are not suitable for hydroelectric installations.

Climatic Effects of Land and Water

Both water and land are capable of absorbing and storing heat, but water is considerably more efficient as a storage medium. As a result, large bodies of water tend to moderate the temperatures in their vicinities very strongly, whereas large landmasses exert only a weak effect on air temperatures. This is particularly noticeable where prevailing winds pass over water before reaching land. The West Coast of the United States and Canada, under the influence of the prevailing west winds off the Pacific Ocean, has a much milder climate, cooler in summer and warmer in winter, than does the East Coast, where the same prevailing west winds come off the continental landmass. Water can also transport heat for great distances, as in the case of the warm Atlantic Gulf Stream, which gathers heat in the tropics and carries it northward to soften (and moisten) the weather in western Europe. London, warmed by winds off the Gulf Stream, has little subfreezing weather in winter, whereas Minneapolis, landlocked in the central United States at a somewhat more southerly latitude than London, has considerable snow and protracted periods of bitter cold. Thus latitude alone is not a precise index of climate.

Microclimate

At an individual building site, even more climatic variables may come into play. The apparent movement of the sun across the site is rigidly fixed according to the geographic latitude, but the effect of the sun's radiation varies according to the orientation and steepness of the ground slope, the infrared absorbency of the ground surface, the presence or absence of shading vegetation, and reflected and reradiated solar heat from surrounding buildings and geological features. The air temperature on the site is further affected by such factors as the altitude of the site above sea level, its proximity to bodies of water, the direction of prevailing winds, and the presence of shading vegetation. Fountains, waterfalls, and trees on the site may diffuse enough moisture into the air to raise the local humidity and depress the local air temperature. Local wind patterns are largely dependent on local obstructions to the passage of wind such as forests, trees, buildings, and hills. Plowed ground or dark pavement is warmed by the sun to a higher temperature than are surrounding areas, thereby increasing the radiational heating of nearby surfaces and causing small updrafts of warm air. Topography may have an important role in local convective airflow: a valley may be more protected from wind than a hilltop, but on still, cool nights, rivers of cold air flow down the valley to form pools in low areas while warmer air rises toward the hilltop. Cities, too, affect local weather. The energy released by vehicles and buildings is gradually dissipated in the form of heat to the outdoors, often warming the air by 5 to 10 degrees Fahrenheit (3°–6°C) above that of the surrounding countryside. The artificially warmed buildings and vehicles of large cities often create considerable convective updrafts that can have significant climatic effects on a regional scale.

Other Solar Phenomena

In addition to its thermal effects—those of warming the earth and creating wind and precipitation—the sun also has important nonthermal effects. It provides visible light; it furnishes energy for photosynthesis in plants; and it radiates ultraviolet light.

Daylighting

The role of sunlight in illuminating buildings will be discussed later in detail, but we should note here that direct sunlight is often far too bright for comfortable seeing. Much more useful during the daytime is the visible light scattered by the atmosphere, or the even, restful illumination of a shaded area. If we need light at night, or under dense cloud cover, we must use alternative sources of illumination.

1.10

Photosynthesis

It would be difficult to overemphasize the value to humankind of the photosynthetic reaction in plants. We could not live without it. The human organism cannot create nutrients from sunlight. Plants, however, produce sugars, starches, and proteins from water, carbon dioxide, nitrogen, and soil nutrients through solar-fueled processes. They take carbon dioxide from the air during photosynthesis and give back oxygen as a waste product. (Animals consume oxygen in their metabolic processes and give off carbon dioxide, thus forming the other major link in a self-sustaining environmental chain.) Simultaneously, people and other animals eat whatever plants they are capable of digesting and/or the flesh of other animals that ultimately were nourished by plants. Animal excrement contains nitrogen, phosphorus, potassium, carbon, and other substances that become available to plants through soil and water, and thus food production is perpetuated through other self-sustaining chains (1.10). Even dead plants and animals have a role to play. Their corpses are broken down by other animals and by microorganisms into basic chemical compounds that become once more part of the soil, available to nourish plants and begin life again.

Photosynthesis also produces useful nonfood products such as wood for construction, fibers for the manufacture of fabrics and paper, decorative plants, flowers, ornamental trees and shrubs, and climbing vines. Photosynthesis is responsible for our entire supply of fossil fuels—coal, oil, and gas—which were formed millions of years ago by the effects of geological heat and pressure on large masses of decaying vegetable matter. Except for geothermal energy, nuclear energy, and tides, all our energy sources are solar in origin: not only direct sunlight but also wind energy, water energy, plant energy, and, of course, fossil fuels.

Ultraviolet radiation from the sun is important for its role in photosynthesis, but it has other roles as well. Ultraviolet radiation kills many harmful microorganisms, an effect that is important in purifying the atmosphere and in ridding sunlit surfaces of disease-carrying bacteria. Vitamin D, essential to human nutrition, is formed by the action of ultraviolet light on the skin. On the negative side, ultraviolet rays are responsible for the rapid and soon fatal burning of human skin exposed too long to sunlight and for the high incidence of skin cancer among light-skinned people who are constantly in the sun. Ultraviolet rays also fade dyes in fabrics, decompose many plastics, and contribute to the deterioration of paints, roofing, wood, and other organic building materials. It is because of these negative effects that there is concern about preserving the high-altitude ozone layer that intercepts most ultraviolet radiation before it can reach the earth.

The earth's geology has a great deal to do with the ways in which we build. Many of our building materials, of course, are mineral in origin: earth, stone, concrete, brick, glass, gypsum, asbestos, steel, aluminum, copper, and dozens of others. In many cases the simplest of these can be obtained directly from the building site or from sources in the neighborhood. The subsoil, subsurface water levels, topsoil, and rocks of a site affect the sorts of excavations, foundations, and landscaping that are likely to be undertaken. The contours of the site—its hills, valleys, and slopes—help determine how water will drain during storms, where erosion of soil may occur, where roadways and paths may run without being excessively steep, what areas will be more or less sheltered from wind, what areas will be exposed most favorably to sunlight, where various sorts of plants will grow best, and where and how the buildings will be built. These are exceedingly complex factors, rich in both positive and negative implications for an architect or engineer.

Certain biological factors of the building site are important, too. Microorganisms are universally present in such forms as the bacteria, molds, and fungi that break down dead vegetable and animal matter into soil nutrients. Higher plants such as grasses, weeds, flowers, shrubs, and trees play important roles in trapping precipitation, preventing soil erosion, providing shade, deflecting wind, and other functions already mentioned under the heading of photosynthesis. Insects can affect building design: Biting insects and food-contaminating insects must be excluded from interior spaces. Building-destroying insects such as termites need to be discouraged from attacking the structure. Native reptiles, birds, and mammals also may figure importantly in the planning process. We may want bird songs to filter into the breakfast room, but not the birds themselves. Mice, rats, raccoons, foxes, deer, squirrels, and the neighbor's dog, to name a few, can be nuisance animals in one's building. But a cow, sheep, or horse may be welcome in a barn, and one's own dog, cat, or hamster in a house.

Nearby buildings often affect what we are likely to build. They may shade certain areas of the site, divert the wind in unforeseen ways, upset natural drainage patterns, or cause areas of the site to lack visual or acoustical privacy (1.11). Buildings or remains of buildings erected on the site by previous builders may have to be dealt with, along with their associated driveways, parking areas, walks, gardens, wells, sewage disposal systems, and underground utilities. Bad land-use practices of previous or abutting owners may have caused problems of weeds or soil erosion.

Environmental factors caused by people include air that is polluted with smoke, gases, dust, or chemical particles; noise from

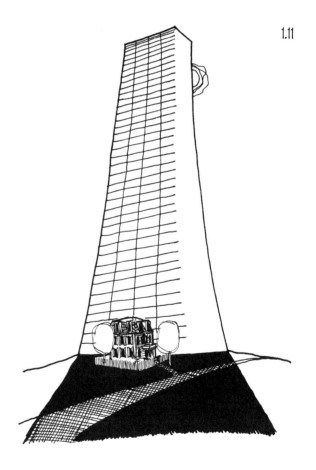

1.11

traffic, industrial processes, a nearby discotheque, or a rowdy family next door; and surface or ground water that is fouled with sewage or chemicals. Sadly, too, a designer must commonly come to terms with the fact that the outdoor environment includes unknown persons who would deface, destroy, or intrude on the building being designed, often before its construction is complete and almost always to the detriment of the building and its occupants.

This, then, for better and for worse, is the outdoor environment, portions of which we may select and modify for human occupancy. It has a warming sun that rises and sets, a procession of seasons, a more-or-less predictable pattern of weather, a unique geology, a varied colony of flora and fauna, and a history of human use and misuse extending through the present and into the future. We must ask ourselves who will occupy and use this environment, what their needs are, and how their needs differ from what this environment can furnish.

Further Reading

David I. Blumenstock. *The Ocean of Air.* New Brunswick, N.J., Rutgers University Press, 1959.

T. F. Gaskell and Martin Morris. *World Climate: The Weather, the Environment and Man.* London, Thames and Hudson, 1979.

2
The Human Environment

The Human Body

The quality of a human environment can be measured only in terms of its effect on the people who experience it. But people, both physically and emotionally, are creatures not easily understood, and evaluations of quality are seldom simple. Even a simple question such as "Is this place warm enough?" does not have a simple answer in quantitative terms, for the same person, under varying circumstances of season of the year, amount of clothing, radiant temperature, relative humidity, and air movement, will find the place exactly "warm enough" at a range of air temperatures extending over many degrees, a surprising spread for an animal whose internal temperature cannot vary by more than a couple of degrees either way without distress. To understand how to evaluate environmental quality, then, we must begin by looking within the body itself to find out how it works.

In its most fundamental mechanical behavior, the human body is a heat engine. The fuel for the engine is derived from food, in the form of proteins, carbohydrates, and fats. The digestive process breaks down these nutrients by means of various chemicals, bacteria, and enzymes into substances that the body can use. These useful substances are then pumped into the bloodstream, which transports them to the living cells throughout the body. Waste products and harmful substances are filtered out in the digestive process and stored for periodic excretion. Urine consists primarily of nitrogenous wastes dissolved in water. Feces, though mainly water, contain the indigestible fibers, minerals, and particles that could not be utilized in the metabolic process.

We need a regular supply of water to facilitate the chemical processes in the body, to move the products of these processes about the body, and to help cool the body. We need air too, because in the critical set of chemical reactions that combust the food-derived fuels to keep the human heat engine operating, oxygen is a necessary reactant. When we breathe air into our lungs, we absorb a portion of its oxygen into our bloodstream. We mix carbon dioxide and water, which are waste products of the combustion, with the air in our lungs before we breathe it out again. Less than a fifth of the air's oxygen is replaced by carbon dioxide in each lungful, but a continuous supply of outside air must be available to the body to avoid oxygen depletion and carbon dioxide narcosis through repeated breathing of the same air (2.1).

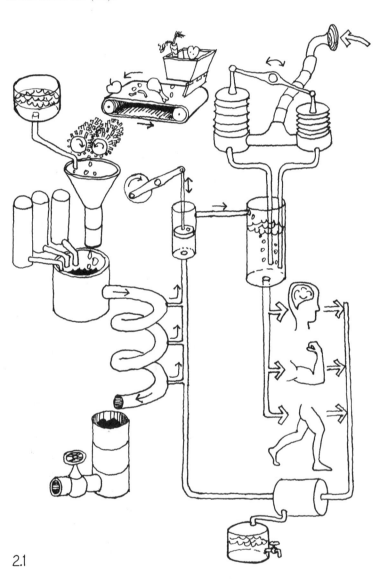

2.1

How the Body Cools Itself

The normal internal operating temperature of the human engine is just under 99° Fahrenheit (37°C), a temperature that must be maintained within narrow tolerances in order to avoid metabolic malfunction. But our bodies are only about one-fifth efficient in converting food energy to mechanical work. They must give off four times as much heat as they use in order to maintain a stable internal temperature. An adult working at a desk produces excess heat at about the same rate as does a 100-watt lightbulb. The same person walking generates two to three times as much heat and, when exercising strenuously, six to ten times (2.2). These necessary rates of cooling are achieved through an admirable collection of physiological mechanisms.

The body is continuously cooled by the heating of respired air, the vaporization of water from the lungs and breathing passages, the convection and radiation of heat from the surface of the skin, and the diffusion of small amounts of water vapor through the skin (2.3). The surface temperature of our skin, and hence its rate of heat loss, is controlled by the dilatation or constriction (enlarging or shrinking) of the small blood vessels of the skin. As the vessels dilate, the flow of warm blood near the surface of the body increases, and the skin temperature rises so as to give off heat more quickly to the surrounding environment. The increased volume of blood, which is a good thermal conductor, also partially displaces fatty tissues, which are poor thermal conductors, near the surface of the body. This increases direct heat loss from the underlying body tissues to the surrounding environment. This very sensitive set of mechanisms, known as the *vasomotor system*, is able to regulate the body's rate of heat loss under a fairly wide range of conditions.

When the rate of cooling by respiration, skin diffusion, skin radiation, and skin convection is insufficient to meet our body's demands, we sweat. Water is exuded from the pores of the skin and evaporates into the atmosphere. The latent heat of vaporization that is required by this evaporation is furnished primarily by the body. Large quantities of heat can be lost in this way. Perspiration is sufficient under most conditions to provide the additional cooling required, but its effectiveness depends on the amount of moisture in the air. If the surrounding air is very dry, perspiration evaporates very quickly, and considerable cooling is possible even when the air temperature is higher than our body temperature. When the humidity of the surrounding air is high, evaporation is slow, and so the rate of perspiration increases as the body attempts to compensate. The situation can be helped to some extent by increasing the rate of air movement past the body: the moving air is more effective not only

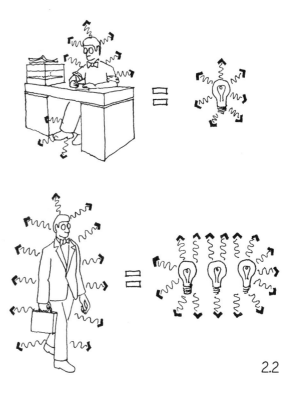

2.2

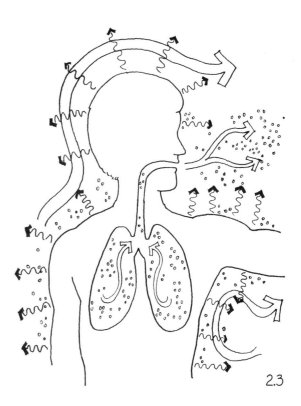

2.3

2.4

2.5

2.6

in evaporating perspiration but also in speeding convective heat loss from the skin, provided that the air temperature is lower than skin temperature (2.4). If the body is in a situation in which none of these strategies is sufficient, however, the deep-body temperature will rise until metabolic function is impaired, bringing heat stroke and death.

Excessive Rates of Body Cooling

Under conditions in which heat is being removed too quickly from the body, heat loss is especially rapid from the back of the neck, the head, the back, and the extremities. Clothing and furniture that are designed to obstruct the flow of heat from these areas are particularly effective in aiding thermal comfort under cold conditions (2.5). Because the body can transfer heat through the bloodstream from one of its parts to another, symptoms of excessive heat loss are sometimes difficult to interpret. Warm footwear may not be of much help for cold feet if rapid cooling is occurring in some other part of the body. Outdoorspeople have a saying, "If your feet are cold, put your hat on." This seemingly odd strategy works in a surprisingly high proportion of cases, because the head, with a high ratio of heat transfer surface to internal volume, is capable of radiating and convecting very large amounts of heat to a cold environment, much as a relatively small automobile radiator can cool a very large engine. The body responds to excessive heat loss from any of its parts by lowering the temperature of the feet and hands in order to keep vital internal organs at an optimum temperature. If rapid heat loss continues, "goose pimpling" occurs, in which the hairs of the skin are erected to trap still air as an insulating layer next to the skin. One's instinct generally leads one, quite correctly, to cut down the exposed surface area of the body by folding the arms, hunching the shoulders, and bringing the legs tightly together. Another helpful response is to exercise in order to raise the level of metabolic heat production to match the rate at which heat is being lost (2.6). If these measures are insufficient, shivering—an involuntary form of heat-generating muscular exercise—commences, and if even this cannot restore equilibrium, the deep-body temperature will begin to fall, a condition known as hypothermia. Hypothermia can be reversed in its early stages by the direct conduction of heat into the body by means of hot food and drink, a hot bath or sauna, or snuggling with a friend, but in its later stages a deepening coma is followed by death.

The human body is not comfortable when it is placed under thermal stress. Excessive sweating is uncomfortable and annoying. So is goose pimpling or shivering. Prolonged overheating or overcooling of the body results in increased fatigue and weakens resistance to disease. A suitable human thermal environment, then, is

18

fundamentally one in which the body is able to give off its excess heat at the required rate without having to resort to sweating, huddling, goose pimpling, or shivering.

Other Requirements for Human Life

Besides food, water, fresh air, and optimum thermal conditions, the human body has other environmental requirements. The most vital of these is adequate sanitation (2.7). The body is susceptible to attack by a very large assortment of bacteria, viruses, and fungi. The skin, respiratory system, and digestive tract are particularly fertile environments for these microorganisms. The basic sanitary requirements for a human environment include the provision of food and drinking water that are free of harmful microorganisms, the prompt removal and processing of excreta and food wastes to render them free of disease-causing organisms, adequate ventilation to carry away air-borne bacteria and excessive moisture, adequate sunlight to dry and sterilize the environment, the exclusion of disease-carrying rodents and insects from buildings, and facilities for washing foodstuffs, dishes, skin, hair, and clothing.

2.7

Inadequate sanitation is costly in human terms: Poor ventilation encourages tuberculosis and other respiratory diseases. Contaminated food and water spread hepatitis and typhoid. Pest-borne diseases include typhus, yellow fever, malaria, sleeping sickness, encephalitis, plague, and various infestations of parasites. These are but a few examples.

Human eyes and ears, the most important sensory organs of the body, have their own sets of environmental requirements. The eye can be damaged if it looks even momentarily at the sun or if it looks too long at a sunlit landscape of snow or light-colored sand. Seeing becomes difficult or painful if the eye must look at a very bright object against a very dark background, and vice versa. Seeing is difficult and less accurate at very low levels of illumination. The eye is able to adjust in order to see objects fairly well at moderately low levels of illumination, but the adjustment mechanism, which probably evolved in order to give humans the ability to see during the twilight period of the day, is very slow, acting over a period of minutes.

The ear is somewhat similar in its characteristics: It can be damaged by sounds of excessive loudness, especially if they occur over a protracted period of time. Hearing is difficult at very low sound intensities or if a strong background of noise obscures the sounds that one wishes to hear. But there is one very important difference between our eyes and our ears: By closing our eyelids, we can shut off nearly all visual stimuli, whereas we cannot stop our ears so

2.8

easily (2.8). We can find visual relief in any but the very brightest environments, but for relief from a disturbingly noisy environment, we have to move to a quieter location.

The human body needs space in which to move—to work, to play, or merely to maintain its muscle tone, skeletal movement, and heart and lung function through exercise. Even when at rest, the body needs to be able to shift about in order to unburden and relax its various components in turn.

The body is soft and requires protection from injury. It needs smooth surfaces underfoot to prevent ankle damage or tripping. It needs properly proportioned stairs to move up or down in a building without falling. It needs guardrails to prevent it from accidentally falling over edges of surfaces. Hard or sharp objects must be kept out of the volumes of space normally traversed by the body in its movements. Fire and very hot objects must be kept away from the delicate human skin. The body must be kept safe from falling objects, explosions, poisons, corrosive chemicals, harmful radiation, and electric shocks, any of which could cause it severe injury or sudden death.

The Environmental Necessities of Human Civilization

To this point, we have considered the human body primarily as a machine that will not run properly except under a certain set of conditions. But of course, a person is much more than just a physical mechanism. People seek out social activities, those contacts with others through which they create, produce, learn, grow, relax, play, and enjoy life.

At the most fundamental level, each person requires a place to sleep, facilities with which to carry out the basics of personal hygiene, a source of water, sources of food, and facilities to prepare the food for eating. But most people live as part of a family and in somewhat less Spartan surroundings, a place called *home*. Family life requires places for procreation and the rearing of children. Preparing and eating food become elaborate processes in the family, a source of enjoyment as well as bodily nutrition and a setting for social interaction at several levels. Home becomes a place for certain kinds of work carried out by various members of the family: pursuing hobbies, studying, writing letters, cleaning and repairing things, managing financial affairs. Home is also a place for play and for entertaining friends. Home is where you hang your hat—along with your coat, your shoes, your wardrobe, your dishes, your books, and all the rest of your belongings. It is meant to be a safe, secure, familiar place, filled with the things of one's life, closed and private at times, open and outgoing at other times, at the option of its occupants (2.9).

Outside the home, we require a variety of other sorts of places. We need workplaces—workshops, warehouses, markets, offices,

2.9

2.10

studios, barns, laboratories—where the goods of civilization are designed, produced, and distributed. Each workplace has to furnish the basic necessities of life, plus the special requirements of the processes that take place there. We need gathering places of various sorts, places of worship, places to exercise, places to play, places in which to be entertained, places in which to view interesting and beautiful things, and places in which to carry out the functions of government and education. Large numbers of people need to be accommodated at once in these types of facilities and all their needs satisfied simultaneously (2.10).

Human society requires mobility. We need to move around in order to get to work or school and to enjoy the various amenities of a city or a countryside. A network for human movement must be provided, starting with the doors of rooms; the hallways, stairs, and elevators that connect them; the entrances that merge the building and the outdoors; and continuing with footpaths, streets, roads, and long-distance mechanisms for moving both people and goods (2.11).

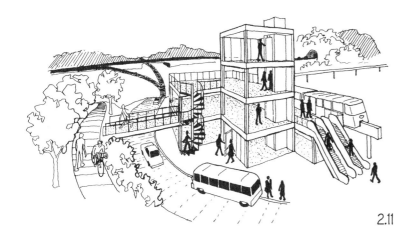

2.11

This requires clear rights-of-way, smooth pavements, functional vehicles, convenient stations of transfer—and understandable information on how to get where one is going.

These requirements of a high-quality human environment are numerous and often exacting. They include the physiological and social requirements that we have identified, as well as psychological requirements that are much more difficult to define. Taken together, they describe an environment that exists nowhere in the natural world. The outdoor environment is too variable, too frequently extreme, too often destructive and unstable, to be hospitable to human life and civilization. In the course of its development, humankind has had to learn not merely to seek sheltered areas of the natural landscape but also to create buildings, which are artificially sheltered and conditioned areas of more constant and comfortable qualities than Nature is capable of providing on its own.

Further Reading

B. Givoni. *Man, Climate, and Architecture*. New York, Elsevier, 1969, pp. 19–95.

3
The Concept of Shelter

Shelter at its most basic is not a human invention; it is something we seek instinctively, as do all animals, in a world that is seldom attuned exactly to our physiological and social needs. On a hot summer day, we picnic under a tree or near a shady waterfall or cascade. On bitter winter days, we gravitate instinctively toward the lee side of any landscape feature that will deflect the wind, especially if a patch of warming sunlight is available there. The experienced outdoor traveler, when selecting a spot on which to roll out a sleeping bag for the night in any season of the year, avoids the low spots and valleys, which channel nighttime flows of cold air and moisture, and, animal-like, beds down on the higher ground, perhaps on an eastward slope, to be wakened and warmed by the morning sun.

In an agrarian society, the search for shelter begins with a judicious use of the natural landscape. People choose building sites for their sheltering qualities—orientation with respect to sun and prevailing winds, good drainage, interesting or useful topographic features, trees and vegetation that give shade or deflect the wind, and sources of clean water. In northern climates, higher ground that slopes toward the south is reserved for growing the most essential crops. Farmers know from personal experience that the earliest frosts of autumn and the latest frosts of spring occur in the low spots of the landscape. They understand that plants in south-sloping fields receive life-giving sunlight of an intensity higher than that of flat or north-sloping fields (3.1). Rural towns are sited, where possible, next to rivers or springs on leeward, generally southerly slopes.

Artificial shelter starts with such gentle manipulations of the landscape as planting a tree for shade or a row of shrubbery for a windbreak. A simple, freestanding east-west wall of piled-up rocks, by means of its vertical profile and its thermal capacity, can create

3.1

3.2

a small zone of shaded coolness immediately to its north in hot weather and a sun-warmed, less windy zone to its south in cold weather (3.2). The wall absorbs some of the sun's heat during the day and releases it gradually after sundown, extending the sheltered zone's period of habitability.

In progressively more elaborate stages of environmental intervention, a paving of stones or a platform of wood provides a drier footing for the inhabitant. A lean-to roof keeps off rain and snow (3.3). East and west walls increase the wind-deflecting capabilities of the shelter and interfere little with the entry of winter sunshine. At night, a fire at the mouth of this simple shelter warms its occupants by both direct and wall-reflected radiation, and a small portion of its heat is stored in the stones to moderate the temperature of the sheltered space even after the fire has died (3.4). One can easily imagine further steps in the improvement of such a rudimentary shelter: the use of fabric or skins to close off the open side after dark or on cloudy days, the moving of the fire to an interior hearth, and so on (3.5). Perhaps many primitive building forms evolved in much this same way, to join later in the stream of development that led ultimately to modern building techniques.

Today's buildings are much more complicated than this primitive example, of course. Each genuine new improvement in shelter wrought by our ancestors was at first a novelty, but soon afterward became standard practice and then, finally, the acceptable minimum as later improvements superseded it. A shelter that represented the height of comfort and convenience to one generation might be considered substandard a generation or two later. We have grown to expect more and more of our buildings, to the point that buildings now are expected to perform functions that are not strictly "sheltering" at all,

3.3

3.4

3.5

such as providing water, removing wastes, and furnishing energy for use in mechanical tools and electronic entertainment devices. Our buildings have become, in fact, comprehensive life-support mechanisms.

Many of the functions we now expect of our buildings were formerly the functions of other devices. Clothing and shelter are to a considerable extent interchangeable in function, but with the passage of time, people have tended to ask less of their clothing and proportionally more of their shelter. Some functions formerly expected of pieces of furniture, such as the provision of enclosed storage for various household articles, are steadily being subsumed by building components such as closets and cupboards. Sinks, bathtubs, cookstoves, and automatic dishwashers, once portable devices, are nowadays fixed parts of a house. Offices were once lit by portable lamps that had to be refilled periodically with oil (3.6). Today, office illumination is usually provided by fixtures that are integral with the building, and the building conducts the energizing electricity directly to the fixtures (3.7).

3.6

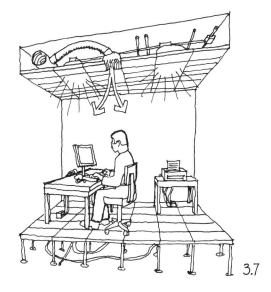

3.7

Functions of a Building

Our concept of what a building should do is much more than what would be found in a dictionary definition of shelter. Functionally, a building is what we expect it to be, and our expectations have grown very large. The list that follows attempts to include all the functional expectations we are likely to have for a building at the present time, arranged roughly in descending order according to the relative importance of each to the support of life:

1. We expect a building to provide most of the immediate necessities for human metabolism:

    A. Clean air for breathing
    B. Clean water for drinking, food preparation, cleaning, and flushing of wastes
    C. In many types of buildings, facilities for the preparation and consumption of food
    D. Removal and recycling of wastes, including excrement, wash water, food wastes, and rubbish

2. We expect a building to create the necessary conditions for human thermal comfort:

    A. Control of the mean radiant temperature
    B. Control of the air temperature

25

    c. Control of the thermal characteristics of surfaces contacted directly by the human body

    D. Control of humidity and the flow of water vapor

    E. Control of air circulation

3. We expect a building to create the necessary conditions for nonthermal sensory comfort, efficiency, and privacy:

    A. Optimal seeing conditions

    B. Visual privacy

    c. Optimal hearing conditions

    D. Acoustical privacy

4. We expect a building to control the entry and exit of living creatures of every kind, from viruses to elephants, including human beings.

5. We expect a building to distribute concentrated energy to convenient points for use in powering various lights, tools, and appliances.

6. We expect a building to provide up-to-date channels of connection and communication with the world outside: windows, telephones, mailboxes, computer networks, video cables, satellite dishes, and so on.

7. We expect a building to facilitate bodily comfort, safety, and productive activity by providing useful surfaces: floors, walls, stairs, shelves, countertops, benches, and the like.

8. We expect a building to provide stable support for the weights of all the people, belongings, and architectural devices in the building and to provide sufficient structural resistance to the physical forces of snow, wind, and earthquake.

9. We expect a building to protect its own structure, surfaces, internal mechanical and electrical systems, and other architectural devices from wetting by precipitation or other water.

10. We expect a building to adjust to its own normal movements, such as foundation settlement, thermal expansion and contraction, and movement induced by changes in moisture content of building materials, without damage to itself or its contents.

11. We expect a building to furnish reasonable protection to its occupants, its contents, and itself against damage by fire.

12. We expect a building to be built without excessive expense or difficulty.

13. We expect a building to be capable of being operated, maintained, and changed in a useful, economical manner.

This list begins with expectations that arise more or less naturally from human needs amid a hostile outdoor environment. From item 8 to the end of the list, however, the expectations are of a different sort. They arise largely from needs created by the building itself and relate only in a secondary way to human needs. A structural beam, for example, is not related in a primary way to the solution of any human need. It is a secondary device supporting a surface (a floor or roof) that is of primary importance to the users of a building. Movement and fire are problems that arise only because the building exists, but unless the building solves these problems of its own, they constitute a danger to its occupants.

The following chapters explain the ways in which buildings meet these functional expectations. They proceed in the same general order as this list, with several exceptions: All building functions having to do with movement of air are discussed together in the chapter entitled "Controlling Air Movement," and the chapter entitled "Keeping Water Out" incorporates the material on all the water-resisting functions of buildings. Various aspects of the function of controlling the entry and exit of living creatures are discussed in several of the chapters; this function is far too diverse to fit logically into a single chapter.

It is noted throughout the book that although we have complex functional expectations of our buildings and complex ways of meeting some of these expectations, most of the expectations can be met by any well-informed designer, even in very large buildings, with architectural devices as straightforward and direct as the instinctively sought, simple shelters of the natural landscape.

How Buildings Work

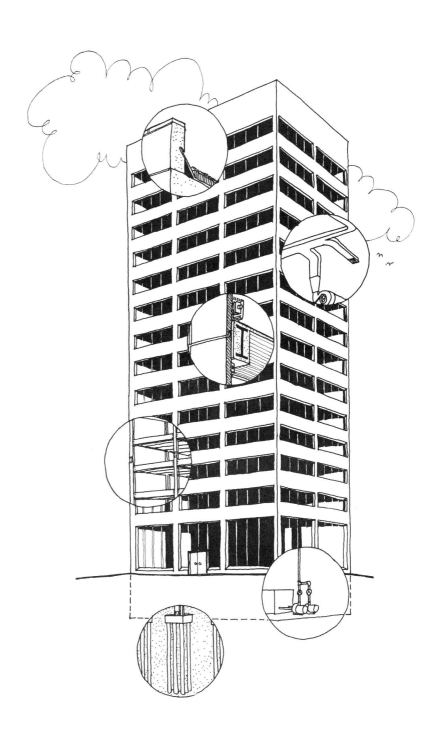

4
Building Function

In order to understand how a building works, we can dissect it and study its various elemental functions. But few building functions take place in isolation. Almost every component of a building serves more than one function, with some components commonly serving ten or more simultaneously, and these functions are heavily interdependent. For example, if we decide to build the partitions in a school building of thin sheets of gypsum wallboard over a framework of steel studs, instead of bricks and mortar, we will affect the thermal properties of the building, its acoustical qualities, the quality and quantity of light in the classrooms, how the wiring and piping are installed, the usefulness of the wall surfaces, the deadweight that the structure of the building must support, the fire resistance of the building, which trades will construct it, and how it will be maintained. Some functions of the school building will be improved by changing from brickwork to gypsum wallboard, and some will be impaired.

A building has its own ecology, a delicate internal balance of connected mechanisms that function not in isolation but as a richly interconnected whole. The accompanying diagram shows how the functions we expect of buildings are linked with one another (4.1). A designer cannot expect to change the way in which one function is served without affecting other functions. Thus our dissection runs the risk of overlooking or obscuring natural linkages among the various building functions and of giving too simplistic a view of how a building works. We will attempt to minimize these risks in the final chapter, which discusses the combination of elemental functions in common components of buildings. Until then, as we read the intervening pages, we constantly ought to be asking questions about the connectedness of things: What are *all* the functional repercussions of a very massive building? Of a light-colored or a dark-colored building? Of a sunny building? Of a building built entirely of wood?

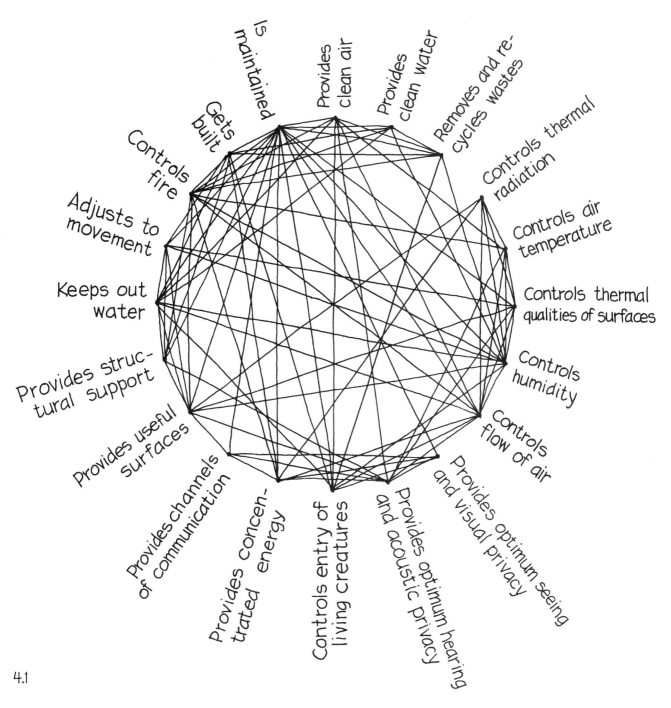

Is maintained

Provides clean air

Provides clean water

Removes and re-cycles wastes

Controls thermal radiation

Controls air temperature

Controls thermal qualities of surfaces

Controls humidity

Controls flow of air

Provides optimum seeing and visual privacy

Provides optimum hearing and acoustic privacy

Controls entry of living creatures

Provides concen-trated energy

Provides channels of communication

Provides useful surfaces

Provides struc-tural support

Keeps out water

Adjusts to movement

Controls fire

Gets built

4.1

Of a building in a windy location? What are all the ways in which we may warm a building, cool a building, or illuminate a building? These questions come naturally to mind in response to themes that recur again and again under various functional headings, and the answers, as they accumulate, begin to reveal the larger functional patterns that underlie every building.

5
Providing Water

Buildings and settlements require an adequate supply of clean water for drinking, cooking, washing, industrial processes, and agriculture. This requires a system that has three basic components: a source of water; a means to purify the water, if necessary; and a way to distribute the water to points of use inside buildings.

Sources of Water

In primitive circumstances people dip water into small containers from ponds, streams, or rivers. If the water is free of harmful substances, they simply drink it on the spot or carry it short distances before using it. If the water contains bacteria or other microorganisms, people soon learn to boil the water, which kills the microscopic life forms, and make tea or coffee to drink.

Where surface water is unavailable or salty, primitive societies usually capture rainwater from roofs of buildings or other catchment areas and collect it in subterranean cisterns, from which it is drawn in buckets or by pumps.

To obtain the purest possible water in quantities sufficient for a city, we attempt wherever possible to harness the atmospheric distillation process by collecting and impounding rainwater and snow melt. For large municipal water systems, we may take over whole mountain valleys as catchment areas and dam them to form storage reservoirs. We closely regulate the human use of the catchment areas and reservoirs in order to minimize water contamination. Large aqueduct pipes carry the water from the reservoirs to the municipality, with gravity usually furnishing the motive power.

Communities that are distant from sparsely inhabited mountains are forced either to draw water of lesser purity from rivers or to tap

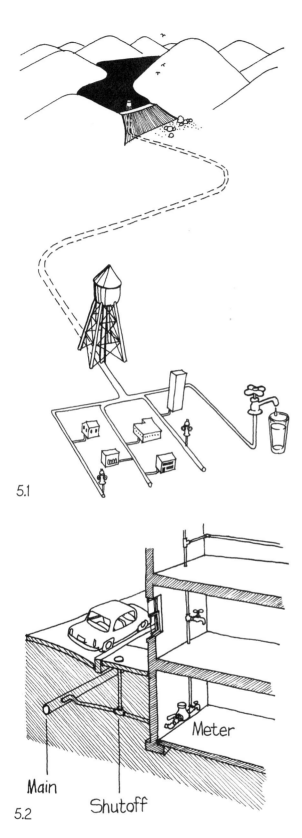

5.1

Main

Shutoff

Meter

5.2

subterranean water flows with wells. Originally, wells were dug by hand, the digger lining the deepening shaft with stones or bricks to prevent cave-ins. It was a dirty, dangerous occupation. Wells today are drilled by heavy, truck-mounted equipment that can grind its way even through solid granite to depths of hundreds of feet if necessary to find a water-bearing stratum in the earth.

Water Treatment

Well-water or water from mountain reservoirs usually requires little or no treatment to make it suitable for human consumption. River water and some waters from other sources require treatment for various contaminants. Sand filters and settling basins remove particulate matter. Aerating the water helps rid it of gaseous pollutants and accelerates the breakdown of organic substances. Chemical precipitation is used to remove such contaminants as iron and lead compounds. Special filters may be necessary to remove hydrogen sulfide, radon, or other dissolved gases. Finally, if necessary, chlorine gas is dissolved in the water in controlled amounts to kill microorganisms. Purification systems that use these mechanisms are available at scales ranging from whole regions to individual houses.

Transporting Water to the Point of Use

Water is transported to, into, and through buildings by placing it under pressure and using this pressure to drive it through cylindrical pipes. Municipal water systems are usually pressurized by gravity: Water is raised above the level of the buildings in reservoirs or water towers. For every foot (0.3 m) of height, the water's own weight exerts a pressure of about 0.43 pounds per square inch (3 kPa). If the water level in a reservoir or water tower is 100 feet above the highest point of use, the pressure at that point is 43 pounds per square inch or 300 kPa.

Water is distributed to the buildings of a city or town through a grid of pipes under the streets. Fire hydrants are connected directly to these pipes or, occasionally, to their own separate underground supply network (5.1).

Plumbing contractors or municipal crews make the connection between understreet water mains and individual buildings (5.2). They install an underground shutoff valve in the service pipe of each building, most often at the curb or sidewalk, so that the local water authority can shut off water service in case of emergency or nonpayment of water bills. The flow of water is usually metered inside the building, and charges are assessed periodically based on the amount of water used. For simplicity, the cost of water is usually calculated to cover the expenses of both water supply and sewage disposal services.

In rural areas and in many small communities, each building must develop its own supply of water. A few fortunate sites possess reliable springs from which pure water can be drawn, but on most building sites we must either catch rainfall or create a well.

Rainwater systems are still the most satisfactory water source in areas of the world where subterranean water lies too deep to tap with wells. Although a special catchment area may be constructed on an unbuilt portion of the site, it is generally more economical to use the roof of the building to collect water. By means of gutters and pipes, the water is brought to a cistern for storage, from which it can be withdrawn by pump or by hand (5.3). Depending on the weather, the size of the catchment area, and the volume of water storage provided, such a system may or may not be able to furnish sufficient quantities of water for use throughout the year. Cleanliness of the water is a constant problem, especially where leaves and bird droppings fall on the catchment area, encouraging the growth of colonies of algae and bacteria in the cistern.

A well is a hole that is dug, driven, or drilled in the ground to reach a porous, subsurface, water-bearing stratum. A well usually provides a supply of water that is more reliable, both qualitatively and quantitatively, than a rainwater system. As the well is being drilled, water is often found within just a few feet of the surface. Such water has probably seeped into the ground in the immediate neighborhood of the well and is therefore subject to contamination by nearby sewage disposal systems, including a building's own, or by barnyards or garbage dumps in the vicinity. Deep wells usually take their water from strata that are fed by surface water that falls to earth tens or hundreds of miles away. The filtering action that occurs during the long horizontal passage through the stratum results in water that is often totally free of bacteria, although it may be laden with dissolved minerals. Most such minerals do not affect the potability or usefulness of the water. Certain calcium salts, however, can cause the internal scaling and eventual obstruction of water pipes and form an insoluble scum when combined with ordinary household soap. Water rich in calcium ions is known as *hard water*. Hard water usually tastes good and deposits little scale in pipes as long as it is cold. When hard water is heated, however, it becomes much more active chemically and quickly encrusts interior surfaces of both the water heater and the hot-water pipes with rock-hard internal deposits. In buildings served with hard water, a *water softener*, which is a simple ion-exchange column, is installed on the pipe that feeds the water heater to replace the troublesome calcium ions with soluble sodium ions. Chemically softened water does not scale

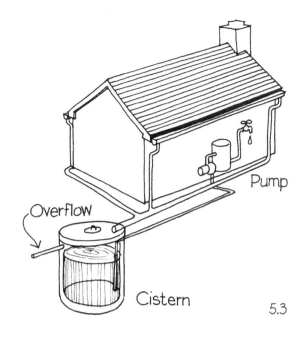

Overflow

Pump

Cistern

5.3

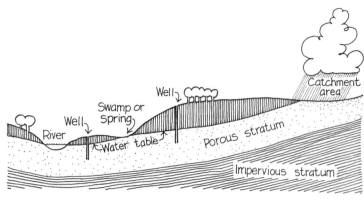

5.4

pipes, and its cleansing properties are similar to those of mineral-free rainwater.

In an ordinary well, the water level lies some distance below the surface of the ground. An *artesian well* is one that taps a stratum pressurized by a flow of water from a higher elevation. Such a stratum is often encountered, but the pressure is seldom high enough to force the water all the way out the top of the well (5.4). In either type of well, a pump must be installed to lift the water and force it through the building's distribution pipes. If the water level in the well is within about 25 feet (7 m) of the surface, a pump at ground level can create a sufficient vacuum in its intake pipe that atmospheric pressure will force the water through the pipe to the surface (5.5). If the water level lies deeper, a pressure stronger than that of the atmosphere is required, and so a pump must be lowered permanently into the bottom of the well to force the water up the pipe. The most common such pump is the *submersible pump*, which contains a sealed electric motor capable of functioning for years without maintenance at the bottom of a well. Electric wires run down the well from the surface of the ground to power the pump, often for hundreds of feet (5.6).

Water Distribution Within the Building

Water requires pressure to move it through pipes. Municipal systems, as previously noted, usually provide this pressure by pumping the water into elevated tanks. Most private water systems provide pressure by pumping the water into a small storage tank in which pressure is maintained by a volume of compressed air in the top of the tank (5.7). The pump engages automatically when the pressure falls to a predetermined minimum level and forces water into the tank until a predetermined maximum pressure is reached. Water driven by air pressure is always available from the bottom of the

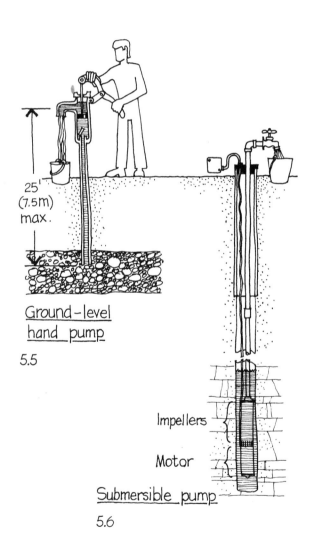

25'
(7.5m)
max.

Ground-level
hand pump

5.5

Impellers

Motor

Submersible pump

5.6

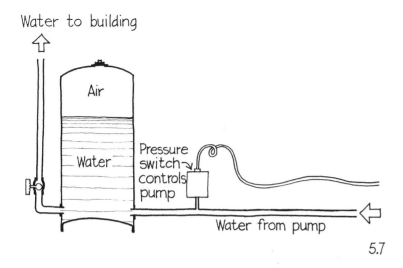

Water to building

Air

Water

Pressure switch controls pump

Water from pump

5.7

tank, whether or not the pump is operating. If filtration or chlorination is required, appropriate devices are coupled in series with the pressure tank.

Cold water is fed either from the pressure tank or from the main water service pipe from the understreet main through a network of *supply pipes* to the various outlets and fixtures inside the building (5.8). A parallel network is usually installed to carry water that has been heated in an insulated tank to make it more suitable for washing. The size of each pipe is determined by the rate at which it must transport water under conditions of maximum probable demand. Thus we find that the pipes in a supply network, treelike, tend to become progressively smaller as we trace them farther and farther away from the water source, toward the points of use. Water supply piping is generally made of copper or hard plastics, which offer smooth, low-friction interior surfaces and a high resistance to corrosion and scaling. Zinc-coated steel pipe, once very popular and lower in cost than copper, is very prone to scaling and is seldom used today. Long ago, lead was used for water-supply piping, until it was discovered that it contaminated the water with poisonous lead-based compounds.

At each fixture, a valve is placed in each supply line so either hot or cold water may be shut off to permit repair of the fixture without interrupting the flow to other parts of the building. Just above each valve, a dead-end, upright branch of pipe is provided to act as an *air chamber*. The air in the chamber cushions the shock created by the almost instantaneous deceleration to zero of the water velocity in the pipe when a faucet is shut off. If such chambers are not provided, a banging noise known as *water hammer* is heard as faucets are shut off, and momentarily high pressures are created in the pipes, causing the possibility of damage to the system.

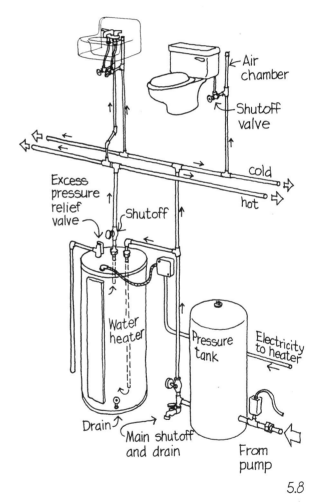

Air chamber

Shutoff valve

cold

hot

Excess pressure relief valve

Shutoff

Water heater

Pressure tank

Electricity to heater

Drain

Main shutoff and drain

From pump

5.8

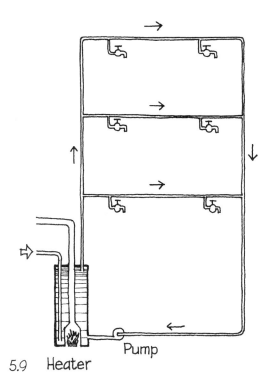

5.9 Heater

Hot water cools off rapidly as it sits in a pipe. In a small building, occupants simply run the water until the cooled water is gone and hot water emerges. Hot-water piping systems for large buildings often have such long runs of pipe from the water heater to fixtures that this strategy would be extremely wasteful of water, fuel, and occupant time. Usually in large buildings, a *return pipe* to the water heater is provided near each fixture. Water circulates up the supply pipe and back down the return pipe to the heater to be rewarmed, with the circulation force furnished by either convection or a small pump (5.9). Thus hot water is always available at each tap within one or two seconds, despite the cooling that takes place in the pipe. Another way of circumventing the problem of cooling in the pipe is not to have a central water heater but to provide smaller heaters at or near each point of use.

Chilled water for drinking was commonly provided at one time by a central chiller and a separate network of supply and return piping analogous to the hot-water system just described. In recent times, however, it has become more economical and satisfactory to chill water in small coolers at each point of use.

All water supply pipes should be thermally insulated. In the case of hot or chilled water, energy is saved and water is conserved if the water does not have to be run for a long time before it emerges from the tap at the desired temperature. Cold and chilled water pipes require insulation jacketed by a vapor retarder, to prevent condensate from forming on the pipes in humid weather.

In tall buildings, municipal water pressure is often insufficient to force water to the fixtures on the upper floors. Here, pumps must be installed in the building to transport the water to the upper reaches of the building. In some cases, these pumps feed the fixtures directly. In other cases, the pumps lift the water to one or more tanks at higher levels of the building, from which it is fed by gravity to pipe networks in the floor below (5.10).

Plumbing Fixtures

Lavatories, sinks, and bathtubs are designed to catch and hold water for washing and to drain it away after use. For cleanliness and durability, they must be made of hard, smooth materials such as porcelain or stainless steel, which can withstand repeated scrubbing over a period of many years.

Toilets (properly called *water closets*) and urinals are designed to flush away body wastes. They are made of glazed porcelain, an extremely smooth, hard material, to ensure that they will not accumulate bacteria-harboring scratches as they are being cleaned. Where supply piping is kept economically small, as in houses, it is incapable of providing directly the quick, copious rush of water

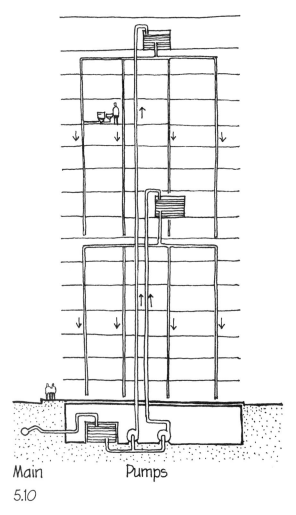

Main   Pumps

5.10

necessary to operate the siphon trap of the fixture, so water is slowly accumulated for each flush in a tank at the back of the fixture. In public buildings, flushing is so frequent that slow-filling tanks are unequal to the demand, and thus larger water supply pipes must be installed to flush the water closets directly. Special valves regulate the strength and duration of each flush.

Avoiding Cross-Connections

Water pressure in supply pipes sometimes fails. It may do so because the water main or pump has been shut down for servicing, because a vehicle has broken off a fire hydrant, or because of the extreme demands for water of fire engines as they fight a major building fire. When such failures occur, the water that is in the pipes and mains drains back away from the building, creating a suction in the pipes. If someone has left a hose running with its nozzle at the bottom of a container, or if the water inlet to a fixture or swimming pool is below the level of the water held in the fixture or pool, the held water will be drawn back into the supply pipes. Such a connection between the supply piping and a source of potentially contaminated water is known as a *cross-connection*. Cross-connections are hazardous because they can result in the ingestion of contaminated water by large numbers of people.

Most plumbing fixtures are designed in such a way that the level of the open water held by the fixture—the wash water in a bathroom sink, for example, or the water in the tank or bowl of a water closet—cannot possibly reach the level of the opening that supplies fresh water to the fixture. A bathroom sink has an overflow port that drains off excess water before it can reach the end of the faucet. The bowl of a tank-type water closet may clog and fill up to its rim, but the water inlet from the building's supply network is safely above both the rim of the bowl and the water level of the tank. These fixtures are incapable of causing cross-connections. But some fixtures cannot be designed in this way. A water closet or urinal in a public building has a supply pipe connected directly to its rim. The end of a hose connected to an outdoor faucet can be left in a swimming pool or a garbage can filled with water. In each fixture where such a cross-connection is possible, a *vacuum breaker* must be installed in the supply line (5.11). Whenever the water pressure fails, the vacuum breaker allows air to enter the line and destroy the siphoning action, thus preventing contaminated water from being sucked into the system. The familiar chrome-plated flush valve on every public toilet fixture contains a vacuum breaker, and appropriate vacuum breakers are manufactured for outdoor faucets, swimming-pool piping, irrigation piping, and other fixtures as well.

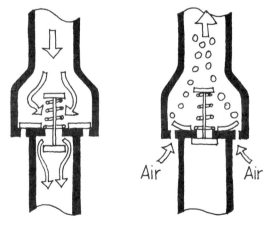

Normal Flow   Reverse Flow
Principle of the Vacuum Breaker
5.11

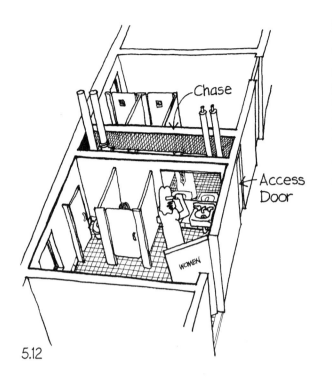

5.12

Providing Space for Water Pipes

Water supply piping occupies space. Small wood-frame buildings often have enough space inside floors and walls to accommodate it. But the walls of buildings with large numbers of fixtures cannot hold all the pipes, and so special *pipe chases*, both vertical and horizontal, must be provided as a part of the building's basic design. Such chases are often built with access doors to allow occasional change and maintenance of the pipes without disrupting the fabric of the building (5.12).

In cold climates, water supply pipes must be kept from freezing to protect them from bursting due to the expansion of water as it turns to ice. Water mains and service pipes are buried below the level to which the soil freezes in winter. Neither plumbing chases nor walls containing water piping should be located at the outside perimeter of a building, because in such locations they may be subjected to subfreezing temperatures. If exterior wall locations are inevitable, care must be taken to place all the thermal insulation in the wall outside of the piping. This ensures that the piping will never be more than a few degrees colder than the air inside the building. Merely insulating the pipes themselves will not keep them from freezing if water stands still in the pipes for an extended time. This is because the surface area of the pipes is very large with respect to the volume of water that they contain. The water in the pipes cools rapidly just because of the huge exposed surface area, even if all the surfaces are covered with insulation.

Bottled Water vs. Tap Water

Most municipal water and well-water from private systems in North America are sufficiently pure for drinking and taste good. Nevertheless, in a major triumph of advertising over truth, many people have been persuaded that they should drink only commercially bottled spring water that is sold at prices that are often higher than those of soft drinks or dairy products. Never mind that some of it is shipped halfway around the world and that it is put up in woefully small containers that constitute an unconscionable waste of material and fuel: bottled water, especially if it comes from a foreign source in an exotic bottle, is stylish and makes its consumers feel good, even though in most cases it is no better in taste and purity than tap water.

Further Reading

Benjamin Stein and John Reynolds. *Mechanical and Electrical Equipment for Buildings* (9th ed.). New York, Wiley, 2000, pp. 531–667.

6
Recycling Wastes

Nature works in closed cycles. What is waste to one organism is food to another, in an endless, intricately interwoven web that ultimately wastes nothing at all except small amounts of renewable energy from the sun. In the wild, an army of insects and microorganisms feed on the excrement and corpses of higher animals, reducing these wastes to soil nutrients that can be utilized by plants. Dead vegetable matter of all types is similarly attacked, broken down, and used again as plant food. In the soil, in the water, and in the air, processes take place continually to ensure that none of Nature's valuable substances is ever left in an unproductive state.

In many agrarian societies, farm families participate actively in these cycles. They mix their animal and vegetable wastes together in piles or bins and *compost* them by allowing earthworms and a host of bacteria to convert them to rich soil. In the soil, energized by sunlight and watered by rainfall, plants grow to feed the family and its animals and to furnish fuel for cooking and heating. The animals provide both food and clothing. The ashes from the spent fuel and the excrement of the animals go back into the soil, replenishing its nutrient content. The land's fertility decreases little over the family's lifetime, if at all.

Even some small, primitive towns are capable of sustaining this sort of relationship to the land. Food scraps and human excrement are carefully gathered and transported by "night soil" collectors to the outskirts of town, where farmers mix them with vegetable wastes and allow them to compost. Then they add the compost to the soil to help it produce food (6.1). If adequate composting practices are employed, the wastes are free of harmful organisms by the time they reach the soil, and diseases will not be communicated through the cycle. Both the health of the community and the richness of its agriculture are maintained.

6.1

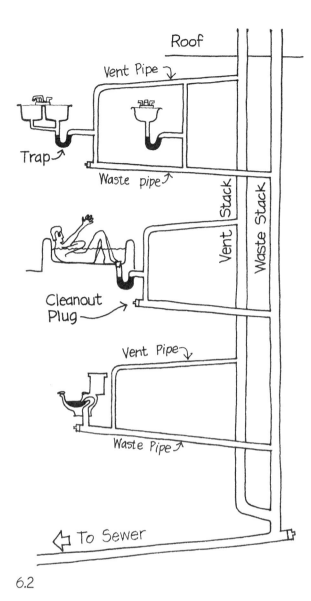

Roof

Vent Pipe

Trap

Waste pipe

Vent Stack

Waste Stack

Cleanout Plug

Vent Pipe

Waste Pipe

To Sewer

6.2

Unfortunately, it is difficult to ensure that adequate composting practices are always employed, and careless handling of night soil has caused disastrous epidemics and plagues throughout history. Most cities do not compost their wastes because most are not fed in any large degree by the farms in the immediate vicinity; their wastes would have to be transported considerable distances for agrarian recycling. Thus we have broken the natural chain of recycling. We expend half our urban water consumption in flushing garbage and excrement from our buildings and then mix this half with the half we have used for washing and other purposes. This is marvelously convenient and keeps our buildings free of disease and odor, but it creates new problems. The water that the municipality just brought to the town at such trouble and expense, sparkling clean and bacteria free, is now *sewage*. It is thoroughly contaminated with odor and potential disease and presents an enormous disposal problem.

Sewage Systems in Buildings

As a part of its own metabolic process, a building must give off its liquid wastes. It is worthwhile to examine both how this is currently done and how buildings might contribute to a more sound system of waste recycling.

Liquid wastes are conducted from sinks, lavatories, tubs, showers, water closets, urinals, and floor drains through a network of *waste pipes* that is drained by gravity (6.2). In order to maintain gravity flow, relatively large-diameter pipes are necessary as compared with the small diameters that are used for pressurized water supply pipes. All waste pipes must run consistently downhill. Normal atmospheric air pressure must be maintained in all sections of the network at all times to avoid the accumulation of higher pressures in some parts of the network that might block flow. Furthermore, because the waste piping handles suspended solid wastes of various kinds, it is prone to clogging, and so access to the pipes must be provided at frequent intervals to allow for cleaning.

A fixture such as a lavatory, sink, or tub empties into the waste piping network through a *trap*, a U-shaped piece of pipe that retains enough water to act as a seal that prevents the odors and gases of decomposition from the waste piping from passing back through the fixture and into the building (6.3). The water seal in the trap can be broken, however, if waste water from the fixture siphons through the trap or if gas pressure or air pressure builds up in the piping. For this reason, a *vent pipe* is attached to the waste piping a short distance downstream from each trap. The vent allows air to enter the waste pipe to break any potential siphoning action, and it releases to the atmosphere any decomposition gases such as methane or hydrogen

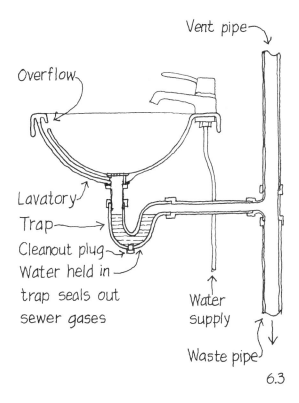

Vent pipe

Overflow

Lavatory

Trap

Cleanout plug

Water held in
trap seals out
sewer gases

Water
supply

Waste pipe

6.3

sulfide. Thus a complete network of waste piping for a building includes two treelike configurations, one that collects the sewage and leads it downward and another, upside down, that allows air to enter the first tree at the tips of its branches. The piping in each tree grows steadily larger from fixture to outlet, to serve the greater number of fixtures at each stage.

The contemporary water closet is simply a large trap that is forced to siphon rapidly during the flushing process so as to transport solid wastes. After flushing, the bowl refills automatically with fresh water to maintain its seal against the entry of sewer gases (6.4). Like any other trap, it must be vented nearby, to prevent accidental siphoning between flushes.

Most new water closets are designed to use less than half as much water per flush as do older water closets. Many areas of the United States permit only this type of toilet in new installations. There are even more water-efficient options available, however: A toilet with a mechanical seal rather than a water trap uses only about 5 percent of the ordinary amount, and a toilet using recirculating chemicals is even more efficient than this. Several types generate no sewage at all. One such type incinerates the excrement with a gas flame or electric element after each use, leaving only a bit of clean ash. Another type is a much-improved version of the traditional out-house, ventilated in such a way that it can be maintained odor

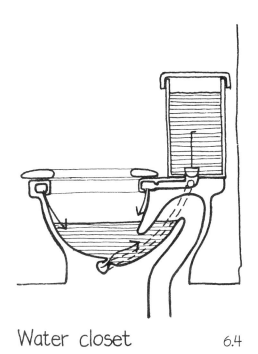

Water closet   6.4

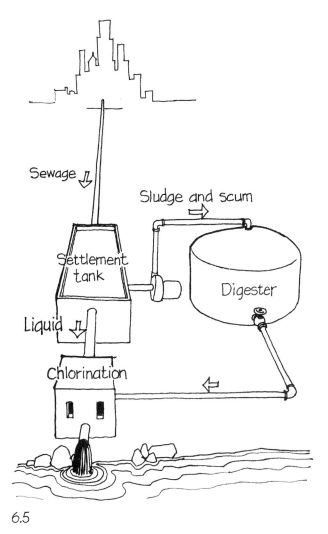

Sewage

Sludge and scum

Settlement
tank

Digester

Liquid

Chlorination

6.5

free inside the house and configured internally so it continuously reduces both excrement and kitchen garbage to a small volume of disease-free garden compost. Such a device may offer one small-scale way of mending a part of the break in the nutrient chain.

Municipal Sewage Disposal

Some towns (as did nearly all not so long ago) do nothing to treat their sewage. They simply discharge it, bacteria and all, into a nearby river, lake, or ocean. But most towns nowadays carry out at least *primary treatment* of their sewage in a sewage treatment plant. They hold the sewage for a time in tanks where the solid material, the *sludge*, settles to the bottom. The liquid in the top of the tank is chlorinated to kill bacteria and then dumped into a local waterway. The sludge is pumped into another tank where it is allowed to ferment anaerobically for several weeks. This fermentation kills most of the disease-causing bacteria in the sludge and precipitates out most of the minerals it contains. Then this "digested" sludge is also chlorinated and pumped into a waterway (6.5).

Through this process, soil nutrients—brought into the city as fruits, vegetables, grains, milk products, and meats and flushed out of the city as sewage—are now deposited not back into the soil, but into waterways. Unlike the soil, which needs the nutrients and is capable through natural processes of finishing their reconversion into food, the waterways cannot complete the cycle. Instead, the increased nutrient content of the water accelerates the growth of waterweeds and algae. Soon the water is choked with plant growth so dense that sunlight can no longer penetrate more than a few inches into the water. Masses of plants die and decay. The decay process consumes much of the oxygen dissolved in the water. Fish suffocate in the oxygen-poor environment, and the waterway itself begins to die. Over a few decades it fills with dead plants and eventually becomes a swamp and then a meadow. By that time, of course, no one remembers that people once swam, boated, and fished there. In the meantime, food-producing farmland is gradually drained of its nutrients. Farm productivity falls, and such plants as are grown there may lack essential human nutrients. Artificial fertilizers must then be applied to the soil to replace the wasted natural fertilizers that are destroying lakes and rivers instead of replenishing the soil.

Many municipal sewage treatment plants are improving the efficacy of their treatment processes, using aerobic digestion and various sorts of chemical treatment and filtration to produce, in some cases, an effluent that is suitable for drinking. In some cities, clean effluent is pumped into the ground to replenish depleted water-bearing strata. In most cases, the nutrients still end up in a river or ocean. A few cities have taken steps to try to recover and use the nutrients. Some dry the processed sludge, bag it, and sell it as agricultural fertilizer. Unfortunately, most sewage contains poisons that are unaffected by treatment processes: heavy metals such as cadmium and mercury, along with various organic compounds. These have raised serious questions about the advisability of utilizing sludge as fertilizer. Other cities subject the effluent from their sewage treatment plants to *bioremediation*, passing it through ponds in which selected aquatic plants feed on the nutrients and absorb heavy metals and other poisons. In some locations, processed sewage is used to fertilize forests.

On-site Sewage Disposal Systems

Buildings that lie beyond the reach of metropolitan sewers must treat and dispose of their own sewage. This was formerly accomplished through the use of a *cesspool*, a porous underground container of stone or brick that allowed the sewage to seep into the surrounding soil. The cesspool was unsatisfactory, however, in that it did nothing to remove disease-causing organisms from the sewage, and it clogged the surrounding soil with solids in a relatively short period of time, after which it was likely to overflow onto the surface of the ground and cause sewage to back up into fixtures inside the building. Its much more satisfactory successor is the nonporous *septic tank* (6.6). The septic tank is configured in such a way that it holds sewage for a period of days, allowing it to decompose anaerobically and to separate into a clear, relatively harmless liquid effluent and a small amount of solid mineral matter, which settles to the bottom. The effluent runs out of the tank and into a *leaching field*, a system of porous pipes or porous tanks, from which it is allowed to seep into the soil (6.7). The sludge from the bottom of the tank must be pumped out every few years, to be hauled away and processed into harmlessness at a remote treatment plant.

A septic tank and leaching field may malfunction and contaminate the water or soil. This can happen for any of several reasons: Perhaps the septic tank is too small for the building it serves. Perhaps the soil in the leaching field is not sufficiently porous or the system is installed too near a well, a body of water, or a steep slope. To guard against such failures, most municipalities and states have stringent regulations requiring soil testing and the utilization of approved techniques of design and construction in the installation of septic systems. It is not uncommon for a potential building site to prove incapable of accommodating a septic system and therefore to be incapable of supporting a building. This can happen if the soil is too impervious to water, the site is too small to contain a sufficient size

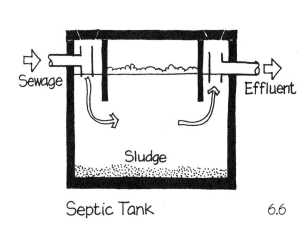

Septic Tank   6.6

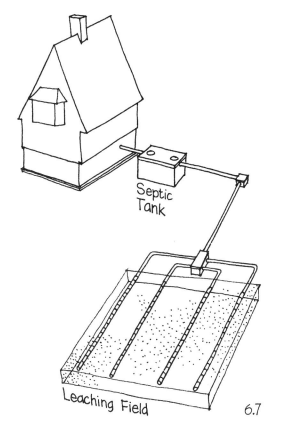

Leaching Field   6.7

of leaching field, or the water in the ground is at so high a level that it would mingle with the effluent and become contaminated.

In an effort to improve small sewage disposal systems, new devices are being introduced into the market each year. Some aim to improve the digestion of sewage in the tank through such expedients as aerating the sewage to encourage the more thorough digestive action of aerobic organisms. Others attempt to improve the leaching process by distributing the effluent more evenly throughout the field or by allowing access to the leaching surfaces for inspection and cleaning.

As water becomes a more precious resource, we are seeing more buildings with systems for separating discarded wash water from toilet wastes. After a minimum of filtration within the building, wash water can serve such secondary uses as the flushing of toilets or the watering of lawns and gardens. Much of the heat from warm waste water could be recovered through a heat exchanger to preheat fresh water before it enters the water heater or to contribute to the comfort heating of the building.

Anaerobic digestion of excrement and vegetable wastes produces methane gas, potentially valuable as a fuel, as a natural by-product. Such insignificant quantities of methane are developed from domestic sewage that it is not worthwhile to build a gas-generating apparatus for home use, but for large-scale farmers and operators of large sewage treatment plants, the possibilities are much greater. Many municipal treatment plants are at present heated, illuminated, and powered by methane gas from their digesters, and some farmers have their own methane-generation systems.

Solid Waste Disposal

Our society also produces enormous quantities of solid wastes, which create different sorts of problems. Paper, plastics, glass, and metals enter our buildings, bearing information and containing goods of various sorts. These substances are soon discarded, along with ashes and cinders, dust and dirt, broken or worn appliances, kitchen garbage, old clothing, industrial by-products, spent batteries, used motor oil, and radioactive and chemical wastes from laboratories and industries (6.8). Hundreds of pounds per person per year of these solid wastes are produced in the United States. Nearly all this material represents either potential links in biological recycling chains (such as food scraps or paper) or finite quantities of nonrenewable resources (such as metals and plastics). Many of the waste substances contain useful energy, and many can be recovered and reused, but the separation and recycling of this mingled refuse is a huge, almost impossible task. Many cities simply burn the mass and bury the ashes in a landfill or bury the mass without burning

6.8

it. The buried organic materials decompose in the soil, giving off substantial quantities of combustible gases such as methane and ammonia. Glass, metals, and plastics simply sit in the soil, wasted.

Most cities in the United States have run out of suitable landfill sites, and legal restrictions have made landfill an increasingly unattractive way of disposing of solid waste in any case. The wastes are taken instead to large incineration plants where they are burned. This vastly reduces the volume of waste to be buried. The plants must be carefully designed, constructed, and operated so that they do not contribute to air pollution. Abandoned landfill sites, most of them having become small mountains, are capped with a thick layer of soil. Vent pipes are installed to allow gases of decomposition to escape. In some cases, useful quantities of combustible gas are collected by a network of pipes and used for heating of municipal buildings. The sites are often turned into parks or golf courses.

An increasing number of municipalities operate recycling programs to recover waste materials such as paper, cardboard, glass, and plastics that can be reprocessed into new products. These programs generally depend on building owners to sort the recyclable materials and segregate them from nonrecyclable wastes, thus avoiding the need for complicated central sorting plants. This means, however, that each house or building needs separate, clearly labeled storage containers for garbage, clean paper, steel, aluminum, glass, and various types of plastics. The solid waste disposal system of the building can no longer be a garbage can or two in a leftover corner but, rather, must be carefully planned and constructed for its purpose. Such programs often result in a reduction of half to two-thirds in the volume of solid waste that must be incinerated. They also save substantial quantities of energy and materials that would otherwise be lost. Some cities utilize the heat of combustion of their rubbish to fuel electric power plants or central heating installations. Others have systems for the automatic reclamation of valuable constituents of rubbish, through either mechanized sorting or pyrolysis. Some cities are even able to extract useful quantities of methane from their old garbage dumps by drilling wells to tap underground pockets of decomposition gases.

Garbage and trash are most commonly collected by hand within buildings, to be transported to containers where they are left for periodic removal by municipal or private trucks. Some buildings have incinerator systems, in which wastes are jettisoned down a chute, to be consumed by a gas- or oil-fueled fire at the bottom. Only the ashes need then be carried away, but the air pollution generated by incomplete combustion in faulty incinerators has caused their use to be strictly regulated in many areas. Garbage grinders macerate and flush food scraps into the sewage system, but the sewage disposal installation, whether municipal or private, must be sufficiently large to handle this additional burden of water and solid material. In some buildings, the laborious manual transport of solid wastes has been largely eliminated through the installation of systems of very large vacuum pipes that suck all the wastes to a central location for incineration or for compression into bales for easier trucking.

Further Reading

Benjamin Stein and John Reynolds. *Mechanical and Electrical Equipment for Buildings* (9th ed.). New York, Wiley, 2000, pp. 669–745.

7
Providing for Thermal Comfort

In chapter 2, we discussed the ingenious physiological mechanisms the human body employs to achieve thermal equilibrium. However, these mechanisms can't cope with the extreme range of temperatures in which we live. To achieve thermal comfort, we must rely on clothing and buildings.

Clothing and buildings are similar in that both use passive devices to control natural flows of heat, air, and moisture vapor for the increased comfort of the wearer or occupant (7.1). They differ in two important respects: First, buildings enclose a volume many times as large as that contained by clothing, in order to house not only the bodies of the occupants but also all the space occupied and traversed in the course of their activities. Second, buildings are usually equipped to take an active as well as a passive role in creating thermal comfort, through the controlled release of energy to create a more favorable indoor climate.

We often characterize the active thermal comfort control systems in buildings as "heating" systems or "cooling" systems. Except in rare cases, however, a "heating" system does not create an overall net flow of heat into the human body but merely adjusts the thermal characteristics of the indoor environment to reduce the rate of heat loss from the body to a comfortable level. A "cooling" or "air-conditioning" system increases the rate of the body's heat loss in hot weather. Though for the sake of convenience, we will continue to talk of heating and cooling systems in buildings, as a matter of strict accuracy it should be remembered that *both* heating and cooling systems are designed to control the rate at which the body is cooled.

The accompanying chart (7.2) shows the alternative means normally available for the voluntary regulation of human thermal comfort. It is divided horizontally into two major sections, one

7.1

49

		Physical Activity	Clothing	Radiation	Air Temperature	Humidity	Air Movement	Surface Contact
Means for cooling the body more rapidly	Passive	• Extend body to maximize surface area	• Open or remove layers of clothing • Saturate clothing with water	• Shade body from warm object • Expose body to cooler object	• Keep sun from heating occupied space • Use thermal mass to cool air • Evaporate H_2O to cool air	• Dehumidify air by condensing water onto cool building surfaces	• Allow wind or convection currents to move past body	• Put body against cool, dense surface • Keep body off warm or insulating surfaces
	Active	• Reduce level of muscular activity	• Liquid-cooled space suit	• Mechanically cool building surfaces	• Mechanically refrigerate air	• Mechanical dehumidification	• Use fan to move air	• Take a cool bath or swim • Ingest cool food or drink • Mechanically cool floors and/or seats
Means for cooling the body less rapidly	Passive	• Contract body to minimize surface area	• Close or put on layers of clothing • Dry out wet clothing	• Expose body to warm object • Reflect back body heat with metallic surface	• Allow sun to heat occupied space • Use thermal mass to release stored heat into air	• Allow sun to evaporate water into air	• Shelter body from wind	• Put body against warm or insulating surfaces
	Active	• Raise level of muscular activity • Snuggle with a friend	• Electric blanket • Electric stockings	• Mechanically warm building surfaces • Build fire	• Heat the air	• Boil water into air	• Reduce fan speed	• Hot bath • Hot water bottle or hot brick • Heat floors and/or seats • Ingest hot food or drink

Voluntary Means for Regulating Thermal Comfort
7.2

7.3

containing means for cooling the body *more* rapidly and the other for cooling the body *less* rapidly. Each major section of the chart is again divided into two horizontal subsections, one for *passive* means, those that do not require the artificial release of energy, and one for *active* means, those that do.

The first two vertical columns indicate the roles of physical activity and clothing. The remaining columns list means of regulating thermal comfort that may be employed in or around buildings, most often by the buildings themselves. These means will be explained more fully in the following four chapters, but note that five separate factors—thermal radiation, air temperature, humidity, air movement, and the thermal properties of surfaces contacted by the body—are involved in creating thermal comfort (7.3).

In a building, these five factors are heavily interdependent. When a floor surface is warmed by the sun, it warms the air above itself, radiates heat to the human body, and conducts heat to the human foot that contacts it (7.4). The warmed air rises above the surrounding air, creating a convective circulation, and the air's relative humidity is reduced as its temperature is raised. Thus a single occurrence—the warming of a floor by a shaft of sunlight—can affect all the factors bearing on thermal comfort. Similarly, an ordinary warm-air heating system heats the air, reduces its relative humidity, blows it past the occupants of a room, and warms the surfaces of the room by sweeping them with warm air. It is impossible to change any one factor without affecting the others in some degree.

Besides this interdependence, there is also considerable interchangeability among these means of thermal comfort regulation. As can be seen in the chart, two sorts of interchangeability are possible: One is between the *columns* in the chart. We can be quite comfortable in a room in which the air temperature is relatively low, for example, if there is a crackling fire radiating generous amounts of heat from the fireplace to the skin (7.5). Summer air temperatures in the high eighties (30°C–32°C) will seem ideal if the humidity is low, a moderate breeze is blowing, only light clothing is worn, and one is shielded from direct sunlight (7.6). There are limits to this sort of interchangeability, but within a rather wide latitude, one parameter may be adjusted to compensate for another without causing discomfort.

A second sort of interchangeability is between horizontal *rows* in the chart, between active and passive means of varying the same parameter of thermal comfort. A breeze passing through a room can substitute for an electric fan (7.7). A thick rug over a concrete floor may eliminate the need to warm the floor with circulating hot water (7.8). When passive means can be used in place of active ones, fuel consumption in the building is reduced. Long-term cost savings are likely, depending on the relative costs of installing and maintaining the passive and active devices.

People vary a good deal with respect to such important thermal factors as metabolic rate, tendency to perspire, amount of insulating fat beneath the skin, ratio of skin surface area to body volume, and

7.4

7.5

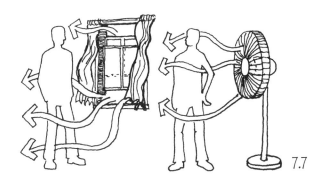

7.7

7.6

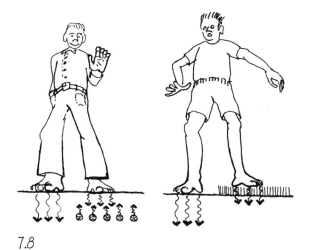

7.8

amount of clothing worn. Additionally, the same person in the same clothing has different thermal requirements at different times of day, as when exercising more vigorously, digesting a heavy meal, or sleeping. As a result of all these variables, each person in a room is likely to have a slightly different opinion about what set of thermal conditions feels most comfortable. In general, the best that can be done is to seek those conditions that satisfy the greatest number of people and to allow the rest to adjust their clothing in order to compensate. In some circumstances in which people remain in one place for an extended period, as on an airplane, in a theater, or in an office or workshop, it is possible to give each person control over at least one thermal factor, by such means as individual air vents, small operable windows, or small electric heaters. In other circumstances, especially in dwellings, one has freedom to move a little farther from the fire, or to sit in a sunny window while others sit in the shade farther back in the room. If the designer of a building takes care to provide such opportunities for individual adjustment, there can be many of them.

Further Reading

Victor Olgyay. *Design with Climate*. Princeton, N.J., Princeton University Press, 1973, pp. 14–23.

8

Thermal Properties of Building Components

Each material used in building construction has its own unique set of physical properties relative to the flow of heat. An important part of a designer's job is to select and combine building materials in such a way as to result in a building whose enclosure performs as much of the building's climate-control function as possible, leaving as little work as possible to be done by energy-consuming heating and cooling systems.

We must distinguish clearly among the three basic mechanisms of heat transfer. *Radiation* is a transfer of heat by means of electromagnetic waves that pass through space or air from a warmer object to a cooler one (8.1). The skin is warmed by radiation when one stands in the sun or near a fire and is cooled by radiation when one stands near a cold wall or under a clear night sky. *Conduction* is a flow of heat through solid material (8.2). Heat is conducted to or from the skin when the skin is pressed against a warmer or cooler object, such as a hot potato or an ice cube. *Convection* is a transfer of heat by means of a moving stream of air or water that is heated by a warmer object and then gives up heat to a cooler one (8.3). The skin is warmed or cooled convectively by exposure to warm or cool air. A common kitchen stove employs all three mechanisms of heat transfer: the broiler warms food primarily by radiation, the oven primarily by convection, and the burners primarily by conduction through the metal of the pan.

Radiation

All objects give off heat in the form of electromagnetic radiation, and all receive heat by radiation from surrounding objects. A source at a very high temperature, such as the sun, radiates much of its heat

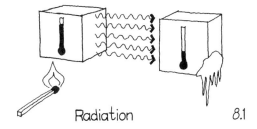
Radiation   8.1

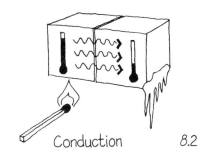
Conduction   8.2

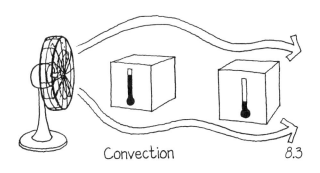
Convection   8.3

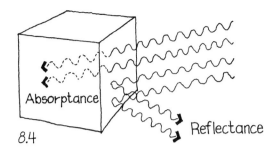

Absorptance

Reflectance

8.4

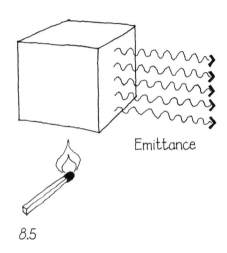

Emittance

8.5

	Solar Radiation		Terrestrial Radiation	
	Absorp. Emitt.	Reflect.	Absorp. Emitt.	Reflect.
Bright aluminum	0.05	0.95	0.05	0.95
Galvanized steel	0.25	0.75	0.25	0.75
White paint	0.20	0.80	0.90	0.10
Fresh whitewash	0.12	0.88	0.90	0.10
Lt. green paint	0.40	0.60	0.90	0.10
Dk. green paint	0.70	0.30	0.90	0.10
Black paint	0.85	0.15	0.90	0.10
Concrete	0.60	0.40	0.90	0.10

8.6

as visible light. Warm sources on the earth are not nearly as hot as the sun and radiate mainly in the infrared range. Infrared (pronounced *infra-red*, meaning "beyond red") rays are an invisible part of the light spectrum and behave exactly like visible light. Any two objects that can "see" each other through a medium that is transparent to light, such as air or a vacuum, exchange radiant energy. When line-of-sight contact between the two objects is blocked, as by the insertion anyplace between them of an opaque object such as a sheet of paper, the exchange stops instantly. This is what happens when you step into the shade of a tree on a sunny day.

The net rate of heat exchange by radiation between two objects is proportional to the difference between the fourth powers of their absolute temperatures. Thus two objects at the same temperature have no net exchange of heat. If one object is a few degrees warmer, there will be a relatively small flow of heat from the warmer object to the cooler one. As the difference in temperature between the two objects grows, the radiant flow grows at an increasingly rapid rate.

The radiative properties of building materials—the ways in which they affect thermal radiation that impinges on them—are of extreme importance to designers. *Reflectance* is the proportion of incoming radiation that bounces off a material, leaving the temperature of the material unchanged. *Absorptance* is the proportion that enters a material and thereby raises its temperature (8.4). The sum of reflectance and absorptance for a given material is always one. *Emittance* is a measure of a material's ability to radiate heat outward to other objects. At any given wavelength emittance is numerically identical to absorptance (8.5).

The range of electromagnetic wavelengths is quite large, and we find that buildings must commonly deal with thermal radiation in two distinctly different parts of the spectrum. Solar radiation, emitted by a source at a temperature of many thousands of degrees, is composed of relatively short wavelengths. Thermal radiation from most terrestrial sources—sun-warmed earth or floors, warm building surfaces, human skin—is emitted at much lower temperatures and therefore at much longer wavelengths. Most common building materials react quite differently to these two ranges of wavelengths, and these differences account for several interesting thermal phenomena. From the accompanying chart (8.6), we note, for example, that a building painted white reflects about 80 percent of the sun's direct thermal radiation. However, it reflects only about 10 percent of the thermal radiation from surrounding sun-heated lawns and pavement, almost the same as if it were painted black. If the building had a bright metallic exterior, it would be much better protected against this terrestrial reradiation of solar heat. It would also radiate less heat to the outdoors in winter than if it were painted white. This low emittance of polished metals at long wavelengths is of particular use in building construction, because it allows us to use bright metal foils as thermal insulators in walls or roofs, provided that we install them adjacent to an airspace. A material can emit or reflect radiation only through a gas that is transparent to the wavelengths of the radiation or through a vacuum. If a metal foil is sandwiched snugly between other layers of construction, it cannot reflect radiation but can only conduct heat directly. Because metal foils are excellent conductors of heat, it follows that they are valuable as insulation only when they have an adjacent airspace on one side or the other, or preferably both.

Conduction

The resistance of a material to the conduction of heat is a measure of its insulating value. The rate at which a building gains or loses heat through any portion of its enclosure under stable indoor and outdoor temperatures is directly proportional to the difference in air temperature between the inside and the outside of the enclosure and inversely proportional to the overall *thermal resistance* of that portion of its enclosure. In general, we try to build walls, roofs, and floors so that they have maximum possible thermal resistance, both for bodily comfort and for conservation of energy. Solid materials have varying resistances (8.7). Metals have very low resistance (which is the same as saying that they are good conductors of heat, or poor thermal insulators), whereas masonry materials have moderately low resistance, and wood has moderately high resistance. Roughly speaking, the thermal resistances of materials are inversely proportional to their densities.

The best resistor of heat flow that is commonly available for use in buildings is air, provided that it can be kept from moving. If we trap the air layer within the hollow wall of an ordinary wood-frame house in a loose tangle of glass or mineral fibers which prevent it from circulating, it will have a very high thermal resistance. The fibers, spun from a dense material, are themselves rather poor resistors to heat flow. Their function is simply to create so much resistance to circulation of the air they have trapped that the air remains still and acts as a good insulator. If the same air is allowed to circulate freely within the wall, it will set up a pattern of convective flow that transfers heat from the warmer surface to the cooler one with surprising efficiency (8.8).

Because window glass has a notoriously low resistance to the flow of heat, most windows are made with *double* or *triple glazing*, in which air is trapped in thin layers between sheets of glass. The visual qualities of the glass are not noticeably different from those of a

Thermal Resistances, R

	$\frac{ft^2 hr\,°F}{BTU}$	$\frac{m^2\,°C}{W}$
1" (25 mm) aluminum	0.0007	0.00012
1" (25 mm) pine	1.25	0.23
4" (100 mm) brick	0.80	0.14
8" (200 mm) concrete	0.88	0.16
3½" (90 mm) glass fiber batt	10.9	1.96
6" (150 mm) glass fiber batt	18.8	3.38
1" (25 mm) polystyrene foam	4.2	0.76
1" (25 mm) polyurethane foam	5.9	1.06
Single glass	0.9	0.16
Double glass	1.8	0.32
Triple glass	2.8	0.50
Well-insulated wall	15.0–19.0	2.7–3.4

8.7

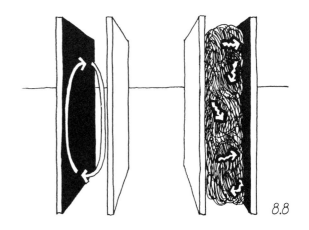

8.8

55

single sheet of glass, but the thermal resistance is greatly increased, though not to a value approaching that of a well-insulated wall. In an effort to increase the resistance of double glazing, manufacturers have tried progressively increasing the thickness of the air layer between the panes. What they have discovered is that thermal resistance increases slightly as the layer is thickened to an inch or so and then fails to increase further as the dimension is further increased. What happens is that when the airspace is very thin, friction between the glass surfaces and the trapped air prevents much of the convective flow that would readily transfer heat from one pane to the other, but the very thinness of the air layer prevents it from having a very high resistance. When the air layer is very thick, it could in theory provide a great deal of resistance, except that the air is given enough space to circulate with relative ease. A maximum overall resistance can therefore be achieved with an air layer of intermediate thickness (8.9). Resistance can be increased somewhat by substituting a gas of lower thermal capacity for the air between the panes or by introducing tangled glass fibers into the airspace. Glass fibers affect the optical quality of the window, however, and so cannot be used where a view is desired. They also reduce the amount of light transmitted, forcing the designer to select an optimum compromise between thermal resistance and light transmission.

The resistance of an open airspace is also affected by the emittances of the surfaces on either side. Much of the heat that travels across an airspace is radiated directly from one surface to the other, independently of the convective transfer of the air itself. Thus a layer of bright, nonoxidizing metal foil, usually aluminum, within or on either side of the airspace, can eliminate most of the radiative transfer. In double glazing, thin metallic coatings can be deposited on the surfaces of the glass facing the airspace, to reduce the emittance of the glass. These *low emissivity (low-e) coatings* thereby reduce the conductivity of the entire assembly. Double glazing with a low-e coating is as effective in slowing the transmission of heat as triple glazing without the coating.

The insulating effectiveness of an airspace or insulating material is also dependent on the position of the assembly and the direction in which the heat flows. In a wall or window, as we have noted, heat flow is horizontal and is abetted by a vertical convective circulation of air. In a roof, heat flows upward in cold weather, and warm air within the roof assembly rises immediately to the cold upper surface to give up its heat, a relatively (and unfortunately) efficient process (8.10). In hot weather, however, the heat flow through the roof is reversed. Air warmed by the hot upper surface tends to remain stratified against that surface rather than circulate toward the cooler surface below, and the heat transfer through the roof is relatively

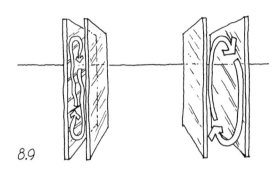

8.9

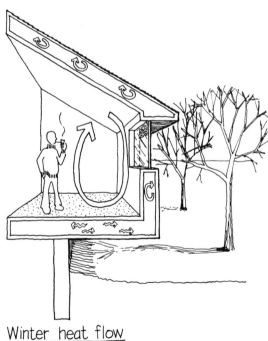

Winter heat flow

8.10

sluggish (8.11). Thus if identical airspaces are provided in the floor, wall, and roof assemblies of a building, convective heat transfer in the winter will be most rapid in the roof, least rapid in the floor, and of intermediate rapidity in the walls. Radiative heat transfer, by contrast, is independent of direction. A reflective foil surface eliminates about half the total outward heat flow through roofs and walls and about two-thirds of the downward flow through floors. Reflective foil attached to the rafters of a house with an airspace above it reduces substantially the downward transmission of heat from a sun-warmed roof into a building in summer. This keeps the attic cooler and reduces the amount of heat that must be removed from the house by a cooling system.

Air serves a small but significant insulating role on the exterior and interior surfaces of buildings. Every surface holds a thin *surface film* of air by means of friction between the air and the surface. The rougher the surface is, the thicker the film and the higher its insulating value will be (8.12). Fur is a very rough surface that traps a considerable thickness of air; its insulating properties are widely appreciated. Surface films are seriously affected by air movement, however. Exterior films are wiped away by high winds, thus accounting for part of the fuel-saving qualities of wind-sheltered building locations. (The other part of the savings comes from the reduced infiltration of cold outside air through cracks in the building.) Convective heat transfer through a surface film is roughly proportional to the cube root of the air velocity past the surface. Expected heat losses from buildings are computed on the basis of maximum prevailing wind velocities in the area.

Walls and roofs of buildings do not usually have uniform thermal resistances across their surfaces, owing to the presence of *thermal bridges*, which are framing members and other components that transmit heat more rapidly than the insulated parts of the assemblies. This is not too severe a problem in wood construction, because wood is itself a fairly good insulator, but metal and masonry construction are often filled with such thermal bridges, which can greatly increase the heat loss through an otherwise-well-insulated assembly (8.13). In existing walls or ceilings, the presence of thermal bridges can often be detected by *pattern staining*, in which cooler areas of the interior surface collect a thicker layer of dust because of the higher electrostatic charge that they carry. In old houses, one frequently sees horizontal stripes on the insides of exterior walls. These occur between the strips of wood lath to which the plaster was applied. The plaster that oozed between the strips of lath conducts heat much more quickly than the plaster that has wood behind it. In cold weather, condensate or frost can form on the portions of interior surfaces cooled by thermal bridges.

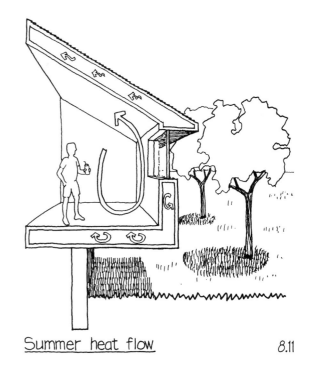

Summer heat flow   8.11

Thermal Resistances, R, of Surface Air Films

	$\frac{ft^2hr°F}{BTU}$	$\frac{m^2°C}{W}$
Interior wall surface	0.68	0.12
Exterior surface, summer wind	0.25	0.05
Exterior surface, winter wind	0.17	0.03

8.12

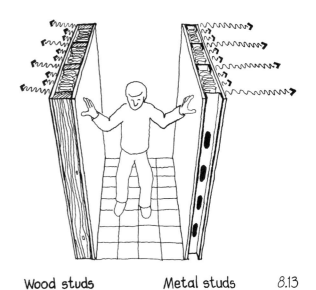

Wood studs   Metal studs   8.13

New approaches to reducing the conduction of heat through exterior building assemblies are gradually coming out of the laboratory and into use. *Cloud gel* is a fluffy, stable material that is the lowest density solid substance created by man. It works much like glass fiber insulation, but it is a much more effective insulator. It is very fragile and must be protected from physical damage, which limits its use to situations in which it is sandwiched between rigid layers that protect it. One such situation is double glazing: Cloud gel between two sheets of glass produces a window with very high resistance to the flow of heat. The gel is so insubstantial that the window appears to be clear glass.

Sheets of glass or metal with a vacuum between them form an excellent insulating assembly. If the interior surfaces have reflective metal coatings, like the interior surfaces of a glass vacuum bottle that is used to carry hot or cold drinks ("Thermos" is one brand of vacuum bottle), heat flow is almost totally blocked. The difficulty is that a vacuum causes atmospheric pressure to exert a tremendous force on the sheets of material that contain the vacuum. Flat sheets must be held apart by rigid spacers at close intervals, and these spacers act as thermal bridges. Furthermore, even the tiniest leak will allow air to enter and destroy the vacuum.

Some designers and builders have experimented with *double-skin* or *double-envelope* buildings that have two independent, insulated layers of exterior walls and roofs, like one building built inside another with an airspace between (8.14). In some instances, the space between the layers is heated in cold weather and ventilated or cooled in hot weather. These buildings produce impressive levels of thermal comfort, but their economy is open to question. Construction costs for walls and roofs are nearly doubled. Floor areas are substantially larger, too: A house 24 feet by 50 feet in plan has a floor area of 1,200 square feet (7.3 m by 16.2 m with an area of 111 square meters). If a foot and a half is added to the thickness of each wall to create a double envelope, the floor area increases by 19 percent, with an associated jump in cost that is nearly as much. Energy expended to heat or cool the space between the layers could be used far more efficiently to heat or cool the inhabited space of the building, with a considerable saving in operating expenses. In large buildings with two layers of windows, the ongoing cost of window washing is doubled. These figures indicate that careful analysis is in order before beginning design and construction of a double-skin or double-envelope building.

Thermal Capacity

Thermal capacity, the ability to store heat, is an important property of building materials. Thermal capacity is roughly proportional to

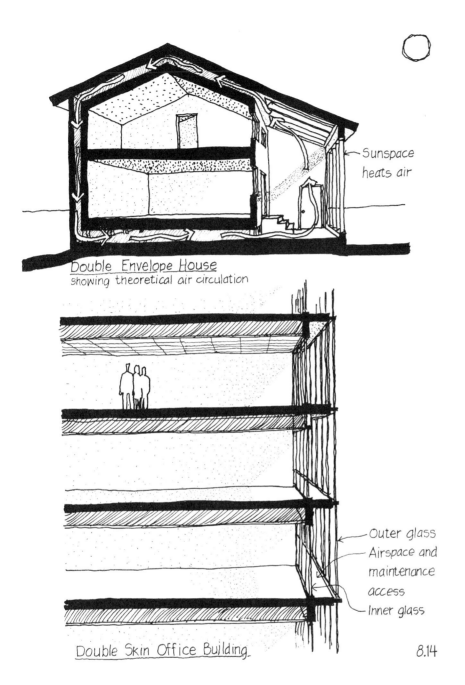

Sunspace
heats air

Double Envelope House
showing theoretical air circulation

Outer glass
Airspace and
maintenance
access
Inner glass

Double Skin Office Building

8.14

mass. Large quantities of dense materials hold large quantities of heat. Fluffy materials and small pieces of material hold small quantities of heat. Thermal capacity is measured as the amount of heat required to raise the temperature of a unit volume or unit weight of material by one degree. Water has a higher thermal capacity than does any other material at ordinary air temperatures (except for certain substances that freeze and thaw at ordinary temperatures). Earth, brick, stone, plaster, metals, and concrete have high thermal

<u>Thermal Capacities</u>

		<u>Per unit mass</u>		<u>Per unit volume</u>	
	BTU lb°F	kJ kg°C	BTU ft³°F	kJ m³°C
Water	1.0	4.19	62	4160
Steel	0.12	0.50	59	3960
Stone	0.21	0.88	36	2415
Concrete	0.21	0.88	31	2080
Brick	0.20	0.84	25	1680
Clay soil	0.20	0.84	20	1350
Wood	0.45	1.89	14	940
Mineral wool	0.20	0.84	0.4	27

8.15

capacities (8.15). Fabrics and thermal insulating materials have low capacities.

In order to appreciate the effect of thermal capacity on building performance, let us consider the hypothetical case of three identical, very well insulated test chambers, each connected to its own warm-air heating system. Into the first chamber we place a thousand bricks, each standing on end with plenty of airspace between it and the surrounding bricks. In the second chamber, we stack a thousand of the same bricks into a solid cube. In the third chamber we place a thousand blocks of dry wood, each equal in size to a brick, standing on end in a loose array identical to that of the bricks in the first chamber. We leave the three chambers open to the laboratory air for several days to make sure that the air and contents of each have equilibrated at an identical temperature. Then we adjust the thermostats in the three chambers to identical settings 30 degrees above the laboratory room temperature, close the chambers, and switch on the three heating systems. For each chamber, a recorder plots a graph of total fuel consumption versus time.

After correcting the three graphs for incidental heat losses from the chambers to the air of the laboratory, a striking pattern emerges (8.16). Initially the rate of fuel consumption to heat the three chambers is approximately equal as the air temperatures are raised the first few degrees. Then the fuel consumption of the third chamber, the one containing the wood blocks, begins to fall off as the thermostat calls for less and less heat. The thermostat ceases to call for heat altogether after a relatively short period of time, meaning that both the air and the wood blocks have reached the temperature of the thermostat setting. Meanwhile, the first chamber, with its loose bricks, continues to require heat and consumes both more fuel and more time than does the third chamber before its temperature

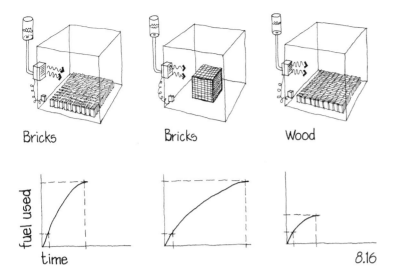

Bricks   Bricks   Wood

8.16

stabilizes at the higher level. While this is going on, however, the second chamber, with its tight stack of bricks, is burning fuel more slowly than the first chamber, and it continues to consume fuel long after both the other chambers are at equilibrium. After a very long time, it, too, reaches equilibrium after consuming exactly the same amount of fuel as did the chamber containing the same volume of bricks in a loose array.

What has happened is that the wood blocks, which have a thermal capacity per unit volume about half that of the bricks, require only about half as much heat to warm them up. The bricks, with their higher thermal capacity, require more heat to warm them to the same temperature, and the amount is the same whether the bricks are arrayed loosely or in a compact volume. The loosely arrayed bricks, however, have many times as much surface area exposed to the air as do the bricks in a cube and are thus able to absorb heat from the air relatively quickly. In the brick cube, the heat penetrating from the surface must warm each layer of bricks in turn, and the bricks in the very core of the cube will not be warmed to the air temperature of the chamber until all the surrounding layers have been warmed. This process is a very slow one.

As an application of this experiment, imagine three identical, well-insulated buildings in a cold climate. The first has thin interior partitions of brick. The second contains the same volume of brick-work, but it is all concentrated in a massive, unused fireplace standing free in the middle of the building. The third has wooden partitions and contains no bricks at all (8.17). When furnaces are turned on in the three buildings, the third building will heat up very quickly; the first will heat very slowly; and the second will reach the desired air temperature after an intermediate period of time but will

61

continue for a very long time to require additional inputs of heat to warm its masonry mass. (Notice that the graphs in figure 8.17 plot temperature versus time, whereas those in figure 8.16 plot fuel consumption against time.)

If heat is introduced into these same three buildings at sporadic but identical intervals as, for example, by sunlight streaming in the windows whenever the sky happens to be clear, the building with wooden partitions will experience wide fluctuations in its air temperature, and the other two will tend to lessen the fluctuations considerably (8.18).

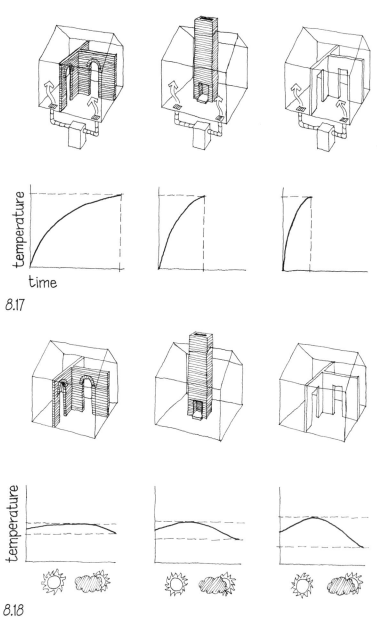

8.17

8.18

62

When a massive fireplace has a fire built in it, some of the sudden and intense heat of the flames is radiated and convected directly into the interior of the building, but a great deal goes to warm the masonry of the fireplace and chimney. This heat is released slowly when the fire is low or after it is extinguished. Some of the heat goes up the chimney to the outdoors and some through the walls of the chimney and fireplace and through the fireplace opening to the interior of the building. By this means, the fireplace itself serves to even out and prolong the flow of heat from a fire. Some fuel-burning stoves are constructed massively of stone or ceramic, for similar reasons. Masses of masonry or water can be used to accumulate heat from solar collectors for release at night or on cloudy days. They can also serve to accumulate heat from electric resistance elements during off-peak hours when electric rates are lower, for use in heating the house during the rest of the day.

Consider an exterior wall of a building that is constructed of a thick layer of a high-capacity material such as adobe, stone, brick, or concrete and is subjected to a difference in temperature between the outdoors and the indoors (8.19). The wall is warmed only slowly by the heat penetrating from the warmer side, as heat is absorbed in turn by each internal layer of the wall. Eventually a stable condition is reached in which the temperature of the colder side of the wall approaches the cold-side air temperature; the warmer side approaches the warm-side air temperature; and a straight-line gradient of temperature exists through the thickness of the wall. Until this stable condition prevails, the wall transmits heat from the one side to the other at a rate lower than what would be predicted solely from the thermal resistance of the wall. Once a stable condition is achieved, however, heat is transferred at the predicted rate. Because materials of high thermal capacity are characterized by low thermal resistances, this rate is quite rapid compared with that of a well-insulated wall.

When the air temperature on one side of a high-capacity wall fluctuates, the wall acts to diminish and delay the fluctuations of air temperature on the other side (8.20a). A very useful example of this is the heavy mud or stone architecture that is common throughout the warm desert climates of the world. During the day, the outdoor air is hot, and heat migrates slowly through the wall or roof toward the interior of the building. Before much of the heat can penetrate the thick construction to reach the interior, however, the sun sets. Radiational cooling of the ground results in rapid cooling of the outdoor air to temperatures below that of the warm exterior of the building. The cooler air cools the exterior building surfaces. Direct radiational cooling of exterior surfaces, particularly the roof, also takes place. Much of the heat that was accumulated during the day

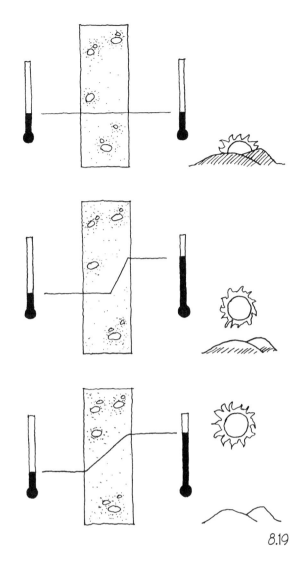

8.19

Exterior
Temperature

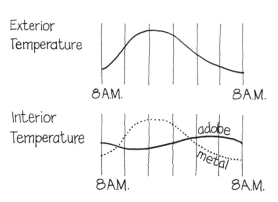

8 A.M.   8 A.M.

Interior
Temperature

8 A.M.   8 A.M.

8.20

in the walls and roof now does a U-turn and flows slowly back toward the cool exterior surfaces, rather than continuing its migration toward the interior. The net effect is that the building interior is cooler than its surroundings during the day and warmer at night, which is precisely the pattern the occupants require to remain comfortable. Thermally optimal thicknesses of walls and roofs for various materials and various climates have been arrived at by centuries of trial and error. In many geographical areas, the effect of thermal mass is enhanced by the whitewashing of exterior building surfaces. Whitewash reflects most solar infrared radiation but is a fairly efficient emitter of long-wave infrared from heated building surfaces to the night sky. Windows are small and are closed tightly during the most intense heat of the day or the most intense cold of the night, so as not to let convective heat transfer work against the actions of the walls and roof.

Contemporary utilitarian buildings in many warm desert areas are constructed with low-capacity roofs made of thin, corrugated sheets of metal or cement-asbestos. The thermal performance of such buildings is radically different than that of the massive buildings of the preceding example (8.20b). The lightweight roofs heat almost instantaneously in the sun. Much of this heat is conducted and reradiated to the interior of the building, quickly raising its temperature to unbearable levels. At night, such roofs lose their heat quickly to the sky and chill the interior space and its occupants by means of both convection and radiation. When such a mistaken choice of materials has been made, its thermal effects can be ameliorated by adding a thick layer of insulation and/or high-capacity material below the roof, preferably with a generous, ventilated airspace just below the roofing to allow the escape of solar heat to the outside air.

Materials of high thermal resistance can often be combined with materials of high thermal capacity to help achieve a desired pattern of thermal behavior in a building enclosure. Heavy, warm-climate buildings can be made to function even more effectively by the addition of a layer of insulation outside the masonry enclosure. The insulation reduces the amplitude of the temperature fluctuations to which the masonry is exposed, making the indoor temperature extremely stable (8.21). The same amount of insulation applied inside the masonry enclosure is considerably less effective. In this configuration the mass of the structure is still fully exposed to solar heat gain and to variations in outdoor air temperature. The insulation on the interior is virtually wasted in dealing only with the small temperature swings of the interior surfaces of the masonry. External insulation offers the additional advantage of protecting the building, particularly the roof structure, from extreme stresses of thermal expansion and contraction.

Even in temperate climates, the addition of thermal capacity inside the well-insulated enclosure that is normally provided helps to level out wintertime fluctuations in air temperature caused by solar heat gains through windows, heat losses through windows, and internal heat gains from fireplace fires, bathing, cooking, and baking. In summer, the added capacity helps to moderate high day-time temperatures.

On the other hand, buildings in hot, damp climates where night temperatures remain high work best when they have as little thermal capacity as possible. They should be designed instead to reflect away solar heat and to react as quickly as possible to cooling breezes and small downward shifts in air temperature. A typical indigenous house in such a climate is elevated above the ground on wooden poles to catch the wind, is roofed with a light covering of thatch, and has walls that are open screens of wood or reeds.

In colder climates, buildings such as weekend ski chalets that are occupied only occasionally during the winter ought to be low in thermal capacity but high in resistance, so that they will warm quickly for occupancy and cool quickly after the occupants have departed, wasting no stored heat on an empty interior. A well-insulated wood frame construction with a wood-paneled interior would be appropriate.

High thermal resistance is a desirable attribute of building enclosures under nearly all climatic conditions, especially in roofs, which are subject to both large solar heat gains and large cold-weather heat losses. In addition to high thermal resistance, high thermal capacity is also desirable where cyclical daily temperature variations need to be smoothed out. The combined effects on the indoor thermal environment of thermal capacity, thermal resistance, radiant gains and losses through windows, gains and losses from ventilation, and gains from heat released within the building are complex, especially when several of these factors vary independently with time. But even in the absence of a detailed mathematical analysis, an informed designer ought to be able to make preliminary selections of materials and design decisions that are thermally correct in a qualitative sense, and reasonably close quantitatively.

Because of the high thermal capacity of the soil, building surfaces that are in contact with earth that lies below the deepest penetration of frost, such as basement walls or walls against which earth is banked, remain within a narrow temperature range throughout the year (8.22). This range is centered on the annual average air temperature at any geographic location. In hot weather, underground surfaces remain cool, and in cold weather, they remain warm relative to outdoor air temperatures. Because of this, the buried portions of buildings are generally much easier and cheaper to cool in summer and

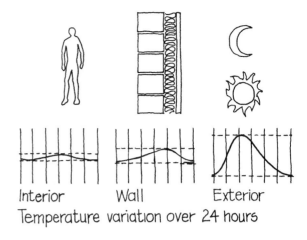

Interior   Wall   Exterior
Temperature variation over 24 hours

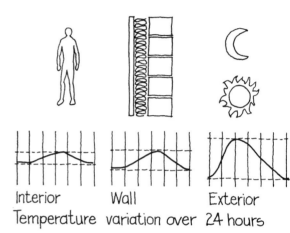

Interior   Wall   Exterior
Temperature variation over 24 hours

8.21

to heat in winter. In order to realize these important advantages, however, underground building surfaces must be insulated to thermal resistance values approaching those considered optimal in above-ground portions of the building enclosure. Where possible, frost penetration into the ground adjacent to the building should be minimized by burying horizontal sheets of foam plastic insulation just below the surface of the soil.

In part because of their thermal advantages, underground buildings have been designed and constructed at every scale in recent years, from small residences to very large office and laboratory complexes. Many buildings are *earth-sheltered*, meaning that they are not really underground, but are built low in the earth and have earth mounded up around their walls. The largest problem that must usually be overcome in underground and earth-sheltered buildings is that of keeping ground water out of the building. Solutions to this problem are presented in chapter 12.

Water Vapor

The interactions of various building materials and water vapor are of extreme importance to the thermal behavior of buildings. Water vapor is a colorless, odorless gas. It is universally present in the air, but in widely varying quantities. The warmer the air is, the more water vapor it is able to contain, but air seldom contains as much vapor as it could at a given temperature. The most convenient way of defining the water vapor content of air is by *relative humidity*, a percentage figure that represents the quantity of vapor that the air *actually* contains divided by the maximum quantity of vapor it *could* contain at the given temperature. A relative humidity (RH) of 60 percent indicates that the air contains six-tenths as much water vapor as it could at the given temperature. This RH can easily be raised in an enclosed space by adding water vapor to the air. This can be done by boiling water to release steam, by washing or bathing, by bringing lots of green plants indoors—or simply by breathing. If the relative humidity is raised to 100 percent, as it sometimes is in a gymnasium shower room or a swimming pool enclosure, the air can hold no more water vapor, and so some begins to condense as fog.

Another way to raise the relative humidity is to reduce the temperature of the room without allowing any air to escape. As the temperature falls, the mass of water vapor in the air remains constant, but the capacity of the air to contain it diminishes, which means that the relative humidity rises. (You will remember that this is what happens to outdoor air as it rises up a mountain, cooling by means of expansion.) If the temperature drops low enough, it will reach

8.22

the *dew point*, the temperature at which the air contains 100 percent RH. If cooling continues below the dew point, the gaseous water vapor will begin to turn to liquid, usually in the form of droplets of fog. Only enough vapor will condense at a given temperature to maintain 100 percent RH, with the remainder staying in the air as a gas. If the temperature is reduced still further, another increment will condense, just enough to bring the air mass to 100 percent RH at the new temperature. The dew point is not, of course, a single, fixed temperature; every mass of air has its own dew point, which is determined by the proportion of water vapor that the air contains. The drier the air is, the lower its dew point will be, and the more moist the air is, the higher its dew point will be.

Air in buildings is frequently cooled below its dew point by coming into contact with cold surfaces. We see this phenomenon in humid summer weather, when condensed moisture appears as "sweat" on a glass that contains a cool drink, a cold-water pipe, a tank of cold water on the back of a toilet, or a cool basement wall. Condensate dripping from pipes and tanks often causes water staining, mildew, and decay in buildings. In cold weather, the most visible evidence of air cooled below its dew point is on cold window panes, which become fogged and sometimes frosted from the condensation of interior water vapor. Although fog and frost on windows are often picturesque, they later collect as liquid on window frames, encouraging rust or decay.

Much more serious damage can be done to a building when water vapor condenses in an insulated assembly, such as an exterior wall. In cold weather, the wall is exposed to warm, relatively humid air on the inside and to cool, relatively dry air on the exterior (8.23). In hot, humid, summer weather, the situation can be reversed when the air inside the building is cooled and dehumidified.

Water vapor in air exerts a partial gas pressure known as *vapor pressure*. The higher the moisture content in the air is, the higher the vapor pressure will be. This pressure drives the water vapor to expand into areas of lower vapor pressure, seeking to create equilibrium. In a condition in which moist air is on one side of a wall and drier air is on the other, water vapor (an invisible gas, remember) migrates through the wall from the moist side to the dry side, driven by a differential in vapor pressure between the two sides. Where there are air leaks in the wall, air currents can also carry water vapor, often in much larger quantities than are carried by vapor pressure differences. Most common building materials offer only slight-to-moderate resistance to the passage of water vapor, and considerable quantities of vapor are pumped through the wall with only slight-to-moderate losses in vapor pressure from the moist side to the dry side. These losses are reflected in a progressive decrease in

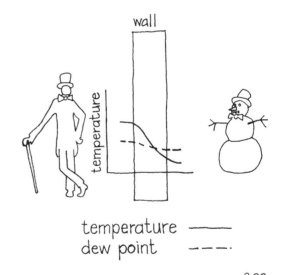

temperature ———
dew point ‒ ‒ ‒ ·

8.23

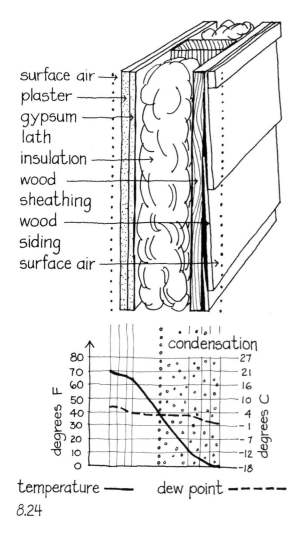

surface air →
plaster
gypsum
lath
insulation →
wood
sheathing
wood
siding
surface air →

condensation

degrees F
80
70
60
50
40
30
20
10
0

degrees C
27
21
16
10
4
-1
-7
-12
-18

temperature ——   dew point -----

8.24

the dew point temperature as the vapor moves from the moist side to the dry side.

Simultaneously, the temperature of the interior of the wall drops gradually from the warmer surface to the cooler one (8.24). The warm-side wall surface, protected by an insulating air film, is slightly cooler than the air on that side. Through the various layers of construction, the temperature drops at different rates, depending on the various thermal resistances of the materials, until at the cool side of the wall, the surface is just slightly warmer than the cold air.

Problems arise within the wall whenever the temperature of the wall at a given location falls below the dew point at that location, causing the water vapor to condense and wet the interior construction of the wall. Whenever moisture condenses from the air, a slight local decrease in the vapor pressure of the air is created, and vapor migrates toward the area of condensation from surrounding areas of higher vapor pressure. By this means the water vapor keeps moving relentlessly to the zone of condensation, and condensate keeps forming, unless either the difference in vapor pressure between the two sides or the difference in temperature decreases sufficiently to halt the condensation. Where air passes through leaks in the wall construction, the same phenomenon occurs. The result is frequently a wall whose thermal insulation is saturated and sagging under the weight of its absorbed water. In this state the insulating material is almost totally ineffective. The wall conducts heat much more rapidly, and the heating-fuel requirements of the building are correspondingly increased. Decay or corrosion of the wall framing is a frequent side effect of vapor condensation, an effect made more serious by the fact that the deterioration often lies concealed from sight until it is extensive enough to cause structural problems.

When migrating water vapor encounters a relatively impervious layer, such as a well-applied coat of exterior paint, the vapor pressure can raise "blisters," literally lifting the paint off the wall. Peeling exterior paint on houses is most frequently seen outside kitchens and bathrooms, where interior vapor pressure is highest.

To avoid these problem situations, a *vapor retarder*, also known, less accurately, as a *vapor barrier*, should be installed as near to the warm side of the construction as possible, but in any case between the main insulating layer and the warm side. A typical vapor retarder is a continuous, vapor-tight sheet of polyethylene plastic or metal foil. For best results in ordinary house construction, it should be applied across the interior face of the wall and ceiling framing after the thermal insulation has been installed. Seams should be sealed with tape or mastic. The effect of the vapor retarder is to prevent water vapor from entering the wall cavity, so as to maintain the dew point within the wall assembly well below the temperature of the wall materials and entrapped air (8.25). This prevents moisture from condensing inside the wall.

In older buildings with vapor problems, it is often not feasible to install a proper vapor retarder. The best that can be done is to plug air leaks in the walls and apply a good coat of paint to the warm-side surface. Special vapor-retarding interior paints are available for this purpose.

Dripping cold-water pipes should be insulated well and then wrapped vapor tight with a plastic or metal jacket. The insulation keeps the jacket well above the dew-point temperature, and the jacket prevents the water vapor from entering and condensing within the insulation.

The tanks of water closets also drip in humid weather. Tanks are available with insulating liners of plastic foam inside the tank; the liner raises the outside surface temperature of the tank above the dewpoint. The porcelain tank acts as a vapor retarder.

A window pane, quite vapor tight already, can usually have its temperature raised above the dew point by installing a second sheet of glass with an airspace between as insulation. This second sheet can be a storm window or part of a double-glazing assembly.

The vapor retarder is *always* installed on the warm side of any building assembly. For a building in a cold climate, this is the inside. For an artificially cooled building in a tropical climate, the warm side is the outside. Buildings in climates that are never very hot or very cold may not need vapor retarders at all.

Membrane roofs in cold climates present a particular problem with respect to water vapor, for the waterproof membrane is quite naturally installed on top of the entire roof construction, which is the cold side, to protect the construction from rain and snow (8.26). This membrane, however, is also a very effective vapor retarder, and it is on the cold side, which is the wrong side, of the thermal insulation. Thus if no additional vapor retarder is provided at the warm underside of the roof, the roof membrane will be subject to blistering from internal vapor pressure, and the insulating and structural materials of the roof deck will be exposed to condensation. And if a separate vapor retarder is provided on the warm side, any residual moisture from rains or concrete work during construction will be trapped between the two layers and is also be likely to cause problems. Until recently there was no adequate solution to this dilemma, but with the introduction of water-resistant rigid foam insulating materials, *inverted roof* construction has become possible (8.27). The roof membrane is laid directly on the structural deck. The boards of rigid foam insulation are then laid over the membrane, where they are held down and protected from the sun by a layer of gravel. The result is a roof in which the membrane is near

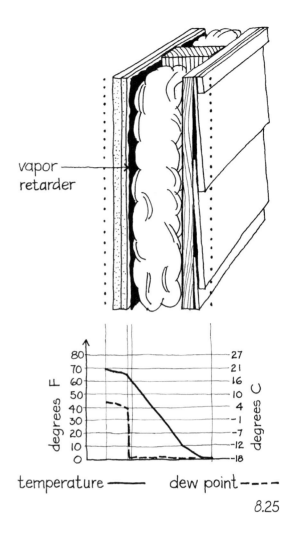

vapor retarder

temperature ——— dew point - - - -

8.25

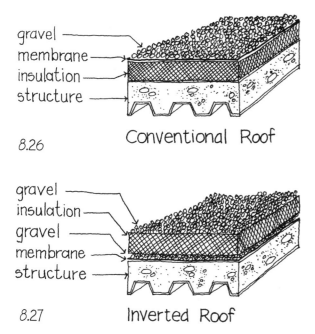

gravel
membrane
insulation
structure

8.26 Conventional Roof

gravel
insulation
gravel
membrane
structure

8.27 Inverted Roof

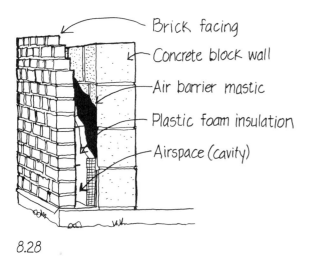

Brick facing
Concrete block wall
Air barrier mastic
Plastic foam insulation
Airspace (cavity)

8.28

the warm side and is maintained at a temperature well above the dew point. As a side benefit, the membrane is also protected from the extremes of outdoor temperature and sunlight that attack and eventually destroy membrane roofs.

Airtightness

Air leaks through walls and roofs waste energy in two different ways: by letting outdoor air in and indoor air out, and by transporting water vapor to places where it condenses. The installation of an *air barrier* in walls and roofs is required by most building codes for these reasons. The nature of the air barrier depends on the type of construction. In a masonry wall, it is often a layer of sticky mastic that is spread over the surface of the interior layer of masonry within the cavity between the interior and facing layers (8.28). In many types of framed walls, it is a continuous sheet material that is wrapped around the outside of the building just before the exterior finish material is applied. To work properly, the air barrier must not allow air currents to pass, but because it is often installed on the cold side of a wall, it must allow free passage of water vapor. There are a number of sheet products that are designed specifically to have these properties. It is also possible in many situations to use a vapor tight air barrier on the warm side of the wall and have it serve also as a vapor retarder.

Thermal Feel

It remains to discuss one more important thermal characteristic of building materials: how they feel when we touch them. This is of no consequence in ceilings, roofs, and outside walls, which are unlikely to be touched by people, but it is an important factor in selecting materials for floors, interior walls, tables, chairs, benches, and beds. Most of us instinctively make correct judgments that certain materials used in certain ways will feel either cold or warm. Seeking a bench in a park on a chilly day, do we select the granite bench or the wooden one? Do we prefer to step from a warm bath onto a ceramic tile floor or onto a deep-pile bathmat? Should the door handle in a 200°F (90°C) sauna be made of steel or redwood? Should a child's playroom have a concrete floor or a wooden one?

Materials that are warm to the touch—wood, carpeting, upholstery, bedding, some plastics—are those that are low in thermal capacity and high in thermal resistance. By means of conduction, the body quickly warms a thin surface layer of the material to a temperature approaching the temperature of the skin, and so the material feels warm. Materials that feel cold against the body have the characteristics of high thermal capacity and low thermal resistance. When we touch a room-temperature surface of metal, stone, plaster, concrete, or brick, heat is drawn quickly from the body for an extended period of time by a relatively large bulk of cooler material, and a cold feeling results. An excellent example of this is the difference between a 72°F (22°C) room and a bath of 72°F water. The room feels pleasantly warm, but the bath feels unpleasantly cool. Air is a poor conductor of heat and has a low thermal capacity, whereas water is exactly the opposite. The body gives off heat to 72° air at a comfortable rate but loses heat much too quickly to 72° water. Similarly, a 72° plaster wall feels cool, and a 72° upholstered chair is quite cozy. A 72° carpeted floor feels comfortable to bare feet, but a concrete floor needs to be heated to a higher temperature from within by electric resistance wires or hot-water pipes, or from without by exposure to sunlight, to achieve the same degree of comfort.

Further Reading

B. Civoni. *Man, Climate, and Architecture*. New York, Elsevier, 1969, pp. 96–155.

9
Controlling the Radiation of Heat

One essential role of a building in providing thermal comfort is controlling the flow of thermal radiation to and from the human body. Sometimes a building must protect the body from an excessive influx of radiant heat from the sun or from sun-warmed objects. At other times, protection is needed to prevent an excessive radiation of heat from the body to a cold outdoor environment. Exchanges of radiation also take place continually between the body and the surrounding interior surfaces of the building, requiring that the temperatures of these surfaces be regulated sufficiently to ensure comfort. In some situations, the active manipulation of radiation is appropriate as the major mechanism in a scheme for achieving thermal comfort for the occupants of a building.

Radiational Intensity vs. Distance from Radiant Source

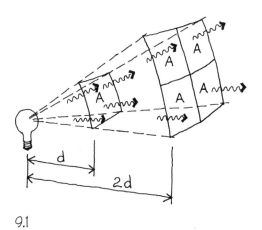

9.1

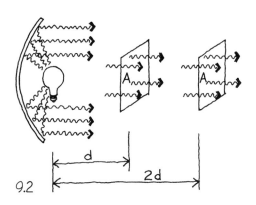

9.2

We have already noted that thermal radiation consists of electromagnetic energy in the infrared range of wavelengths and that it behaves very much like visible light. A point source, such as the incandescent filament of a lightbulb, radiates heat to a nearby object at a rate that is inversely proportional to the square of the distance between the filament and the object (9.1). (The sun operates by this inverse-square law in heating the earth.) It is possible to receive a very high influx of infrared by placing one's hand close to the bulb, whereas if the hand is withdrawn to a point several feet away, the heating effect is scarcely noticeable.

If the same bulb is placed in front of a parabolic reflector, most of the diverging rays of the filament can be focused into a parallel beam of moderate radiant intensity (9.2). Within this beam, the rate of radiant flow is constant without respect to distance, except for the energy absorbed by dust particles in the air and by the air itself, and for losses caused by inaccurate focusing of the beam.

A surface of infinite extent also radiates to a point object at an intensity that is independent of distance. A bird flying 500 feet (150 m) above the middle of the Sahara Desert receives just as intense radiation from the hot sands as a traveler on foot does.

9.3

Mean Radiant Temperature

Usually we are surrounded by objects of differing surface temperatures. Suppose that you are sitting in a high-backed, upholstered chair, facing a cozy fire to your right and a large window that frames a view of a frozen lake to your left (9.3). The chair serves as a barrier to radiation, so that no significant quantity of radiation is being given or received through the back surfaces of your body. The flames and glowing coals of the fire are high-temperature objects, larger than point sources but smaller than infinite surfaces, which radiate heat rapidly to your body. The window is a large, cold object to which your body radiates heat. Above is a large ceiling that is somewhat cooler than your body that causes another net outflow of your body heat. The floor and walls exert radiant cooling effects similar to that of the ceiling. In such a situation, it is not immediately apparent whether the sum of these radiant flows on your body is, overall, a net gain or loss of heat.

In order to assess the net overall radiant flow, we measure the temperature of each surface (the fire, window, ceiling, walls, and floor) and the solid spherical angle subtended by each surface with respect to your body. The *mean radiant temperature* (MRT) to which you are exposed is an average of the temperatures of each of the surrounding surfaces, weighted according to the spherical angle subtended by each and the thermal emissivity of each. In our example, perhaps 40 percent of your body is shielded by the chair. Your body "sees" the intensely hot fire as about 3 percent of its spherical field of thermal "vision" (9.4). The cold window surface might constitute 15 percent, and the ceiling, walls, and floor the remainder. The fire is the only source of net radiant heat flow to your body in this example. Because it subtends an angle of only 3 percent of a sphere with respect to your body, it must be very hot if it is to overcome the cooling effect of the cooler surfaces that occupy 57 percent of your body's field of thermal "vision."

MRT is not in itself a sufficient measure of the thermal comfort that may be expected in response to the radiant conditions in an environment. Everyone is familiar with the experience of being

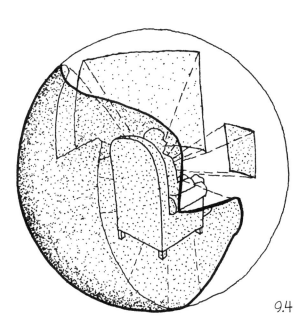

9.4

9.5

roasted on one side by a bonfire while being frozen on the other by radiation to a cold night sky. The MRT may be appropriate for comfort in this case, but the distribution of heated surfaces around the body is not (9.5). To prevent excessively rapid gains or losses from any one area of the body, there must be a balance among the temperatures of the surfaces to which the body is exposed. A balance is also required among heat gains and losses by convection, conduction, and evaporation. In a building with uninsulated walls or very large windows, regardless of the temperature to which the air is heated and in spite of a warm fire in the fireplace, one may be uncomfortable in cold weather because of the excessive radiant flow from the body to the large, cold surfaces of the building. Similarly, the frigid air from an air conditioner will not be sufficient to produce comfort in hot weather if the body is exposed to direct sunlight coming through a window or skylight. If the indoor MRT is high in winter, air temperatures can be somewhat lower, thus reducing heat losses through the enclosure of the building and saving heating fuel. In summer, a building of high thermal capacity is likely to have cool interior surface temperatures, allowing comfort at higher air temperatures, with attendant savings in cooling costs.

Manipulating Radiant Temperature

If we wish to raise the mean radiant temperature in a particular interior location, we can pursue any or all of the following strategies:

1. We can allow the sun to penetrate to that location. The sun is a fickle heating device, but a pleasant and economical one. We use it almost instinctively, as does a dog or cat who dozes happily in a shaft of sunlight in the winter.
2. We can help the building's heating system to warm the interior building surfaces to a higher temperature by installing better thermal insulation in the walls and ceilings and multiple layers of glass and/or insulating curtains or shutters in the windows. Good thermal insulation of a building pays off in increased radiant comfort, as it does in every other respect.
3. We can use highly reflective surfaces to reflect body heat back to the body. (This is how a reflective-foil emergency blanket works.) This strategy has almost never been used in buildings, but it has considerable potential for use if heating fuel becomes more scarce, especially if the reflective surfaces can be incorporated into furniture. This is an intriguing area for architects and furniture designers to explore.

74

4. We can heat very large surfaces, such as floors or ceilings, to temperatures a few degrees above the skin temperature of the body.

5. We can heat small surfaces, such as electric filaments, gas-heated ceramic tiles, metal stoves, or fireplaces, to temperatures hundreds of degrees above the skin temperature of the body.

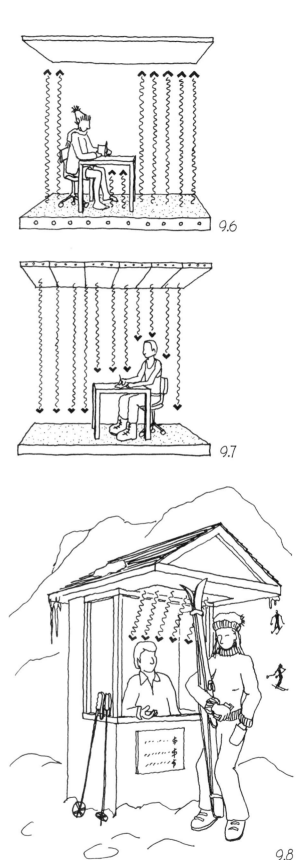

9.6

9.7

9.8

These last two strategies merit further explanation. Schemes for heating floors or ceilings are fairly commonplace. They usually employ electric resistance wires, warm air circulating through multiple ducts, or warm water circulating through coils of plastic tubing. (Heating of walls is not usually attempted, because we tend to drive nails and screws into walls for hanging pictures and shelves.) Formerly, floors for radiant heating had to consist of copper pipes embedded in concrete slabs. More recently, systems based on plastic tubing have made it possible to turn even wooden floors into radiant heat sources. Floor systems are attractive because they warm the feet by conduction and set up convection currents that heat the air in the room quite evenly. But they have several limitations: Tables and desks cast infrared shadows that hamper the ability of the warm floor to heat hands and arms (9.6). The efficiency of such systems is reduced by rugs and carpets. Because of the considerable thermal capacity of the floor materials, they are incapable of reacting quickly to small or sudden changes in the demand for heat inside a building.

Ceiling systems have their own problems. The air warmed by a warm ceiling tends to remain at the ceiling, leading to lower overall efficiencies and a stratum of cool air at floor level, a defect made worse by the infrared shadows that tables and desks cast on people's legs and feet (9.7).

Small, high-temperature infrared heat sources with focusing reflectors are highly effective if installed so as not to cast shadows. They are especially useful where high air temperatures cannot be maintained, as in large industrial buildings or even outdoors, because they can produce heat instantaneously when it is needed and beam it precisely to where it is needed (9.8). Open fires and stoves are less efficient radiant heat sources because of their omnidirectional, inverse-square radiation and because of the relatively large amount of fuel that they convert to warm air rather than radiant energy.

Because of its similarity to solar radiation, infrared heat from either low- or high-temperature sources feels very pleasant on the bare skin. Swimming pools, shower rooms, and bathrooms are particularly appropriate locations for radiant heating systems.

Radiational Cooling

Our means for lowering the mean radiant temperature of an interior location are somewhat more restricted than our means for raising it. We cannot, for example, cool our bodies by exposing them to a small surface at a very low temperature. Whereas we can easily heat an electric filament or gas flame to a temperature a thousand or more degrees above body temperature, there are only a few hundred degrees with which to work between body temperature and absolute zero, and devices for producing very low temperatures are expensive to build and operate. Furthermore, a very cold surface quickly frosts over with moisture that condenses from the air, thereby losing most of its effectiveness because of the insulating properties of the frost. Even a moderately cold surface becomes moist and unpleasant in warm summer weather, which is why we do not actively cool floors and ceilings except in rare cases when we can control the humidity at a level low enough to eliminate condensation. What we can do instead is to shade roofs, walls, and windows against the summer sun, surface them on the exterior with highly reflective coatings whenever practical, insulate them well, and provide enough thermal capacity in the interior surfaces of the building to ensure the maintenance of cool temperatures throughout the day. We can also, in some cases, open a building to the night sky, allowing our bodies and the warm surfaces of the building to radiate heat into space.

To implement many of these strategies for manipulating mean radiant temperatures upward or downward, we must utilize the building's enclosure and take into account its interactions with outside thermal forces. Among these, the most important are the inflow of solar and terrestrial radiation and the outflow of radiation at night.

The roof of a building is a barrier against excessive summertime solar radiation, especially in the tropical latitudes where the sun passes directly overhead. The roof surface itself is of extreme importance. A surface that is highly reflective of solar infrared radiation is heated very little by the sun, whereas an infrared absorptive roof surface can reach extremely high temperatures. The transmission of solar heat from the roof to the ceilings inside the building can be reduced by the use of thermal resistance, thermal capacity, and/or ventilation of spaces within the roof structure (9.9). Under inclined roofs, the convective draft of the heated air can provide the ventilating force to remove the heat, if the roof is appropriately designed (9.10).

In tropical latitudes, the sun passes so high overhead that north and south walls of buildings receive relatively little solar radiation, but east and west walls need protection of the same general sort as that for roofs described in the previous paragraph (9.11). In more

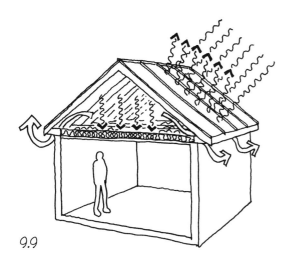
9.9

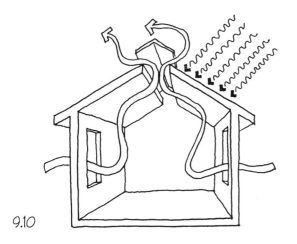
9.10

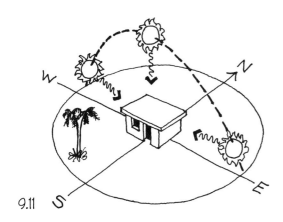
9.11

76

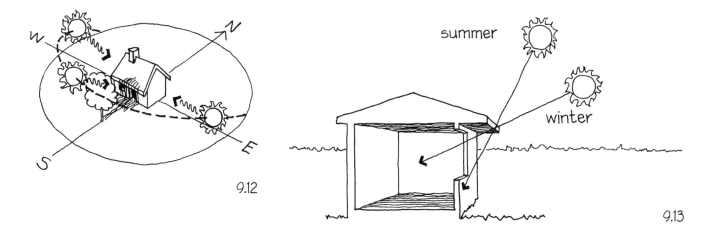

9.12

9.13

northerly locations, the roof and the east and west walls require protection against the summer sun, and also the south wall. For low buildings, deciduous shade trees and vines are a preferred method of sun control, especially because they shed their leaves and allow most sunlight to penetrate during the cold months. A roof overhang or horizontal shading devices at each floor can block the high summertime sun from south-facing walls but still admit light and heat from the low winter sun (9.12, 9.13).

In cold weather, of course, such solar radiation as can be absorbed by roofs and walls is usually a welcome addition to the heat content of the building. Some designers have gone so far as not to insulate the south-facing sides of buildings. This is a misguided effort, for cloudy weather and short hours of daylight bring relatively few hours of sunshine in winter, with the result that for about three-quarters of the winter hours in a typical northern climate, a south-facing surface is losing more heat than it gains. A more productive strategy is to insulate south-facing wall surfaces well and to utilize large south-facing windows to trap solar heat, closing them off with insulating shutters or heavy curtains or shades (preferably reflective of long-wave infrared) when the sun is not out. The well-insulated wall surfaces do not gain appreciable heat when the sun is out, but their heat losses are reduced or eliminated by the solar heating of their exterior layers.

The same highly reflective exterior surfaces that are useful in reducing solar heat gain in the summer can also help reduce building heat losses in winter because of their low rate of emission of radiant heat. Polished metals are the only common building materials that are inefficient emitters of low-temperature infrared. White paint, excellent as a barrier against solar radiation, does little to slow the emission of building heat in cold weather.

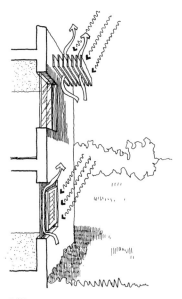

9.14

In warm weather, sunlight entering through windows can produce an undesirable heating effect on the interior of the building by warming interior surfaces that in turn warm the air of the room and radiate heat to its occupants. Where possible, it is best to intercept the sunlight outside the glass, with trees, vines, roof overhangs, louvers, or awnings (9.14). In this way the heat absorbed by the shading device is reradiated and convected largely to the outdoor environment rather than the interior. Outdoor shading devices are difficult to adjust from inside the building, however, and they are vulnerable to the destructive forces of Nature. Some architects, moreover, are unwilling to accept the appearance of exterior shading devices on their buildings. For these reasons, interior shading devices such as roller shades, Venetian blinds, and curtains are often used instead. The effect of these interior devices is largely to absorb solar radiation and convert it to convected heat in the interior air while shading occupants and furnishings inside the building. Interior shading devices are therefore relatively ineffective in reducing the solar heating of air inside a building. They are, however, effective in protecting individuals from high radiant heat gain from the sun and in reducing visual glare from direct sunlight.

Ordinary window glass transmits more than 80 percent of solar infrared radiation but absorbs the majority of the longer-wave infrared from sun-warmed interior surfaces. In cold weather the glass loses most of this absorbed heat by convection to the outside air. The glass does serve, however, to prevent the passage of heated air from the sun-warmed interior back to the outdoors, and it is primarily for this reason that greenhouses, parked automobiles, and flat-plate solar collectors are heated so dramatically by the sun.

Heat-absorbing and *heat-reflecting glasses* are frequently used in buildings to reduce summer air-conditioning loads. However, the heat-absorbing glasses, usually gray or brownish in color, are not as effective as one might first assume from published solar-absorption figures. A glass that absorbs 60 percent of solar heat, for example, does not transmit only 40 percent to the interior. The 60 percent that is absorbed must ultimately go somewhere, and roughly half is radiated and convected to the interior of the building and half to the outdoors, giving a net overall reduction in solar heat gain of only about 30 percent (9.15). Such a reduction may be perfectly sufficient, of course, for many applications. Of much higher efficiency are the heat-reflecting glasses, which bounce back most of the sun's heat without absorbing it. But a large wall of reflective glass can reflect enough sunlight to overheat adjacent buildings and outdoor areas quite seriously and to cause severe visual glare problems in neighboring streets and open spaces. A designer using reflective glass must exercise restraint and good judgment to avoid such problems.

If sufficient care is given to window orientations, much of the expenditure of materials, equipment, and fuel energy to deal with problems of solar heat gain through windows can be avoided. In temperate, northern hemisphere locations, north-facing windows lose radiated heat in all seasons of the year, especially in the winter. East-facing windows gain heat very rapidly in summer because the sun shines into them at a very direct angle, but this gain occurs only in the mornings, when some influx of heat is often welcome after a cool night. South-facing windows receive solar heat for most of the day in summer, but at a low intensity, because the high sun strikes the glass at a very acute angle. In winter, the sun arrives at a low angle through south-facing windows for the entire day, bringing a warmth that is usually beneficial to the occupants of the building. West windows receive heat rapidly on summer afternoons, when the building is already warm, and generally overheat the rooms in which they are located. This effect is especially unfortunate in west-facing bedrooms, which reach maximum temperature at bedtime in summer. It is further aggravated if the west walls of the house are poorly insulated, allowing the interior wall surfaces to heat up and emit radiant heat. Shade trees planted to the west, or deep awnings over the windows, can be of considerable help in correcting existing problems of western exposure. In tropical latitudes, of course, east and west windows gain huge amounts of solar heat and should be shielded by exterior shading devices.

Radiational outflow of heat from a building is at a maximum on clear, dry nights and is especially rapid from roof surfaces that "see" large portions of the night sky. Roofing materials frequently cool by nocturnal radiation to temperatures that are appreciably below surrounding air temperatures. In areas where nighttime air humidities are generally low and skies are clear in hot weather, water may be cooled by contact with the roof at night and then stored in an insulated tank for use in cooling the building during the day. Building surfaces may be cooled directly by the water if the humidity is low enough, or the water may be used to absorb heat from the coils of a mechanical air-conditioning system.

A more direct use of night radiant cooling is the construction of roofs of high thermal capacity in hot, dry climates. The roofs lose heat rapidly at night and become quite cool, which enables them to absorb a great deal of the sun's heat during the day without allowing much of it to get to the interior of the building. The most direct application of all, however, is simply to sleep outdoors at night in warm weather, as is commonly done on flat rooftops in many areas of the world, thereby overcoming the heating effect of the air

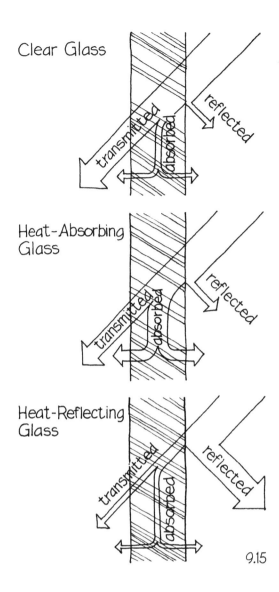

Clear Glass

Heat-Absorbing Glass

Heat-Reflecting Glass

9.15

9.16

by radiating heat directly from the body to the infinite blackness of space (9.16).

Because of the opacity of glass and most plastics to long-wave thermal radiation, neither closed windows nor glass-covered or plastic-covered solar collectors are very efficient in radiating heat to the night sky. Open windows are more effective than closed ones, but a large proportion of what a window "sees" is usually warm trees, earth, and surrounding buildings, and not cold sky. The black plate of a solar collector "sees" mainly sky, but it is a very inefficient cooling device unless its glass covering is removed. Perhaps the most efficacious of all simple radiant cooling devices is water ponded on a flat roof. The water "sees" virtually nothing but sky, and the radiational cooling effect is enhanced by additional evaporative cooling from the surface of the pond.

Further Reading

J. F. van Straaten. *Thermal Performance of Buildings.* New York, Elsevier, 1967.

10
Controlling Air Temperature and Humidity

The roles of air temperature and humidity in human thermal comfort are easily grasped. In cool air the body loses heat too quickly for comfort, and in hot air, too slowly. We seek a happy medium. If the air is too humid, skin evaporation is too slow for comfort. If the air is too dry, the skin and the respiratory surfaces of the lungs are dried too rapidly, and static electricity becomes a nuisance. Thus we expect our buildings to regulate air temperature and humidity, along with thermal radiation and air movement, within fairly close tolerances.

Passive Control of Air Temperature and Humidity

The enclosure of a building, quite independently of any mechanical heating or cooling systems, does a great deal to modify the temperature and humidity of the interior air. Humidity is reduced in a well-designed building by the exclusion of both ground dampness and precipitation. Beyond that, humidity is dependent on ventilation with outdoor air at a humidity different from that of the existing interior air, the generation of atmospheric moisture by the building's occupants, and the raising and lowering of air temperature within the building enclosure. A rising air temperature automatically results in a lowering of relative humidity, and a falling temperature results in a rising humidity. At times, water vapor is taken from the air by condensing on a cold building surface such as a window pane, a water pipe, a basement wall, or a concrete floor slab, which reduces humidity.

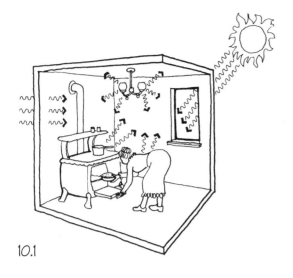

10.1

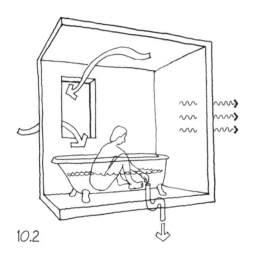

10.2

The air temperature in an unheated, uncooled building is affected by a number of factors. Heat *enters* the building by means of

- the metabolic heat of its occupants (a considerable quantity in auditoriums, classrooms, arenas, and crowded stores);
- the heat generated by their activities (cooking, bathing, running machinery, operating lighting devices; all these are potentially large sources);
- direct solar radiation, especially through windows and openings;
- terrestrial reradiation of solar heat;
- inward conduction of heat from outside air through walls, windows, and roof; and
- entry of warmer air from outside through windows, doors, and ventilating systems (10.1).

Heat *leaves* the building by means of

- the exhaust or leakage of heated air to the outdoors;
- outward conduction of heat to outside air;
- radiation of heat from the building to cooler outdoor surroundings, especially the night sky; and
- the discharge of heated waste water into sewers (10.2).

The effects of these sources and flows of heat on the interior air temperature of the building are highly dependent on the thermal characteristics of the building enclosure. Consider the effects of just two parameters of an enclosure, thermal resistance and thermal capacity. From these two parameters four extreme combinations of thermal characteristics (10.3) can be contructed through

1. high resistance, high capacity (a heavy concrete building wrapped in insulation);
2. high resistance, low capacity (a well-insulated wooden building);
3. low resistance, high capacity (an uninsulated concrete building); and
4. low resistance, low capacity (an uninsulated wooden building).

The air in a building based on combination 1 heats up slowly in response to its internal sources of heat and reaches an equilibrium temperature that fluctuates rather slowly and belatedly as these sources change. It is affected relatively little by outdoor conditions. The air in a building built according to combination 2 is also affected relatively little by outdoor conditions but heats up rapidly and its temperature fluctuates fairly quickly. The air temperature in a building whose thermal characteristics match combination 3 is strongly influenced by outdoor conditions, but its responses are sluggish and attenuated. The uninsulated wooden building, corresponding to combination number 4, has but a small advantage with respect to air temperature over a wind-protected outdoor space. Its interior air temperature adjusts to a value rapidly approaching the outdoor temperature at any given time. These are oversimplified cases, of course. Designers control many more parameters of interior air temperature, although these two, thermal resistance and thermal capacity, are among the most potent.

It is worth our while to examine what happens over the span of a cold but sunny winter day to interior air temperatures in a hypothetical, unheated building of moderately well insulated wooden construction with a large south-facing window of double glass (10.4). At midnight, the outdoor temperature is lower than the indoor temperature and the interior surfaces, particularly the glass, are therefore cooler than the indoor air. As indoor air approaches these surfaces, it is cooled and becomes more dense. It falls along all four walls, losing more heat as it goes, to collect as a cold stratum along the floor. Warmer air rises in the center of the room to replace it, but

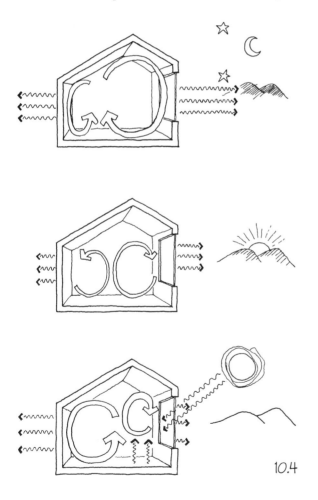

10.4

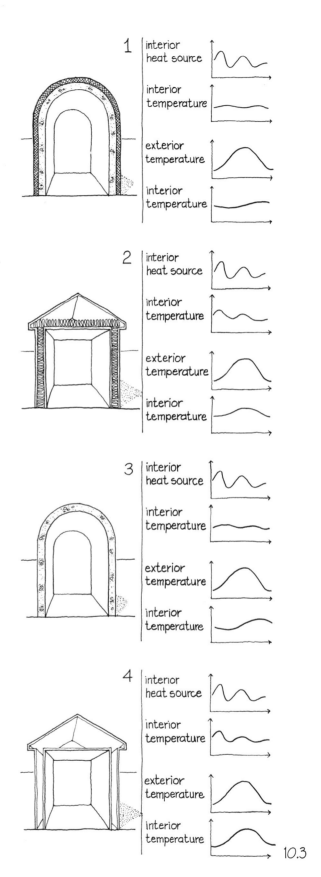

10.3

83

it, too, is cooled in turn by the ceiling and walls and sinks at the perimeter toward the floor. The air near the ceiling is warmer than the air near the floor; if the room were taller, this stratification of air temperatures would be even more pronounced. Toward dawn, the heat stored in the air of the room and in the interior materials of the building enclosure is largely exhausted, and the interior temperature slowly approaches the outdoor temperature.

As the sun rises in the sky, outside air temperatures rise slightly, and direct solar radiation warms slightly the eastward- and southward-facing exterior surfaces of the building. Most of this new warmth is convected from the exterior surfaces into the still-cool outdoor air, but it does help, along with the increased outdoor air temperature, to slow down the rate at which interior heat is conducted outward through the walls and roof. This situation prevails throughout the day, with continuous but moderate losses from the interior to the outdoors. Meanwhile, sunlight is entering through the window, striking and warming parts of the interior walls and floor. These warm surfaces heat the adjacent air, which rises to be replaced by descending, cooler air, which is then also heated. A new pattern of convection is set up, with an upward flow over the sun-warmed surfaces and a downward flow where heat is lost through the walls, especially on the cooler sides away from the sun, and down the inside surface of the warmer but still-cool glass. The interior air temperature rises, reaching a peak in the early afternoon, after which the setting sun, falling outdoor temperatures, and the night sky radiation combine to begin a net cooling of the interior that is most rapid in the early evening and is already growing slower by midnight.

There are several ways in which the thermal performance of this building enclosure could be improved considerably. The enclosure could be better insulated to cut down its rate of heat loss, using either permanent insulating materials or rugs, tapestries, and curtains. Heat losses could be further reduced by minimizing the building's ratio of exposed surface area to enclosed volume. This could be accomplished by reproportioning the building until it more closely resembled a cube or, better yet, a sphere, but severe reproportioning might force an offsetting reduction in the area of glass that could collect solar heat. Thermal performance could also be improved by tightly sandwiching the building between other heated buildings (10.5). A heavy curtain could be drawn across the window, or the shutters closed, when the sun was not in the sky, to slow the outward conduction of heat through the glass. This would make it profitable to enlarge the window still further, to gain still more solar heat, but such an enlargement might result in gross overheating of the space at midday—unless the thermal capacity of the building interior were increased to absorb some of this daytime heat gain and hold it

10.5

until evening. By these means, a considerably different daily cycle of temperatures could be achieved on those days when the sun shines. On cloudy days, some heat is gained through the window from the diffuse light penetrating the clouds, but this effect is weak. The building remains rather cool throughout the 24-hour cycle.

Active Heating

When a heating device is added to this simple building, it adds a warm updraft, usually of considerable strength, to the convective circulation pattern. If the device (some coiled tubing filled with circulating hot water, let us say) is placed in the center of the room, where a weak updraft already exists, it will accelerate the existing pattern of circulation while gradually raising the temperature of the air, especially near the ceiling (10.6). Cool downdrafts from the window and wall surfaces will cross the floor before being warmed by the coils. A better location for the heating device would be under the window, to counter the strong downdrafts that come off the glass and prevent them from reaching the floor (10.7). By this means, the rapid rise of the warm air would also be slowed somewhat. A gentler pattern of circulation would be established that avoids excessive accumulations of warm air in the unoccupied zone near the ceiling or of cold air in the zone around the feet and ankles of the occupants. The higher the levels of thermal insulation in the shell of the building, the weaker these convective air movements will be, and the less critical it becomes to locate the source of heat below a window.

The heat-producing capacity of the heating device has a great deal to do with the level of comfort that can be achieved in the room. If we know that the room will lose 5,000 BTU (5,000 kJ) per hour to the outdoors at a given indoor temperature and under a certain set of weather conditions, we also know that we must add 5,000 BTU (5,000 kJ) per hour to the interior air to replace this loss. If this is done with a heating device that can produce heat only at the rate of 10,000 BTU (10,000 kJ) per hour, the device needs to operate only 50 percent of the time to achieve the necessary output, using some time pattern such as ten minutes on, ten minutes off, and so forth. During the ten minutes the device is on, the average room temperature will rise from slightly below optimum to slightly above optimum, and the cold drafts will be effectively stopped. During the ten minutes the device is off, the temperature will fall to slightly below optimum before the device goes on again. This in itself may be of very small consequence to the occupants' comfort; of greater seriousness is the loss of the circulating action of the heating device during the time it is off. The warmer air in the room will migrate toward the ceiling, and the more dense cool air will flow to the floor,

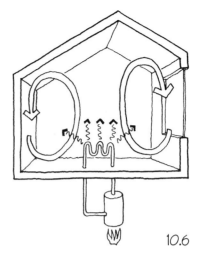

10.6

10.7

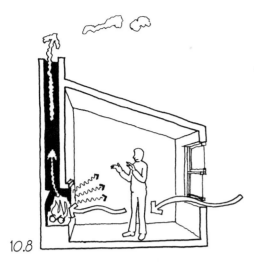

10.8

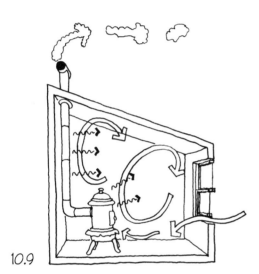

10.9

chilling ankles, feet, and children who are playing there. It is preferable to have a continuously operating heating device whose output can be adjusted to 5,000 BTU (5,000 kJ) per hour, so that its stirring and mixing action can continuously prevent cold drafts and uneven temperature distributions.

Heating Fuels

A wide variety of heating devices and systems are used today. The most primitive and psychologically nourishing is the open fire of wood or coal, but its heating effect is mainly radiant, and most of its warmth, along with considerable quantities of inducted room air, is lost up the chimney (10.8). An enclosed stove of metal or ceramic is considerably more efficient with respect to both radiation and convection. Some modern, thermostatically controlled stoves are highly efficient (10.9). Heat losses up the chimney are relatively low in stoves, but, as with open fires, considerable heat is lost through the room air that is drawn into the flame for combustion, unless combustion air is piped directly from outdoors to the base of the flame. If a room has neither a separate supply of combustion air nor enough leakage around windows and doors to supply combustion air through the room, an open fire or stove is apt to become smoky, and the oxygen in the room air may become seriously depleted.

Electric resistance heaters are unobtrusive, cheap to buy and install, easy to control, can produce (in various models) any desired mix of radiated and convected heat, need no combustion air, and cause no loss of heated air to the outdoors. They convert electricity to heat with complete efficiency. Their overriding disadvantage is that, except where cheap hydroelectric power is available, electricity is several times more expensive than any other available fuel. In terms of resource utilization, when electricity is generated from fossil fuels or nuclear energy, for every unit of heat released through electrical resistance into a room, two or three units are discarded into waterways and the atmosphere because of losses in electrical generation and transmission, making electric heat, overall, roughly half as efficient in terms of fuel consumption as is the direct combustion of fuel in heating devices inside the building.

Coal was once the preferred fuel in central heating systems. It is relatively difficult to distribute from mines to buildings, however, and difficult to handle within buildings. Its combustion produces a heavy, dusty ash that must be transported away for disposal. Coal is also relatively difficult to burn efficiently and cleanly. For these reasons, coal as a heating fuel has been largely supplanted in the United States by oil and gas.

Oil fuel is much easier and cleaner to handle than coal because it can be pumped from delivery trucks directly into a building's fuel tank and drawn from the tank automatically to the burner. Gas is the cleanest and easiest fuel of all, for it is usually piped directly to the burner from a main distribution pipe buried beneath the street. Originally most fuel gas was produced locally by distilling coal and was distributed through purely local networks of piping. Today natural gas is much more common than locally produced artificial gas and is often piped for thousands of miles directly from the well-head to the consumer.

Solar Heating

Solar energy is attractive as a source of heat because it is free of cost, nonpolluting, and, unlike any other fuels except wood and wind, renewable. Its disadvantages are several: It arrives at the building site at a very low intensity. It is available for only a fraction of the time during the heating season, because of short hours of daylight and frequent cloudiness. And for the majority of existing buildings and a large proportion of potential building sites, its availability is severely limited by surrounding buildings, trees, and geographic features and by an unfavorable orientation of the building or building site with respect to the sun.

Because of the relatively low intensity of solar radiation, large areas of building surface must be devoted to its collection in a solar energy system. Focusing collectors, which must move automatically to track the daily motions of the sun, are generally too cumbersome and expensive for use on buildings. Instead, we catch the sun either with large areas of windows or flat-plate collector panels. Although neither windows nor flat-plate collectors can produce the high efficiencies and high output temperatures of focusing collectors, either is capable of gathering useful quantities of heat at temperatures adequate for the comfort heating of buildings.

If windows are used to gather solar heat in the northern hemisphere, they should be oriented within a few degrees of true south, to catch a maximum of winter sunlight (10.10). To avoid wintertime overheating during sunny periods and to store heat for nights and sunless periods, thermal storage capacity must be provided within the enclosure of the building, using large volumes of masonry, concrete, or water, or smaller volumes of particular chemical salts that store heat efficiently. The system will work best if the storage materials are directly exposed to the sunlight entering the windows. Nighttime heat losses through the glass must be minimized by the use of insulated shutters, heavy curtains, or special window glazing that is highly reflective of long-wave infrared. A suitably designed roof overhang or exterior horizontal sunshade blocks the high summer sun from entering and heating the building while admitting the full rays of the low winter sun.

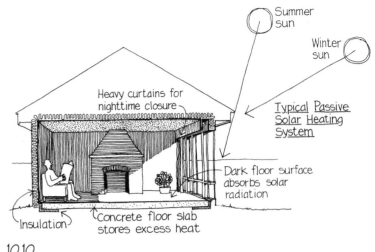

Summer sun

Winter sun

Heavy curtains for nighttime closure

Typical Passive Solar Heating System

Dark floor surface absorbs solar radiation

Insulation

Concrete floor slab stores excess heat

10.10

Window-based solar heating systems usually have no moving parts and are therefore classified as *passive* systems. A system that admits sunlight directly to the occupied space of the building, such as the one described above, is called a *direct-gain* system. Direct-gain systems have several serious disadvantages: They allow interior air temperatures to fluctuate over a wide range. The direct sunlight inside the room is far too bright for reading or other tasks. And the sun's rays cause fading and deterioration of rugs, upholstery, curtains, and wood.

One way of limiting these problems is to gather solar heat with an *attached sunspace* (10.11). The sunspace is fully exposed to sunlight and becomes too hot for comfort when the sun is out. The surplus heat is drawn into the inhabited part of the building by convection or a fan. The sunspace may be used as a greenhouse or solarium, although it is often too hot for either of these uses unless thermal storage is added. This can take the form of a masonry wall, containers

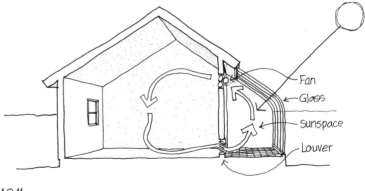

Fan

Glass

Sunspace

Louver

10.11

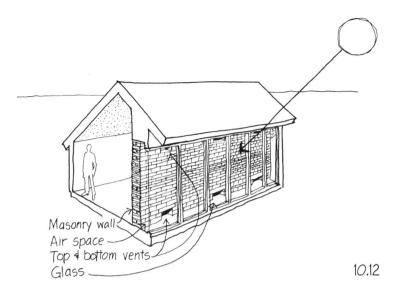

Masonry wall
Air space
Top & bottom vents
Glass

10.12

of water, or a subfloor bed of rocks through which sun-heated air is drawn either by convection or an electric fan.

Another approach is to place a heavy wall of masonry, concrete, or water-filled containers just inside the south-facing glass (10.12). This *Trombe wall* (named for its inventor) shades the interior of the building from the sun and absorbs and stores solar heat. When the air in the building is cooler than the wall, it gains heat from the wall.

All these approaches to passive solar heating add substantial cost to the building for additional window area, thermal storage, and insulating window closures. None of them gives very close control of interior air temperature. None will eliminate the need for a conventional heating system to provide comfort during long cloudy spells. With the additional money that would be spent on passive solar heating, one can add considerable thermal insulation to the ceilings, walls, and floors of a building, and install a moderate area of very efficient windows, preferably facing south to collect small but useful amounts of solar heat. This *superinsulated, sun-tempered* approach can result in a building that uses about the same amount of heating fuel as a passive solar building while offering better control of air temperature and direct sunlight.

Active solar heating systems generally pump either air or liquid through flat-plate collectors to carry away the absorbed heat (10.13). The heat is stored in liquid, rocks, or salts in an insulated container inside the building, from which it may be withdrawn as necessary by the building's heat distribution system. The collectors are usually installed at an angle that is calculated to lie approximately perpendicular to the midwinter noontime rays of the sun. The construction of the collector can be quite simple: one or two cover plates of glass or plastic admit the sunlight and trap its heat; a dark-colored metal

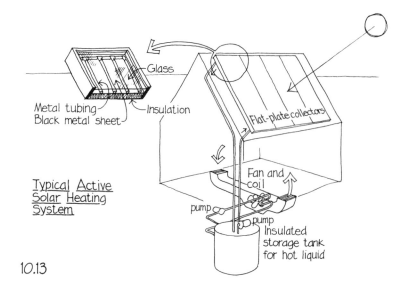

Glass

Metal tubing
Black metal sheet

Insulation

Flat-plate collectors

Fan and coil

pump

pump

Insulated storage tank for hot liquid

Typical Active Solar Heating System

10.13

surface absorbs the heat; air or liquid traverses interior pipes or ducts that are attached to the metal surface to carry away the heat; and an insulated back on the collector minimizes the waste of heat.

It is virtually impossible to design an active solar heating system that can provide all the heat required by a building under all weather conditions. A series of cloudy days in midwinter can exhaust the useful heat from even the largest storage container. As with a passive solar heating system, a backup heating system is required, using fossil fuel, wood, or electricity for fuel. The backup system must have sufficient capacity to heat the building during a prolonged sunless period. This means that it is as expensive to install as is a heating system in a similar building with no solar heating system. Thus it is inherently much more expensive to construct a building with an active solar heating system than without it. As with passive solar heating, better insulation of the building can often achieve the same heating fuel savings at the same or lower initial cost.

Wind Energy

Wind energy, though it is most abundant in the cold months of the year and is often available at night, is unlikely to be a feasible alternative to solar or fossil-fuel heating in most buildings. Aside from its sporadic nature, wind is simply too diffuse an energy source and too difficult to capture. Even a small, well-insulated dwelling requires a very large windmill, difficult to maintain and subject to storm damage, to generate enough energy for wintertime heat in a temperate climate. The cost of the mill would be of the same order of magnitude as the cost of the dwelling.

Heat Distribution

Several different media can be used to distribute heat from a central source to the various spaces in a building. Steam was once popular and remains in use in many buildings today. It is produced in a boiler, circulated under pressure through insulated pipes, and condensed in cast-iron "radiators" (in reality, their effect is largely convective), in which the latent heat of the steam's vaporization is released to the air of the room. The condensate is then pumped back to the boiler through a network of return pipes (10.14). Steam heating systems are reasonably efficient, but they are difficult to control precisely because of the rapidity with which the condensing steam gives off heat.

Hot-water distribution, commonly called *hydronic heating*, is much easier to control (10.15). It involves the circulation of much greater quantities of water than in a steam system, because only the sensible heat of the water is transmitted to the air, not the copious latent heat of vaporization. But by regulating both the temperature of the water and its rate of circulation, a very even and controlled release of heat to the air can be achieved, resulting in a high degree of comfort for the occupants. Hot-water systems are silent when properly installed and adjusted.

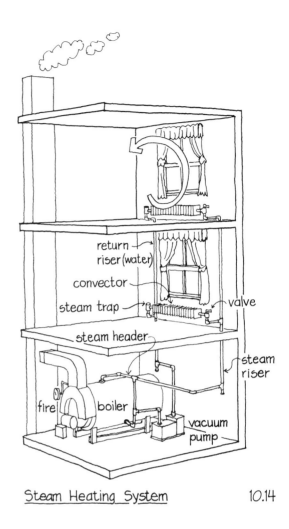

Steam Heating System   10.14

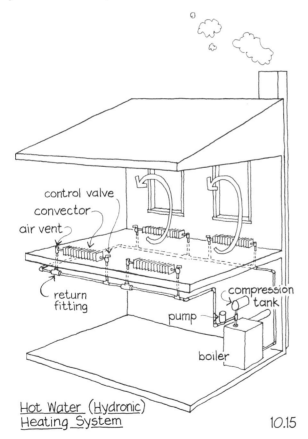

Hot Water (Hydronic) Heating System   10.15

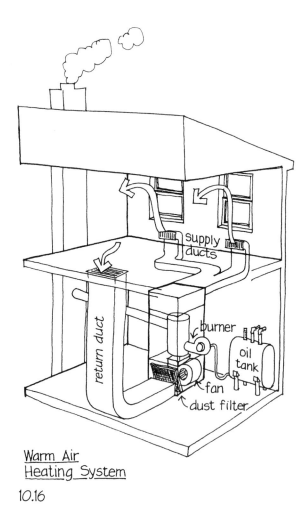

Warm Air
Heating System

10.16

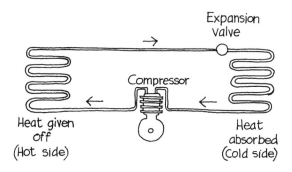

Compression Cycle

10.17

Warm-air systems for the distribution of heat are not as quiet as hot-water systems are, especially if high air velocities are used. Unless constantly maintained, they can circulate dust as well as air through a building. Their ductwork is bulky and difficult to house, compared with water or steam piping. But warm-air systems have strong advantages: Control of comfort conditions can be at least as good as with hot-water systems, through the simultaneous control of air temperature and air volume, and especially through the greater ability of the moving stream of air to stir and redistribute the air in a room. This is particularly important in tall spaces where excessive stratification might otherwise be a problem. Air systems have the further attribute of being able to incorporate filtration, humidification, ventilation, and cooling functions, using the same ductwork. Any desired proportion of fresh outdoor air can be added to the circulated air at the furnace, and in hot weather, the burner can be shut off and cooling coils activated for the circulation of cold air.

The central warm-air system originated simply as a large stove in the middle of the basement, with grilles in the floors above to allow the heat from the stove to convect to upper levels of the building. The uneven temperatures and airflows of this system were improved by the addition of supply-and-return ductwork, by means of which convecting air could be directed to the places where it was most needed. With the further addition of a fan to drive the air, ducts are reduced to a more manageable size and hulk; filters can be installed at the furnace to clean the air as it circulates; and better mixing of room air is possible (10.16).

Cooling Systems

Either of two basic systems may be employed to produce cool air in buildings. The most commonly used is the *compression cycle,* in which a gaseous working fluid, usually a chlorofluorocarbon, is compressed and liquified. This causes the fluid to become very hot. The hot fluid passes through a coil of copper tubing (10. 17). In residential-scale systems, this hot-side coil is cooled by blowing outdoor air past it with a fan. In large-building cooling systems, the heat from the hot-side coil is absorbed by pumping water past the coil. The heated water is pumped to an outdoor *cooling tower,* either on the rooftop or alongside the building, where it trickles over an open latticework against a current of fan-blown outdoor air. This causes the water to release heat to the air through both evaporation and convection, a combination that is considerably more powerful than the convective-only cooling of the residential-scale system. The water from the bottom of the cooling tower, having lost the heat that it had absorbed from the coil of hot fluid, is pumped back to the coil, where once again it

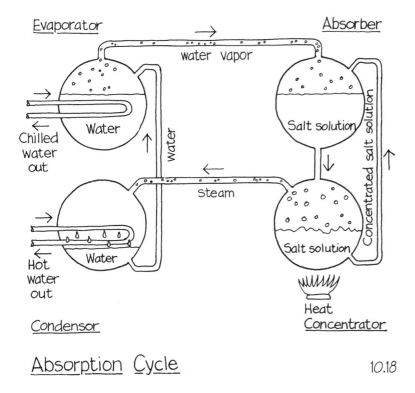

Evaporator → Absorber

water vapor

Chilled water out

Water

Salt solution

water

steam

Hot water out

Water

Salt solution

Concentrated salt solution

Heat Concentrator

Condensor

Absorption Cycle   10.18

absorbs heat. Meanwhile, the compressed, cooled working fluid (which is still slightly warm) is released through an expansion valve into another coil of tubing where, at a lower pressure, changing from a liquid to a gas, it becomes very cold. After vaporization is complete, the working fluid returns to the compressor to begin the cycle again.

Either water or air is cooled by circulating it past the cold-side coils. It is distributed throughout the building, where it absorbs airborne heat from occupants, machinery, lights, and building surfaces before being returned for another cycle of chilling.

As an alternative to the compression cycle, an *absorption cycle* may be used (10.18). A concentrated solution of a hygroscopic chemical, usually lithium bromide salt, absorbs water by evaporating it from a vessel. The water in the vessel becomes very cold as a result of the evaporation. Water is chilled by circulating it through coils in this vessel. The chilled water is circulated to cooling fixtures throughout the building. Meanwhile, the diluted salt solution must be continually drawn off from the absorber vessel and reconcentrated by boiling before it returns to renew the cycle. The steam that boils off is condensed with water from a cooling tower and then returns to the evaporator vessel. The heat to boil the salt solution may be furnished by steam or a flame fueled with gas or oil.

Notice that both these systems, the compressor and the absorption chiller, have a "hot" side and a "cold" side. For cooling we

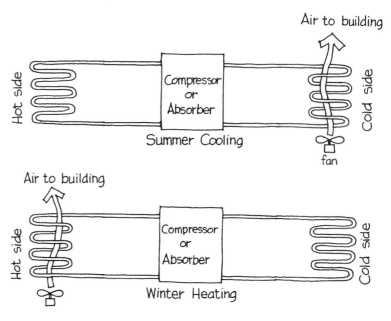

Air to building

Hot side

Compressor
or
Absorber

Summer Cooling

Cold side

fan

Air to building

Hot side

Compressor
or
Absorber

Winter Heating

Cold side

Principle of the Heat Pump

10.19

circulate air or water past the cold side of the system. But it is equally possible to harness the hot side as a source of heat in cold weather, and this is often done. In this application such a system is known as a *heat pump* (10.19). A relatively small amount of energy is used to "pump" a relatively large amount of heat "uphill" from a colder substance (usually water, the ground, or the outdoor air) to a warmer substance, the air inside the building. Heat pumps are manufactured in sizes ranging from units that may be installed in windows, to units suitable for heating and cooling a house, to large units for larger buildings. A heat pump is often at the heart of a *total energy system*, which concentrates the waste heat from an electric generating system to heat the same buildings that are served by the generators.

Dehumidification

When humid summer air is cooled in the coils of an air conditioning system, it usually reaches a temperature below its dew point. This raises two problems: condensed moisture must be removed from the cooling coils, and the cooled air has an uncomfortably high relative humidity of 100 percent. The condensed water drips from the coils into a metal pan from which it is removed by drainage piping. The humidity of the air is reduced by mixing the chilled air with the warmer air of the building interior. If very close control of humidity is required, the chilled, humid air may be passed through a heating coil to raise its temperature a few degrees and reduce its humidity before it enters the inhabited space of the building.

Air-Conditioning Systems

The simplest central air-conditioning system is a *constant air volume* (CAV) system, in which a fan circulates air through heating and cooling coils and a system of ducts that delivers it to all the rooms in the building (10.20). The heating coils are activated only when the building requires heat; in a small system, they often are replaced by a firebox in which gas or oil is burned. The cooling coils in a residential-scale air-conditioning system are cool-side coils of refrigerant connected directly to the compressor. In a larger building, the cooling coils carry water that has been chilled by refrigerant coils from a nearby compression or absorption chiller. Electrically controlled flaps called *dampers* exhaust a percentage of air from the return ductwork and admit an equal percentage of fresh air from outdoors to ventilate the building.

In larger buildings, a CAV system, which is controlled by a single thermostat, is usually incapable of maintaining comfortable temperatures simultaneously in parts of the building that are exposed to different amounts of sunlight and that contain differing amounts of heat-producing machines such as computers. One way of overcoming this problem is to divide the building into *zones*, each of which has similar needs for heating and cooling, and to install a separate CAV system for each zone, delivering hot and chilled water to all the CAV *fan rooms* from a central boiler and chiller plant. In each fan room, a fan moves air through heating and cooling coils and circulates it through the ductwork in its zone.

A *variable air volume* (VAV) system allows for more individual control of temperature than a CAV system. A VAV system closely resembles a CAV system, but each zone of the building has its own thermostat that operates a damper to control the amount of conditioned air that is admitted to the local ductwork in that zone. If a zone needs more cooling, a thermostat opens its damper and more cool air is circulated. If it needs less, the damper will close partway, and less air will be circulated. The fan, coils, and main ductwork are identical to those for a CAV system.

In large buildings whose temperatures must be closely controlled in a large number of zones or rooms, still other types of systems may be installed. A *dual duct system* circulates both heated and cooled air to a control box in each zone, where a thermostat regulates the relative proportions of the two that are mixed and delivered to the rooms. A *terminal reheat* system circulates chilled air and hot water to each zone. The air is delivered through a thermostatically

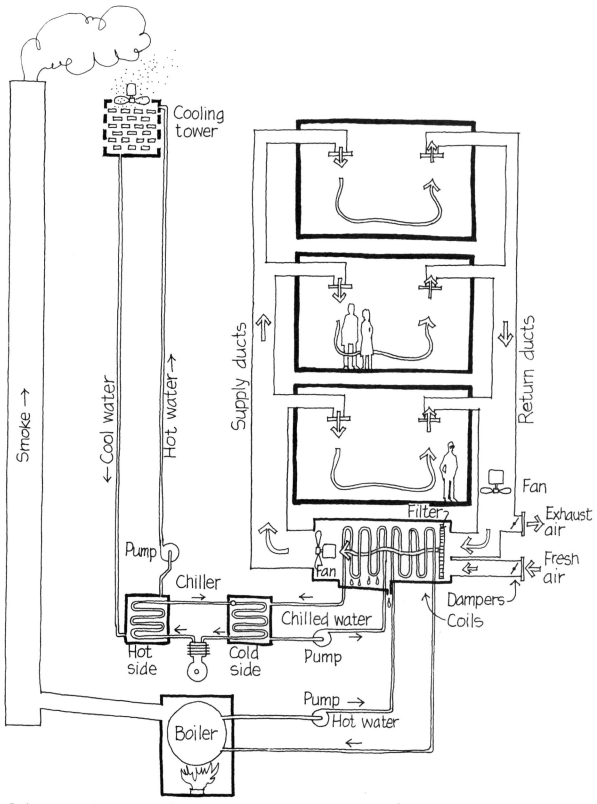

Cooling tower

Smoke →

← Cool water

Hot water →

Supply ducts

Return ducts

Fan

Exhaust air

Fresh air

Dampers

Coils

Filter

Fan

Pump

Chiller

Chilled water

Hot side

Cold side

Pump

Pump →

Hot water

Boiler

Schematic Diagram of a Constant Air Volume (CAV) System

10.20

controlled hot-water coil that heats the air to the desired temperature. Dual duct and terminal reheat systems are more expensive to install and operate than are CAV or VAV systems, so their use is usually restricted to such demanding environments as laboratories, electronics factories, and hospital operating rooms.

Another type of system allows individual temperature control in each room of a building by circulating chilled or heated water from the central unit to the rooms. In each room, a *unit ventilator* on an outside wall circulates the room air plus a percentage of fresh air from outdoors through a filter and a water coil (10.21). When chilled water is circulated through the coil, condensate forms on the coil and drips off into a metal condensate pan, from which it is removed by drainage piping.

Small, electric-powered unit air conditioners, mounted in windows or in exterior walls, are widely used to cool both new and existing rooms and buildings (10.22). They are easy to select, easy to install, and easy to service or replace. However, they are not as efficient as a large central unit, particularly if the central unit is powered by a fuel other than electricity. And they are generally noisy and cause unpleasant drafts in the room because of the high velocities at which they distribute air.

In moderate climates, unit air conditioners are commonly configured so that room air may be circulated through either the cold-side or hot-side coils. This allows each unit to act as a heat pump that can cool the room in hot weather and heat it in cool weather. In very cold weather, the heating cycle cannot operate economically because not enough heat can be "pumped" from the cold outdoor air to the warm interior of the building, and so electric resistance coils must be activated to take over the heating function.

Evaporative Cooling

In dry, hot climates, a simple, inexpensive *evaporative cooler* is often sufficient to maintain comfortable conditions in a building. Air is circulated through a wet pad, from which it absorbs moisture in the form of water vapor (10.23). The air is cooled by the latent heat of vaporization that it furnishes to the water. Evaporative coolers are not effective in humid climates, because the air is already so moist that it does not take up very much water and the cooling effect is correspondingly weak.

Evaporative cooling can be used to cool exterior roof surfaces and thereby to slow or prevent the flow of solar heat through to the rooms below. Sprays of water above the roof are most effective in reducing roof temperatures, but a shallow pond on a flat roof works nearly as well.

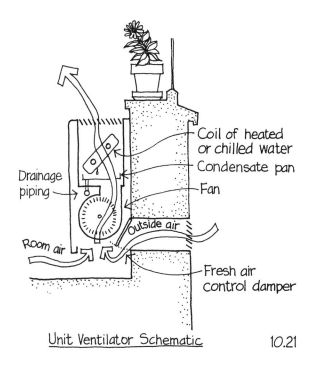

Coil of heated or chilled water
Condensate pan
Fan
Drainage piping
Room air
Outside air
Fresh air control damper

Unit Ventilator Schematic   10.21

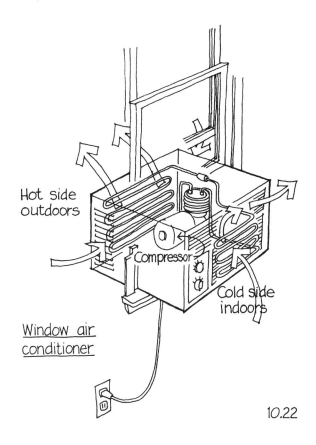

Hot side outdoors
Compressor
Cold side indoors
Window air conditioner   10.22

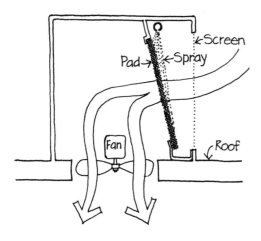

Evaporative Cooler

10.23

Humidity Control

Active control of the air's humidity is often needed in conjunction with its heating or cooling. In winter, heated air becomes extremely dry, to the point that wood components of buildings and furniture shrink and crack excessively, leaves of plants wither, static electricity causes unpleasant shocks, our skin becomes uncomfortably dry, and the mucous membranes of our nose, throat, and lungs are dehydrated and become more susceptible to infection. These conditions can be alleviated by introducing additional moisture into the air. Air-temperature levels can then be reduced slightly without affecting thermal comfort, because of the slower rate of evaporative heat loss from the skin. Thus higher indoor humidity in winter can lead to lower heating fuel expenditures. If a warm-air heating system is used, moisture can be added to the air as it passes through the furnace by means of water sprays or absorbent pads or plates that are automatically and continuously supplied with water. With other heating systems, containers of water can be placed on convectors, or electric humidifying units can be installed in rooms to boil or atomize water into the air. High levels of indoor humidity must be avoided in older buildings because they can lead to serious condensation problems in walls without vapor retarders and at the sills of single-glazed windows.

In summer, the outdoor air humidity is often so high as to reduce skin evaporation to uncomfortably low levels and to encourage various types of mildew and fungus growth in buildings. When air is chilled by a cooling device, its humidity is raised, often to the point that water condenses on the cooling coils and drips off. This is the principle on which an electric dehumidifier works. The same phenomenon occurs, as we have seen, in an air-conditioning system in which moisture must be continually drained from the cooling coils.

Air moisture can play an important role in the habitability of outdoor spaces. A splashing fountain or a lawn sprinkler can perceptibly chill dry outdoor air by vaporizing water into it. Golf courses, sidewalk restaurants, and other inhabited outdoor areas in desert climates are sometimes cooled with nozzles that generate mists. On the other hand, in areas where mosquitoes are a problem, a warm, dry, sunny lawn or courtyard furnishes an environment that does not appeal to mosquitoes, whereas a sprinkled lawn or damp garden brings them in swarms.

Further Reading

Benjamin Stein and John Reynolds. *Mechanical and Electrical Equipment for Buildings* (9th ed.). New York, Wiley, 2000, pp. 371–527.

Edward Mazria. *The Passive Solar Energy Book.* Emmaus, Penn., The Rodale Press, 1979.

11
Controlling Air Movement

Clean, oxygen-rich air for breathing is the most pressing environmental requirement for human life. Continuously moving air is also a primary requirement for thermal comfort, to convect away excess body heat and evaporate perspiration. Although the air in a rural outdoor environment contains such natural pollutants as odors, bacteria, pollens, spores, molds, and dust, we usually perceive it as being pure, and all but the most allergic persons find it optimum for breathing.

Air movement in the outdoors varies over a broad range. On the occasional summer day when there is little or no wind, a sweltering, suffocating, claustrophobic sensation is felt. A light breeze has a pleasant, exhilarating, cooling effect. With increasing wind velocity, convective and evaporative heat losses from the skin can become excessive, particularly if the weather is cold. At very high wind velocities, chilling of the body is extreme; respiration may become difficult; solid objects are picked up and carried by the wind; and structural damage to trees and buildings is likely.

In cities, manufactured pollutants crowd the air: carbon monoxide, carbon dioxide, nitrogen oxides, hydrocarbons, sulfur dioxide, hydrogen sulfide, soot, ash, dust, and odors. Most of these substances are generated by the combustion of fuels in vehicles and heating plants, and others are given off by industrial processes. In the confined spaces of buildings, air loses some of its oxygen and gains carbon dioxide through repeated respiration by human lungs. Bacteria and viruses accumulate. Odors build up from sweating, smoking, toilet functions, cooking, and industrial processes. Gaseous pollutants such as radon and formaldehyde may be given off by building materials. The vapor content of the air is raised by breathing, sweating, bathing, cooking, washing, drying, and

11.1

unventilated gas-burning appliances. Dust and dirt particles float suspended in the air. The temperature of the indoor air may rise above comfortable levels because of solar heat gain, electric lighting, body heat, or the incidental heat given off by industrial processes, cooking, or washing. Air movement is restricted by the walls, floors, and ceilings of the buildings and may become uncomfortably sluggish. Thus buildings require ventilation systems to ensure an optimum velocity of air movement inside and to dilute and replace contaminated air with new air of acceptable temperature, dryness, and cleanliness.

At the same time, the air in buildings often contains odors that we find pleasant, such as the aroma of baking bread, the scent of flowers, or the evocative pungency of incense in a cathedral, and too-rapid ventilation can spoil the experience. But in buildings that are especially prone to dampness or natural overheating, or in rooms that generate heat and odor, such as restaurant kitchens, gymnasium locker rooms, bars, chemistry laboratories, livestock barns, auditoriums, or foundries, rapid rates of air replacement are necessary. Lower rates are usually sufficient for most residential occupancies, lightly occupied offices, warehouses, and light manufacturing plants. Regardless of the volumetric rate of ventilation, however, indoor air speeds must not be so high as to blow belongings about the room (11.1).

Natural Ventilation

Any building ventilation system, from the simplest to the most complex, has four basic components:

1. An air source of acceptable temperature, moisture content, and cleanliness
2. A force to move the air through the inhabited space of the building
3. A means of controlling the volume, velocity, and direction of the airflow
4. A means of recycling or disposing of contaminated air

The simplest ventilation system in buildings is an inadvertent one: it utilizes the outdoor air as its source, the wind as its motive force, the cracks and seams on the windward side of the building as orifices that introduce the fresh air at a controlled velocity and volume, and the leeward cracks and seams as orifices that leak stale indoor air back to the outdoors (11.2). In tightly constructed buildings, this infiltration ventilation is slow, but in buildings with loose-fitting windows and doors, it can become excessive under windy

11.2

outdoor conditions, causing drafty rooms and wasting energy in cold weather through the leakage of heated air to the outdoors. In general, infiltration should be minimized by the weatherstripping of doors and windows, the provision of a continuous air barrier around the perimeter of a building, and the airtight sealing of construction seams. Even when such measures are employed, some air leakage is inevitable, but it functions as a useful, minimum-level air replacement system for a simple building.

Most schemes for natural ventilation of buildings use windows to control the volume, velocity, and direction of airflow. For this reason, most types of windows are designed to be adjustable to any degree of openness. In most areas, an insect screen must be incorporated into every opening window, to keep out bugs, birds, and small animals while still admitting air and light. Where security is a potential problem, as in banks, jails, mental hospitals, and buildings in high-crime areas, steel bars or heavy metal screens may also be fitted to the openings.

Various patterns of window operation have particular advantages: A *casement window* opens to the full area of the window opening, and its swinging sash can function to divert passing breezes into the room (11.3). A *double-hung window* can open to only half its full area, but the half can be at the top, the bottom, or a part of each (11.4). An *awning window* or *horizontal pivoting window* admits air while keeping out rain, a function that other window types can perform only if protected by a broad roof overhang or a separate awning (11.5).

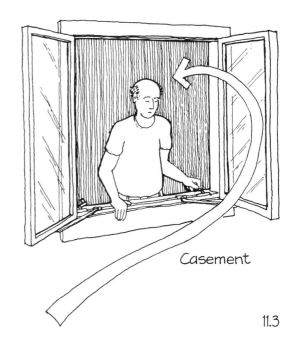

Casement

11.3

Double-hung

11.4

Awning   11.5

101

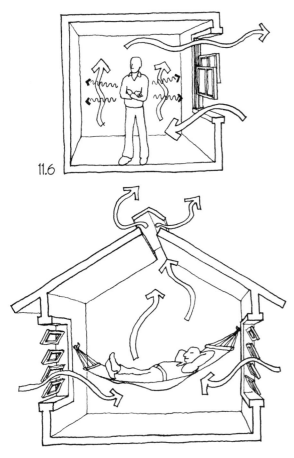

11.6

Convective Ventilation

11.7

Either or both of two motive forces may be employed for natural ventilation: one is convection and the other is wind. Air flows through a building because of the tendency of air to migrate from a higher-pressure area to a lower-pressure one. In convective ventilation, differences in pressure are created by the difference in density between warmer air and cooler air, which causes warm air to rise (11.6, 11.7). In wind-powered ventilation, the air flows from a higher-pressure area in one side of a building to a lower-pressure area on another. For wind-powered ventilation, it is most efficient to have windows on at least two sides of a room, preferably in opposite walls (11.8). Where only a single wall abuts the outdoors, a casement window can be helpful in creating a pressure differential that induces interior airflow (11.9). The building should be sited and configured in such a way as to best intercept the winds prevailing in the seasons when ventilation is most necessary.

The rate of convective ventilation is proportional to the square root of both the vertical distance between openings and the difference in temperature between incoming and outgoing air. Openings must be relatively large, as convective forces are not usually so strong as wind forces. Impediments to airflow, such as insect screens, should be eliminated wherever possible. It is often desirable to design for both wind and convection, placing some openings low on the windward side and some high on the leeward side of the building, to allow both sources to work together.

Openings other than windows are often used for natural ventilation. *Roof ventilators*, *roof monitors*, and opening *skylights* are

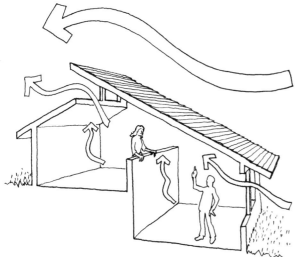

Wind-powered ventilation

11.8

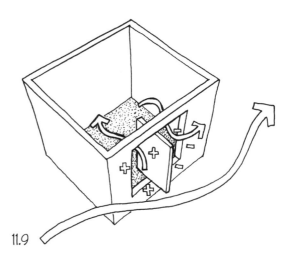

11.9

especially useful (11.10). Some types of roof ventilators are designed to be spun by the wind, creating a centrifugal flow to draw air from the room below. Others rely on convective flow or a hood shaped to cause the wind to create an area of low pressure behind the hood that draws interior air up and out. In any of these devices, control dampers are advisable to reduce or close off the opening as required.

A door ought not to be relied on for essential building ventilation, unless it is provided with a doorstop or other mechanism to hold it open at any desired angle. Otherwise a door is incapable of controlling the amount of air flowing past it.

Ventilation of Combustion Products

Fuel-burning devices such as stoves, furnaces, and fireplaces require oxygen for combustion. This oxygen is often drawn from the room in which the device is located. If the device has no flue or chimney, products of combustion will mix with the room air to replace the oxygen consumed by the flame. A gas cookstove works in this way, consuming oxygen and releasing carbon dioxide and water vapor into the air of the kitchen. Some gas-burning fireplace units are designed to release their combustion products into the room. Although they have safety devices to protect against the release of toxic combustion products, many building professionals advise against their use.

Devices that consume larger quantities of fuel—especially fuels other than natural gas, many of which produce toxic gases as combustion products—must be provided with chimneys. A *chimney* is a convection-driven, vertical ventilation tube powered by heat of the combustion products that it exhausts to the outside air. Thus the room that furnishes the oxygen for the flame of a device connected to a chimney is left at a reduced air pressure with respect to the outdoors, a differential that causes outdoor air to be sucked in through any available cracks or openings. The result is a continuous and often surprisingly large draft of outdoor air through the room. In warm weather this draft may be welcome, but in cold weather it negates a considerable portion of the heating effect of the fuel-consuming device on the room. If the cracks and openings through which the air enters are plugged, the fire will become sluggish and smoky, and the chimney will refuse to work properly, leading to a depletion of oxygen and a buildup of smoke in the room itself, a situation that is both uncomfortable and dangerous. The solution is to provide a duct that allows sufficient outdoor air for combustion to be drawn directly from the outdoors to the base of the fire, without passing through the room.

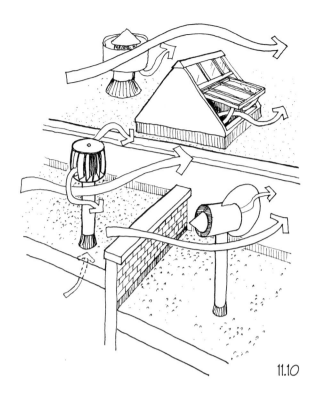

11.10

11.11

Controlling Air Movement Around Buildings

Outside a building, a designer's concern with natural air movement is usually one of reducing the speed of the wind. In streets, on sidewalks, or in courtyards, yards, plazas, gardens, playgrounds, parks, or patios, wind velocities must often be reduced if the area is to be habitable, even in warm weather (11.11). In winter in northern climates, drifting snow frequently presents problems where wind blows around and between buildings. Wintertime heat losses from a building are greatly increased by wind, due partly to the greater infiltration of air and partly to the more efficient transfer of heat between the exterior skin of the building and the rapidly moving outdoor air. When for any of these reasons wind speeds around buildings must be reduced, the most effective protective device is a long, high barrier erected perpendicular to the direction of the wind and upwind from the building or outdoor area to be sheltered (11.12). A solid barrier such as a wall creates a small area of relative calm in its wake. Porous barriers and *shelter belts* of evergreen trees are especially effective, allowing through just enough low-velocity air to fill the low-pressure area behind and divert the full force of the wind for a considerable distance (11.13).

Tall buildings create particularly severe wind problems. Natural wind velocities increase with height above the ground. This exposes the upper stories of a tall building to strong forces that may disrupt the cladding of the building. These wind forces also require careful consideration when bracing the building against lateral structural loadings. At ground level around a tall building, exceptionally strong wind currents are created by the rapid movement of air from the high-pressure windward side of the building to the low-pressure areas behind. If an open space is provided beneath a tall building at ground level, the flow of air through the opening will be so rapid as to make walking difficult when winds are moderate to strong, and doors in the opening either will not open or will open with

11.12

11.13

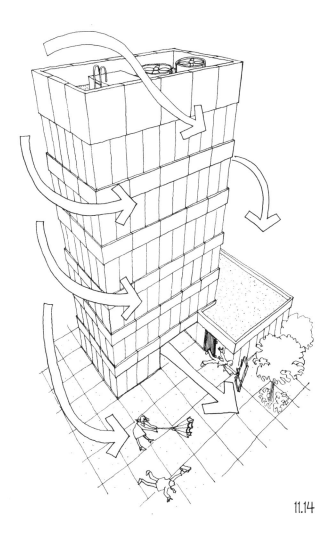

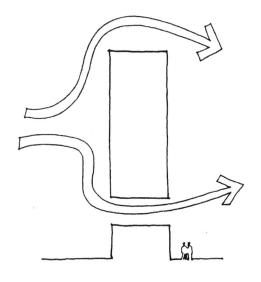

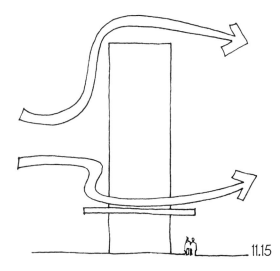

11.14

destructive force when unlatched (11.14). Ground-level wind problems can be largely avoided either by providing very large openings completely through the building a story or two above the ground or by using projecting horizontal roofs at this level to direct the strongest wind currents around the building before they can reach the ground (11.15). Neighboring buildings create local anomalies in wind flow that make extensive wind-tunnel testing advisable before constructing any tall building in order to determine the full structural loads that must be resisted by the skin and skeleton of the building as well as any ground-level wind problems that could bedevil pedestrians and drivers.

Mechanical Ventilation

Built-in fans are useful for room ventilation when reliable, positive airflow is required (11.16). In residential kitchens and baths, simple

11.15

11.16

fans dump interior air directly or through a short run of ductwork to the outdoors (11.17). This air must be replaced by air leaking in from outdoors in various parts of the house. When the house is being heated or cooled, this involves a considerable loss of energy, so that such fans should be used as little as possible.

Fans in more elaborate ventilation systems are connected to twin systems of ductwork for better air distribution throughout the building (11.18). One system of ducts pulls away stale air while another distributes clean air. Such systems are usually combined with heating and cooling systems in such a way that the clean air is distributed at a proper temperature for thermal comfort. Except in buildings where high hazards of chemical, bacterial, or radioactive contamination exist, these systems filter and recirculate most of the interior air they take in, continuously adding a predetermined fraction of outside air and exhausting a similar fraction to the outdoors. The majority of the heating or cooling energy that has previously been expended on the air can be recovered by means of a *regenerative wheel*, a rotating device made of metal mesh that uses its large thermal capacity to transfer heat from one duct into another (11.19), or by means of an *air-to-air heat exchanger* (11.20). The mesh in the regenerative wheel is warmed in winter by outgoing air in the exhaust duct, then releases this heat to incoming air when it rotates into the supply duct. In summer, the same process cools incoming air. The air-to-air heat exchanger shown here passes outgoing air through a number of very thin passages that alternate with passages that carry incoming air. Heat passes through the walls of the passages from the warmer air to the cooler.

An alternative scheme for the ventilation of buildings employs one or more unit ventilating fans at the outside wall of each room

11.17

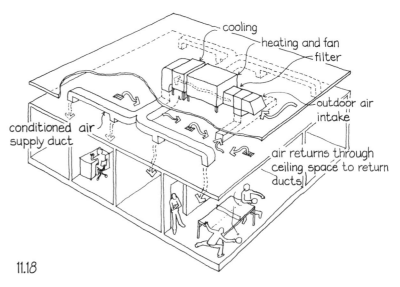

11.18

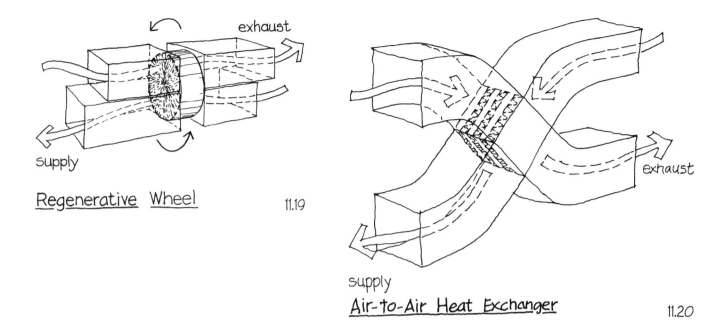

Regenerative Wheel 11.19

Air-to-Air Heat Exchanger 11.20

to circulate the room air and replace a fraction of it with outdoor air. A window or through-the-wall air conditioner works in this way, as do central heating or cooling systems that use coils of hot or chilled water to temper the air in room ventilation units.

Air is usually filtered in a building's ventilating devices by means of a thin, porous pad of fiber that traps dust particles from the air that is blown through it. Much better dust filtration can be achieved with *electrostatic filters*, which first add a static electric charge to the particles in the air and then pass the air across metal plates that hold the opposite charge. The dust particles are drawn to the plates and held there.

Most odors can be absorbed by activated charcoal filtration. The air may also be "scrubbed" with sprays of water to remove dust in some large ventilation systems. Many bacteria can be killed by employing ultraviolet lamps to irradiate the air. Such lamps need not be in the ductwork but are often placed directly in the rooms they serve, particularly in institutional kitchens, sickrooms, and overcrowded dwellings, where they are effective deterrents to airborne disease. Because eyes and skin are damaged by ultraviolet light, ultraviolet lamps must be mounted high in the room and shielded from sight.

Natural Air Renewal

Nature renews outdoor air in many ways. Sunlight kills bacteria in the air. Green plants remove carbon dioxide and replenish oxygen. Rainfall washes the air, and gravity draws out the heavier particulate contaminants. Wind mixes and transports the air, diluting and distributing contaminants. The microscopic hairs on the surfaces of plant leaves catch and hold airborne dust. But there is a limit to the efficacy of these processes, especially when climatic conditions are not ideal. It is important that we not ask too much of the atmosphere as a converter of air contaminants. Fuel burning must be minimized through energy conservation and through as much use as possible of nonpolluting sources such as hydroelectric and solar energies. Combustion devices must be made and maintained in such a way as to burn cleanly and thoroughly. Fuels that do not burn cleanly must be preprocessed to remove contaminants, or filters must be installed in the chimneys to trap the contaminants after combustion. Industrial air exhausts should be filtered for chemicals and kitchen exhausts for grease, so that only easily biodegradable gases reach the atmosphere. Exhaust and inlet openings in any group of buildings need to be located in such a way that they work with prevailing winds and do not mix outgoing air with incoming air. City streets must be kept broad and open enough so that they are continually flushed by the wind.

Despite all these measures, our buildings produce massive amounts of carbon dioxide and release it into the atmosphere. They do this by burning hydrocarbon fuel, both within the building and at remote power plants that produce electricity for the buildings. Carbon dioxide, once thought to be benign, is now known to be a primary cause of the *greenhouse effect*, the trapping of solar heat by the earth's atmosphere. This effect is apparently causing a warming of the earth that will have disastrous effects such as severe weather, melting of polar ice caps and subsequent flooding, and melting of glaciers. Ultimately, we must find ways to release energy that do not also release carbon dioxide.

It is of utmost importance that we maintain and increase our inventory of lawns, gardens, forests, meadows, cultivated fields, and clean waterways, in which reside the green plants that consume carbon dioxide and produce atmospheric oxygen. Air and sunlight are the only necessary substances that enter our buildings free of charge, but even they are not totally free. That is, they are obtained at the cost of human vigilance to ensure that they will always be available.

Further Reading

Victor Olgyay. *Design with Climate*. Princeton, N.J., Princeton University Press, 1973, pp. 94–112.

Benjamin Stein and John Reynolds. *Mechanical and Electrical Equipment for Buildings* (9th ed.). New York, Wiley, 2000, pp. 331–69.

12
Keeping Water Out

Elaborate and expensive precautions are taken in buildings to prevent the entry of even a drop or two of water, because water is an agent of destruction. Water chills the skin, destroys the insulating value of clothing and building fabric, and raises the moisture content of the air in buildings to unhealthy levels. Water is the universal solvent, dissolving many materials used in building interiors and encouraging the staining or corrosion of others. Water is a necessity for all forms of life, including bacteria, molds, mildew, other fungi, plants, and insects. A leaking building is not only uncomfortable and unsanitary, but it is also destined for an early death through corrosion, decay, and insect attack.

A Theory of Watertightness

In order for water to penetrate the enclosure of a building, three conditions are necessary:

1. Water must be present at the surface of the enclosure.
2. There must be an opening in the enclosure through which the water can pass.
3. There must be a force to move the water through the opening.

These conditions are so simple as to be self-evident, yet they constitute a complete basis for the systematic exclusion of water from a building. Unless all three conditions are satisfied, water cannot enter. By eliminating any of the three conditions at a given location on the building enclosure, a watertight condition can be ensured.

The Presence of Water

Water is present in and around a building in many guises. Rain and snow impinge directly on the skin of a building and collect on the ground around it, bringing surface runoff and subsurface water into contact with its foundations. Water can be tracked into a building by people or vehicles. Inside a building, atmospheric moisture can condense on cold surfaces and drip onto the floor. Piping, plumbing fixtures, cooking, washing, bathing, and industrial processes may cause leakage or spillage of water. Building materials that are put in place wet, such as concrete, brickwork, tile work, and plaster, release large amounts of water vapor as they dry, frequently causing copious condensate to run from windows and cold-water pipes.

Openings

Buildings are amply provided with openings through which water can pass. Some, such as movement joints, joints between pieces of cladding materials, and cracks around doors and window sashes, are intentional. Other openings are unintentional but inevitable: shrinkage cracks in concrete, lapses in workmanship, defects in materials, holes for pipes and wires, and cracks and holes created by the deterioration of building materials over time.

Forces That Can Move Water

Water can be driven to penetrate a building by any of a number of forces. *Gravity* constantly pulls water downward and causes hydrostatic pressures where water is allowed to accumulate to any depth. *Air pressure differentials* caused by wind action can drive water in any direction, including uphill. *Capillary action* can pull water in any direction through porous materials or narrow cracks. Even the *momentum* of a falling raindrop is sufficient to drive the drop and its spatter deep into an opening.

The problem of preventing water penetration is aggravated in many cases by the wintertime freezing of water into ice. Ice may clog normal drainage paths and cause ponding of water on roof or ground. The expansion that occurs during the transformation of water into ice can open paths through the building enclosure and is a common factor in several kinds of building deterioration.

Let us examine a building, starting from the top and moving to the bottom, to see what sorts of strategies are employed to prevent water penetration.

Roofs

A roof that is dead level or that rises at a slope of less than one in four sheds water slowly and therefore offers maximum opportunity for water penetration. Such *low-slope roofs* are commonly covered with a continuous, impervious membrane. This may consist of layers of felt bedded in tar or asphalt, metal sheets soldered together, sheets of synthetic rubber or plastic heat-fused or cemented tightly together, a synthetic rubber compound applied in liquid form, or, in primitive buildings in relatively dry climates, a thick layer of clay soil. These continuous roof membranes, seemingly the simplest and most fool-proof way to keep out water, constitute in reality the least reliable roofing mechanisms that we can employ. They are highly suscep-tible to puncture, especially from materials or tools dropped during construction. They are exposed to extreme thermal stress from sum-mer sun, winter cold, daytime–nighttime temperature shifts, and air temperature differentials between indoors and outdoors. Some-times they crack from the resulting thermal movement. They are incapable of passing water vapor, which sometimes leads to blister-ing and rupture of the membrane. A slight hole in the membrane caused by any of these mechanisms is likely to admit prodigious quantities of water into the building, because water drains slowly, if at all, from a low-slope roof, and slow drainage presents maximum opportunities for gravity and capillary forces to do their work. Never-theless, there is often no alternative to a membrane roof, and if care is taken during construction, thermal movement joints are provided at appropriate intervals, and a warm-side vapor retarder is installed to avoid problems of vapor pressure, a membrane roof can give long and satisfactory service.

A *steep roof*, one that slopes at a substantial angle, is much easier to waterproof than a low-slope roof. The steeper the slope is, the faster the water will run off, the less likely it is that the wind will drive water up the slope of the roof, and the easier it is to keep out water. Almost any material will shed water if it slopes steeply enough, as can be proved by holding a washcloth or flat sponge under a water faucet at various inclinations. Whatever material is used on steep roofs, it is usually installed in small units known as *shingles*.

Shingles of many materials—slate, limestone, wood, asphalt-impregnated felt, fired clay, sheet metal—are used in different parts of the world. Each shingle is a small unit, easily handled and applied by the roofer, easily replaced later if defective, and free to adjust to thermal or moisture stresses in the roof structure. Each shingle allows water to pass off three of its four sides under the forces of gravity and wind, but the shingles are laid in such a way that the next lower shingles catch and drain the water quickly in turn, and so on to the lower edge of the roof (12.1). The weakness of a shingle roof is its susceptibility to water driven up the slope or across the slope by a very strong wind. This is countered by a twofold strategy of providing a sheet material beneath the shingles, usually

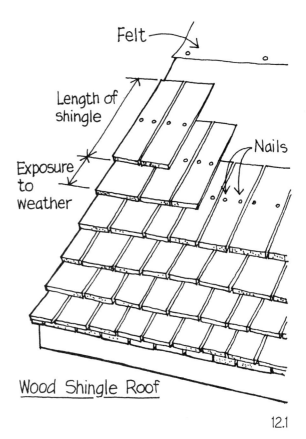

Wood Shingle Roof

12.1

12.2

asphalt-impregnated felt paper, to block the passage of air through the roof plane, and by sloping the roof steeply enough that a larger component of gravity is brought into play against the upward flow of water. Through experience, safe minimum roof slopes have been determined for shingles of various materials under various wind conditions, and leakage is unlikely even in a heavy storm if these criteria are satisfied. In windswept locations—seashores and mountaintops—it is often wise to use even steeper slopes than those recommended or to increase the overlap of the shingles.

The adhesive force of water is utilized as the major water-resisting mechanism of a *thatch roof* (12.2). If a thick layer of straw, leaves, or reeds slopes at a sufficient angle, the drops of water adhere to the fibers and run downward along them to the lower edge of the roof, just as water can be transferred from a beaker to a test tube in the laboratory by pouring it along a glass rod. A thatch roof absorbs considerable water and must dry out between storms to minimize decay. Therefore, thatch is never laid over a solid roof surface but instead is tied to spaced, horizontal poles or strips of wood over a well-ventilated attic. The sheer thickness of the layer of tightly packed stalks is sufficient to dissipate wind energy that might otherwise drive rain through without the use of a sheet material beneath.

On one- and two-story buildings, broad roof overhangs can shelter walls and windows from rain. The walls of taller structures cannot be protected from direct attack directly by rain, making roof overhangs superfluous.

Edges of roofs are particularly problematic. Water may creep under the roofing material or penetrate the tops of parapet walls. The problem is worse on steep roofs and some low-slope roofs because all the water gathered by the roof drains to the edges of the roof for disposal. In most cases, steep roofs simply lap over the walls, so that the roof water drips well outside the wall, a simple and effective expedient. The dripping roof runoff erodes the soil below, however, often enabling water to penetrate into the basement, washing away soil from around and beneath foundations, and spattering earth onto the building walls. At a minimum, a trench filled with gravel should be provided beneath the eave to prevent erosion and provide drainage (12.3).

An alternative approach to is to catch the roof-edge runoff in *gutters*. The gutters slope slightly to drain into vertical pipes called *downspouts* or *leaders*, which in turn discharge either onto splash blocks, into a municipal storm sewer network, or into dry wells (gravel-filled pits) to be absorbed by the ground. But such systems tend to clog with leaves, dirt, pine needles, and other debris and are a nuisance to clean, a problem that can be alleviated somewhat by installing coarse screening over the gutters.

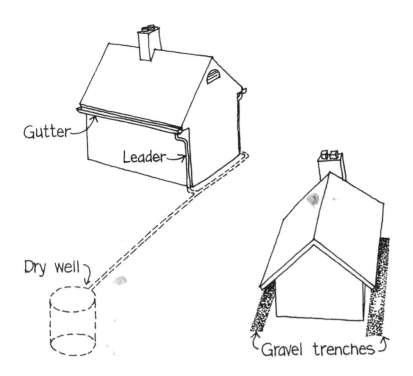

Gutter

Leader →

Dry well ⌐

Gravel trenches

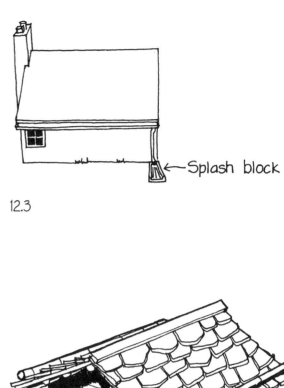

← Splash block

12.3

Snow causes particular problems at the edges of steep roofs in cold climates. One problem is caused by snow's tendency to slide off, tearing away gutters and endangering people and objects below. It is better to reduce the danger by holding the snow on the roof with small metal or wood fences installed for that purpose (12.4). Furthermore, snow is a fairly good thermal insulator, and heating fuel can be saved by retaining it in place. The supporting roof structure must be strong enough to hold a considerable depth of snow without distress.

A second problem is caused by the melting of snow on steep roofs, especially where the thermal insulation of the building is inadequate. Heat passing from the warm interior of the building gradually melts the snow from beneath. The snowmelt water runs down the roof until it reaches the overhang and the gutter, which are much cooler than the roof over the interior spaces, and in many cases colder than the freezing temperature of water. The water refreezes into ice on the overhang, clogging the downspout and gutter. A pool of water collects above this *ice dam* (12.5). Unfortunately, shingled roofs are not resistant to standing water. The water penetrates around and under the shingles and is often first noticed when it discolors the interior wall surfaces and drips from the heads of the window openings just under the roof. The remedies for ice dams are improved attic insulation and also ventilation openings under the eaves and at the roof ridge, to carry away quickly any heat that gets

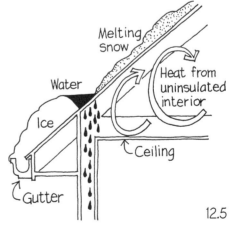

Snow logs on
Alpine barn roof

12.4

Melting
Snow

Water

Heat from
uninsulated
interior

Ice

Ceiling

Gutter

12.5

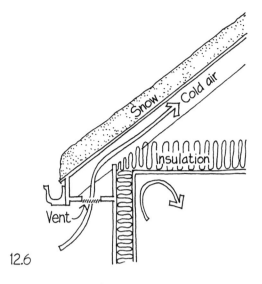

12.6

through the insulation (12.6). If for some reason these measures are impossible or ineffective, the last few rows of shingles at the lower edge of the roof may be replaced by an impervious membrane, or electric melting cables may be installed at the eaves.

Edges of low-slope roofs may or may not overhang the walls, or they may join a parapet wall (12.7, 12.8). In any case, it is important that the edge of the roof membrane be raised at least a few inches (100 mm or more), in order to keep water from spilling over it and down into or onto the structure beneath. The membrane is turned in two folds of 135 degrees each with a cant strip to avoid having to make a crack-prone 90-degree fold. The vertical edge of the membrane is protected. with overlapping sheet metal *flashings* or is tucked into a *reglet*. Rainwater may be carried away by interior roof drains evenly spaced across the expanse of the roof or by *scuppers* (12.7) and downspouts around the exterior walls.

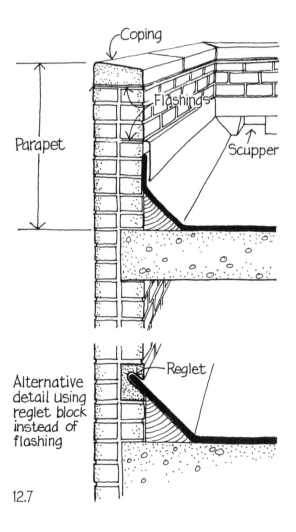

12.7

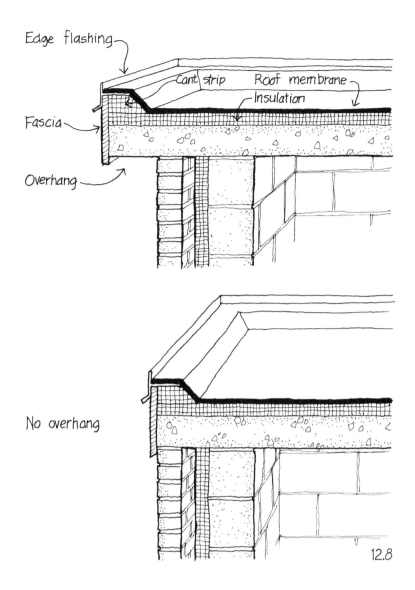

Edge flashing

Cant strip   Roof membrane
Insulation

Fascia

Overhang

No overhang

12.8

Walls

Walls, being vertical, are not subject to water pressures induced by gravity unless a crack or joint in the wall slopes toward the interior of the building. Gravity, moreover, works to the advantage of walls, stripping water off them before it has much time to penetrate. But wind forces on walls are usually much greater than those on roofs, driving raindrops hard against wall surfaces, moving water sideways and sometimes upward across the surfaces, and pumping water through even the most minute openings where the air pressure is lower on the inside than on the outside. We often build walls of more porous materials than roofs, and we invariably riddle our walls with cracks or joints between pieces of material and with holes to accommodate windows and doors, so that water penetration problems are frequently encountered.

Masonry materials all absorb and transmit water to some extent. Mortar joints that have deteriorated over the years afford particularly easy paths for water to pass. Water adheres to the interior surfaces of the pores of the materials, and if, as in most cases, the adhesive force between the water molecules and the wall material is greater than the cohesive force between the molecules themselves, the water will be drawn in by capillary action. A strong wind can increase the rapidity of absorption. A possible solution to this problem would be to apply an impervious coating, such as a heavy paint or a synthetic rubber, to the outside face of the masonry. This would repel rainwater quite effectively, but it would also stop the outward migration of water vapor, thus leading to rupture of the coating and subsequent peeling and leaking. The coating would also be susceptible to tearing because of thermal movement in the underlying wall.

A more reliable approach to making a masonry wall watertight is to assume that some water will penetrate the outer layer of masonry but to provide a continuous gap just behind the outer layer to break any capillary path that might conduct water to the interior of the building. This is the logic of the masonry *cavity wall*, in which the outer *wythe* (vertical layer) of stone or brick held a couple of inches (50 or 60 mm) from the inner wythes by means of stiff metal ties (12.9). The effectiveness of the cavity depends on keeping it free of mortar droppings during construction and providing *weep holes* at frequent horizontal intervals to drain water from the continuous flashing at the bottom of the cavity. Sheet metal or plastic flashings also must be installed around window and door frames to avoid capillary paths across the cavity. An incidental benefit of the cavity wall is that it transmits heat much more slowly than does a solid wall, and foam plastic thermal insulation is usually installed in the cavity to enhance this effect.

If water penetrates into brick, stone, or concrete and freezes there, it can cause *spalling*, the chipping off of flakes from the surface by the expansion of water as it freezes. Spalling was a major force in the destruction of concrete walls and pavements until it was discovered that concrete deliberately produced to contain microscopic air bubbles (*air-entrained concrete*) provides expansion space for the water as it freezes and so virtually eliminates spalling. Obviously, spalling can also be eliminated by keeping water off the wall with roof overhangs or other protective devices.

Panel Walls
We often clad walls with large pieces of less porous materials such as panels of granite or dense precast concrete, or sheets of metal or glass.

116

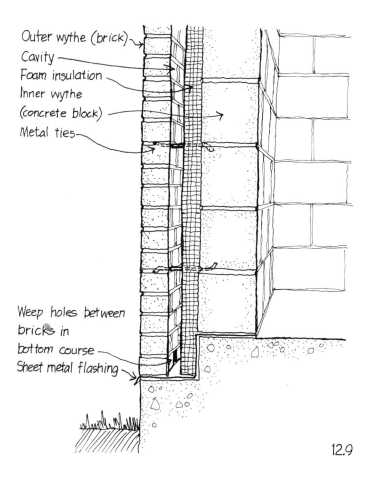

Outer wythe (brick)
Cavity
Foam insulation
Inner wythe
(concrete block)
Metal ties

Weep holes between
bricks in
bottom course
Sheet metal flashing

12.9

With these materials, the problem is not one of stopping an overall slow seepage, as it is with masonry walls, but of preventing leakage through the joints between pieces. Such large panels cannot be fitted tightly together because of their relatively large amounts of thermal expansion and contraction and because of the unavoidable inaccuracies in their manufacture and installation. Quarter-inch to three-quarter-inch (6 mm to 19 mm) gaps must be provided on all sides of each panel, and these gaps must be made resistant to the passage of water.

The easiest way to make these gaps watertight, though not the most reliable, is to fill each gap with an airtight, watertight *sealant*, a liquid synthetic rubber that is injected against a foam plastic *backer rod* and hardens into a continuous elastic plug that adheres to both sides of the gap. Alternatively, a molded synthetic rubber gasket can be tucked into the gap (12.10). In theory, the sealant or gasket expands and contracts readily with any movement of the panels, all the while maintaining its tight seal against wind and water. In practice, even the best sealant or gasket joints will deteriorate over a period of years, particularly if they are exposed to the

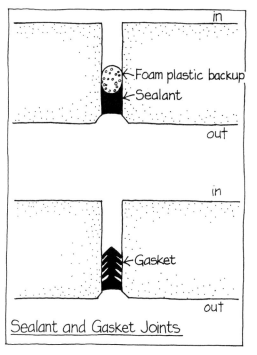

in
Foam plastic backup
Sealant
out

in
Gasket
out

Sealant and Gasket Joints

12.10

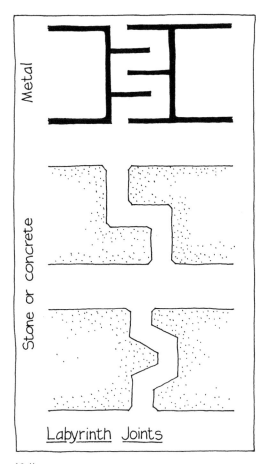

Metal

Stone or concrete

Labyrinth Joints

12.11

weather, and will ultimately crack or lose their grip on the panels. Joints sealed with anything but the finest workmanship will fail much sooner; often they leak from the moment they are installed.

More reliable joints between wall panels are produced by reducing or eliminating the joint's dependence on a sealant material for its water resistance. Going back to our theory of watertightness, this means that either water must be kept away from the joint or the forces that can move water through the joint must be neutralized. It is nearly impossible to keep water completely away from joints in walls. Thus we must turn our attention to neutralizing the forces that might move the water through such joints.

The three primary forces that move water through wall joints are the momentum of impinging raindrops, capillary action, and differential air pressures. The momentum of raindrops can be effectively stopped by means of a simple *labyrinth* consisting of interleaving baffles arranged in such a way that a drop cannot be thrown through the joint without striking a surface that blocks its passage (12.11). Notice that the baffles in a labyrinth do not touch one another. Rather, they are spaced far enough apart that a drop of water cannot bridge between them, thus preventing capillary entry as well as kinetic entry. It is important that labyrinth joints drain freely, to get rid of the water that they normally trap in the performance of their function. Corners and intersections of panels must be designed especially carefully, to drain the vertical joints without flooding the horizontal ones.

Air pressure differentials are created wherever wind strikes a building surface. The windward exterior face of a building is often at a higher air pressure than are the rooms just behind that face. Under this condition, water present in a joint in the wall, even a labyrinth joint, can be carried into the building by the force of moving air. In order to stop the movement of air through the joint, we could apply a sealant to the exterior edges of the joint, but any imperfection in the sealant would allow a stream of moving air to carry water into the building (12.12). If instead we apply the sealant to the interior edges of the joint, the sealant will be exposed to air but not to water, which is excluded by the labyrinth. Even if the sealant is defective, for example, if it does not adhere perfectly to one side of the joint, only small volumes of air are likely to pass, not enough to transport water through the labyrinth. Furthermore, the sealant joint in this case is protected from the deteriorating effects of sunlight and water and, if suitably detailed, is accessible from inside the building for inspection and maintenance. A reliably waterproof joint is thus achieved with a minimum of means.

The same effect can be achieved without the use of sealant by providing a continuous layer of air behind a facade of unsealed, labyrinth-jointed exterior panels to create a wall that works by the *rainscreen principle*. The backup wall behind the airspace must be airtight, must be sealed to the panels around the edges of the facade, and must be strong enough structurally to resist the expected wind pressures on the building. Very small amounts of air passing back and forth through the joints serve to maintain the air pressure in the airspace at exactly the same level as the wind pressure outside at any instant. This effectively eliminates any air-induced movement of water through the joints. In this arrangement, the panels form a *rainscreen* to divert raindrops. The backup wall forms an *air barrier*. The space between is a *pressure equalization chamber* (PEC) that prevents the formation of air pressure differentials between the inside and outside of the joints in the rainscreen (12.13). The backup wall can be made very simply—of concrete blocks surfaced with an airtight mastic, for example, or of light wood or steel framing with sheathing panels covered by an air barrier of asphalt-impregnated building paper cemented together at the seams.

In the example of rainscreen cladding shown here (12.14), a multistory building is faced with panels of thick sheet aluminum. No joint sealant is used. The open joints between the panels are configured so that they systematically neutralize all the forces that might move water through them. Gravity is defeated by sloping the horizontal surfaces of the joints toward the outdoors. Capillary

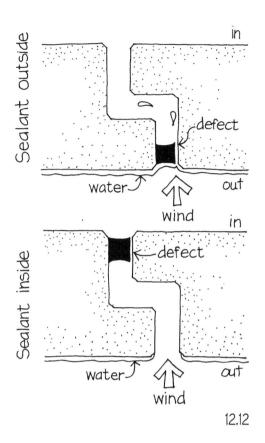

12.12

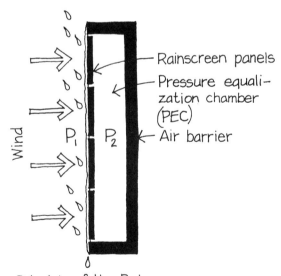

Principle of the Rainscreen

Wind pressure $P_1 = P_2$, pressure in PEC

Therefore wind cannot force water through joints in rainscreen.   12.13

119

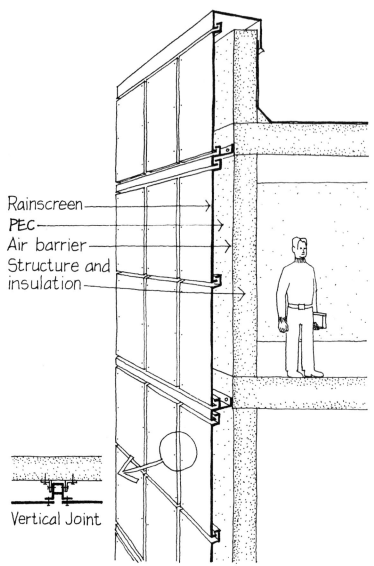

Rainscreen
PEC
Air barrier
Structure and insulation

Vertical Joint

Building With Rainscreen Wall
(after Anderson and Gill)

12.14

action is eliminated by keeping the panels a sufficient distance apart at the joints. Labyrinth joints keep out water that is carried by momentum. Air pressure differentials are neutralized by the pressure equalization chamber behind the panels. The PEC is divided into compartments by the horizontal aluminum components at each floor line and by the aluminum ribs that support the vertical edges of the panels. This compartmentation is desirable because wind pressures vary considerably across the face of a building, particularly near the corners and the top edge. If the PEC were not compartmented, air could rush through it from an area of higher pressure to one of lower pressure, drawing water through the joints in the higher-pressure area. The PEC should be allowed to drain freely at the bottom to rid itself of any water that might somehow get past the rainscreen.

The rainscreen principle can be applied effectively even to very small exterior details such as door and window frames (12.15). The exterior sill should have a sloping top surface, or *wash*, to divert water away from the door or sash, and it should project over the wall below, with a groove called a *drip* to prevent clinging water from working its way back into the wall beneath the sill. A *capillary break* should be provided where the sash meets the sill, to keep water from being drawn through the crack by capillary action. If the sash is weatherstripped on the interior side of the capillary break, the capillary break will also serve as a pressure equalization chamber, making it very difficult for wind to drive water through the crack. The weatherstripping is the air barrier that maintains pressure in the PEC.

Automobile makers utilize rainscreen detailing routinely around the edges of doors, trunk lids, and hatches (12.16). Gaskets are used as air barriers and are placed well inside the large gap between the door and the body of the car, behind a PEC.

With horizontal wood siding or shingles, horizontal overlapping is sufficient to make the wall watertight except under unusually severe conditions of wind-driven water. The siding or shingles should be

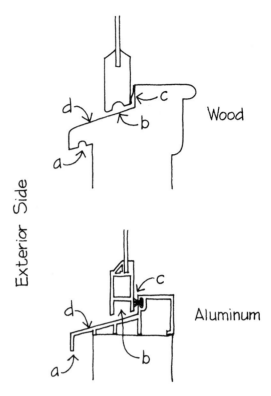

Exterior Side

Wood

Aluminum

<u>Window Sill Profiles</u>

a   Drip
b   Capillary break
c   Weatherstripping (air barrier)
d   Wash

12.15

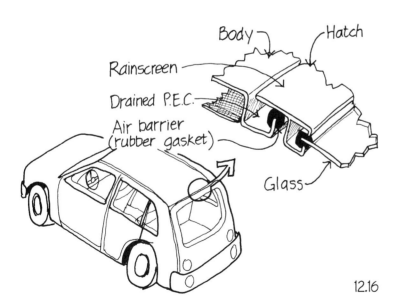

Body
Hatch
Rainscreen
Drained P.E.C.
Air barrier (rubber gasket)
Glass

12.16

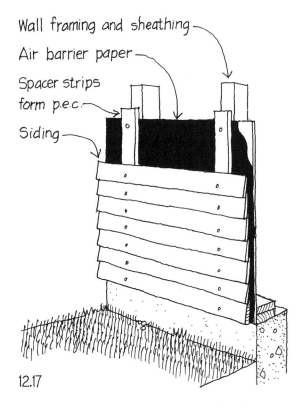

Wall framing and sheathing

Air barrier paper

Spacer strips form p.e.c.

Siding

12.17

backed up by a barrier to the passage of air such as a sheet of asphalt-impregnated felt or bonded plastic fibers. For best performance, the siding or shingles should be spaced out, away from the air barrier, with strips of wood (12.17). When configured in this way, the siding becomes a rainscreen and the space is a PEC.

There have been many water leakage problems in the wetter climates of North America with a siding system called *exterior insulation and finish system* (EIFS). EIFS consists of a layer of rigid plastic foam insulating boards covered with a very thin coat of synthetic stucco that is reinforced with a glass fiber mesh. In the buildings that have experienced the worst problems, the insulating boards are adhered directly to the air barrier layer that is attached to the wall (12.18). Leakage can occur either because of damage to the thin stucco layer or because of poor workmanship in making sealant joints where the stucco joins window and door frames. This leakage would be of relatively little consequence if there were a drained airspace behind the insulating boards, because then the system would function essentially as a rainscreen wall (12.19). However, when the insulating boards are attached directly to the wall of the

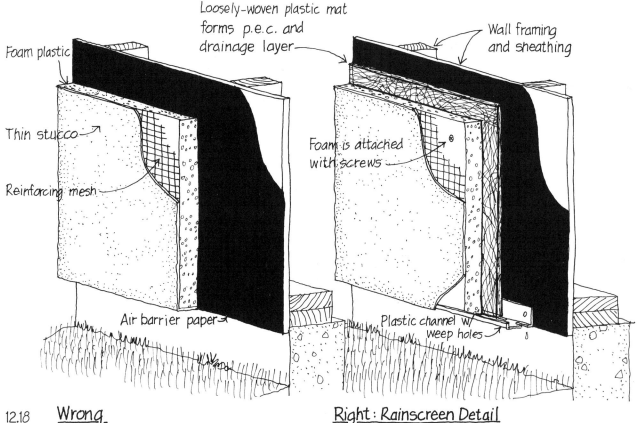

Loosely-woven plastic mat forms p.e.c. and drainage layer

Foam plastic

Wall framing and sheathing

Thin stucco

Foam is attached with screws

Reinforcing mesh

Air barrier paper

Plastic channel w/ weep holes

12.18 <u>Wrong.</u>

<u>Right: Rainscreen Detail</u> 12.19

building, there is no place for moisture to go once it has leaked in. It remains in the wall, causing rot, rust, mildew, and mold. Thousands of houses have had to have entire walls removed and replaced, and repair costs total tens of millions of dollars.

Splashing mud from the drip line of a roof poses only a problem of unsightliness in the case of concrete or masonry walls, but soil microorganisms can cause severe decay problems in wood siding. A wise precaution is never to allow wood to be closer than six inches (150 mm) to the ground. A clearance of eight inches to a foot (200 to 300 mm) is even better. Moisture from the soil may rise up through foundation walls of masonry or concrete by capillary action, to cause dampness and decay in ground floor rooms. A flashing through the wall just above the ground line cures this problem.

Floors and Basements

The strategy of keeping water out of a building by keeping it away from the building surfaces is nowhere better applied than to the portions of a building that reach into the ground. A building that is constantly exposed to standing or running water must rely on expensive and inherently unreliable methods of preventing the water from penetrating, whereas a building on a well-drained site needs only a minimum of precautions in order to stay dry. An adequate roof drainage system is required to carry runoff a safe distance from the building before discharging it. The surface of the ground should be sloped away from the building so that surface runoff is directed away from and around the building, rather than against it. Perforated piping should be laid in a gravel-filled trench outside the foundation, just below the level of the basement floor. Water that might otherwise build up around the foundation seeps through the gravel and the perforations into the pipes (12.20). If subsurface water conditions are severe, more perforated pipes should be installed at intervals beneath the basement floor slab. From the system of perforated pipes, water is conducted away by a nonperforated pipe. If the site is a large, sloping one, this pipe can slope downhill until it emerges from the ground, to drain the water away by means of gravity. On a small or flat site, the pipes drain by gravity into a *sump*, a small, cylindrical pit in the floor of the basement. An automatic electric pump in the sump discharges accumulated water back to the surface of the ground or to a storm sewer.

If the water table is low and drainage is good, a simple *dampproof coating* of asphalt on the exterior of the basement wall is sufficient to keep moisture out. Under more severe conditions, a continuous membrane must be installed around the entire basement and must

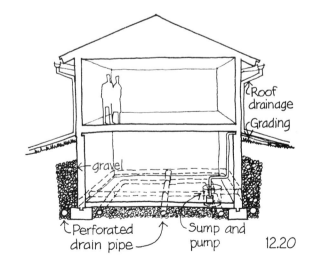

Roof drainage

Grading

gravel

Perforated drain pipe

Sump and pump

12.20

be maintained free of defects while the excavation is being back-filled. A built-up membrane of asphalt and felt, similar to that used on a flat roof, or sheets of synthetic rubber cemented carefully at the seams may be employed, or a continuous layer of clay may be placed against the walls. When using the felt or rubber membranes, particular attention must be paid to the junctions between floor and walls, and to joints in the walls, in order to avoid real or potential leaks.

To keep water pressure from building up around a basement, the gap between the basement walls and the surrounding, undisturbed soil should be filled with gravel. Better yet, a layer of *drainage composite* should be placed on the outside of all the walls and should terminate at the bottom by wrapping over the perforated drain pipes. Drainage composite is a thin mat of decay-resistant plastic that has a very open internal structure through which water moves freely. When water in the soil approaches the basement wall it penetrates the drainage composite, within which it falls by gravity to the drain pipe.

The best way to insulate a concrete or masonry basement wall is to place panels of closed-cell polystyrene foam, which does not absorb water, on the outside of the wall between the drainage composite and the dampproofing or waterproofing layer. The portion of this foam plastic insulation that is visible above the surface of the ground can be finished with either a proprietary coating furnished by the foam manufacturer or with wire mesh and stucco.

If a basement must be insulated on the inside, it should have suitable provisions to keep the walls dry, as outlined above. Polystyrene foam insulating panels should be adhered directly to the inside wall surfaces, with wood strips over them to create a ventilated airspace. The finish wall materials—usually gypsum board or wood panels—are nailed or screwed to the wood strips with gaps at floor and ceiling to provide ventilation (12.21).

If no basement is constructed, either a *crawl space* or a concrete *slab-on-grade* is built instead. The soil level in a crawl space should be high enough that it will not accumulate water that may seep in from outside, and a sheet plastic membrane should be installed over the soil in the crawl space to keep ground moisture from being released into the air. The perimeter walls of the crawl space should be insulated, and the crawl space should be heated in the winter and air conditioned in the summer to control its humidity (12.22). Most building codes still contain a provision that a crawl space should be naturally ventilated with screened openings around its perimeter. This is a mistaken approach, because humid summer air carries moisture into the crawl space, where it condenses on the ground-cooled surfaces and leads to the decay of floor framing. Similarly, a basement should be kept tightly closed and air conditioned in the summer, or at least provided with a dehumidifier. If naturally

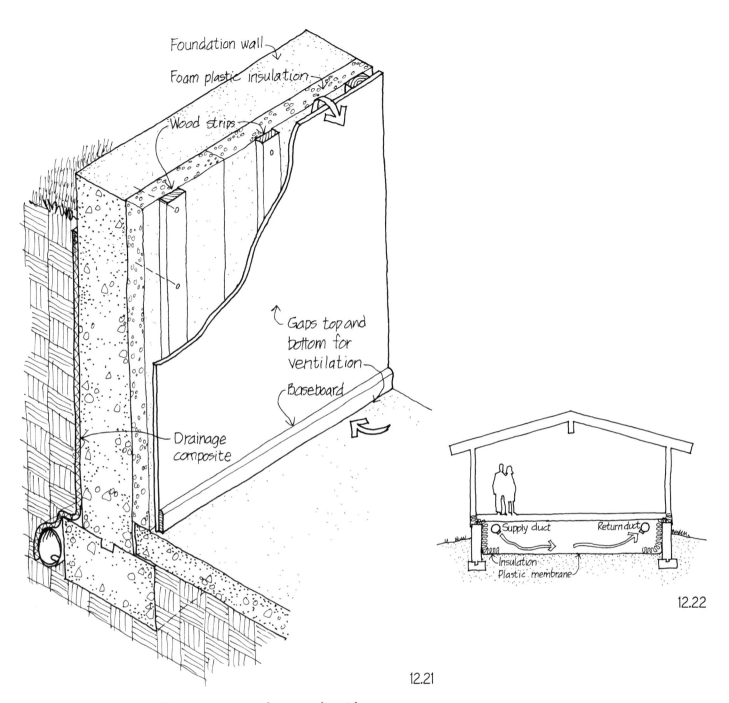

Foundation wall

Foam plastic insulation

Wood strips

Gaps top and bottom for ventilation

Baseboard

Drainage composite

Supply duct   Return duct

Insulation

Plastic membrane

12.22

12.21

ventilated, a basement will become extremely wet in humid summer weather.

In the case of a concrete slab-on-grade, a thick drainage layer of crushed rock beneath the slab will prevent water from building up, and a continuous membrane between the crushed rock and the slab will block the upward migration of water vapor from the soil. Moisture is likely to condense on top of the cool slab in humid weather unless the building is closed and either air-conditioned or dehumidified.

Frost Heaving

When moist soil freezes, it expands slightly. Although this expansion is not severe, it is sometimes enough to crack pavings, slabs, or foundations. Much more serious damage is possible when soil moisture migrates toward the surface because of a difference in vapor pressure between the air in the pores of the soil and the free air above the surface of the ground. In cold weather, the deeper one digs, the higher the soil temperature will be. Thus moisture vapor moving upward during subfreezing weather encounters cooler and cooler soil until a level is reached at which the soil temperature is equal to the freezing point of water. Here long ice crystals form and grow vertically, pushing against the soil with enormous force as they do so. Upward soil movement of several inches (50 mm or more) is quite common under these circumstances, and pavements and foundations can be severely damaged. This phenomenon is known as *frost heaving*. In a foundation, it is usually prevented simply by placing the bottom of the foundation below the level to which the soil freezes in winter. With pavements, a generous layer of uniform-sized stones beneath the slab generally suffices to carry away moisture and allow for any freezing expansion. In subarctic climates this is not always sufficient. Pavements laid on plastic foam thermal insulation, which maintains the underlying soil temperature above freezing, are usually satisfactory.

Flat outdoor areas of any kind—roadways, tennis courts, dead-level roofs, athletic fields, sidewalks, patios—can never be made perfectly flat and planar. Because of the limitations inherent in tools, measuring devices, and materials, low spots and high spots always occur in the surface, even under the most carefully controlled conditions. This results in the accumulation of puddles during precipitation, leading to the premature deterioration of the material under the puddled areas. For this reason we seldom attempt to build a perfectly flat surface outdoors but instead introduce enough of a slope into the surface to drain the lower spots. A slope of about one in fifty, or one-fourth of an inch of drop per foot of horizontal run, is generally sufficient to leave a reasonably well made surface free of standing water. Low-slope roofs are usually pitched toward their roof drains at this slope. If a dead-level roof is attempted, however, more durable and expensive roofing materials must be used to withstand the deleterious effects of the standing water that must be expected. Symmetrical surfaces such as roadways and athletic fields are not usually sloped in a single direction but are gently crowned in the center and fall off equally toward both sides (12.23).

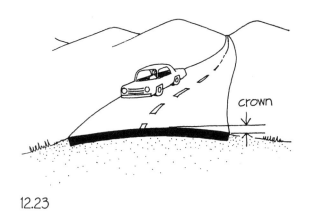

crown

12.23

Interior Sources of Water

Unwanted water can originate inside a building from leaking plumbing or heating systems, splashover from sinks and baths, and condensation on cold surfaces. Leaky pipes can be prevented only by careful installation. Plumbing installations that tend to develop leaks, such as interior roof drains and built-in shower receptors, are provided with underlying metal or plastic sheet membranes to gather stray water and funnel it into the drain pipes. Where splashover is expected, impervious surfaces and, if necessary, floor drains should be installed to keep water out of the fabric of the building. Condensate dripping off water tanks and cold-water piping is a frequent cause of building damage in humid climates. Piping and tanks should be insulated and provided with a vapor retarder.

Condensate running down the interior of window panes results in a decaying or rusting sash. Double glass has an interior surface temperature sufficiently high to avoid condensation under most circumstances. The metal frames of windows and doors sometimes accumulate condensate in cold weather. If such frames have hollow internal spaces, condensate may form inside and cause damage unless it is drained continually to the outdoors through drain holes or unless the hollows are completely filled with sealant or mortar to prevent moist air from occupying the space. Condensation on the exposed indoor surfaces of metal frames can usually be avoided by providing a *thermal break* in the frame section, to enable the indoor surface to be maintained at a temperature above the dew point (12.24).

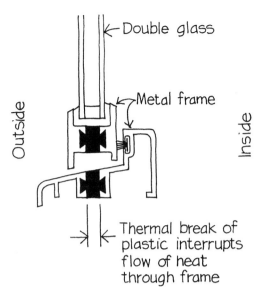

Thermal Break Window Frame Profile

12.24

Further Reading

Edward Allen. *Architectural Detailing: Function, Constructibility, Aesthetics.* New York, Wiley, 1993, pp. 5–36.

J. M. Anderson and J. R. Gill. *Rainscreen Cladding.* London, Butterworths, 1988.

13

Seeing and Illumination

We gather most of our information about the world through our eyes. Eyes are organs capable of sensing a portion of the spectrum of electromagnetic radiation that we call light. We perceive the longest visible wavelengths as red in color and progressively shorter wavelengths as orange, yellow, green, blue, and violet (13.1). "Colorless" light, which we perceive as white, is in reality a balanced mixture of all the wavelengths, whereas black is an absence of light.

Light and Seeing

Useful light originates from either the sun or artificial sources. Because our eyes evolved for the purpose of seeing in sunlight, they perceive sunlight as being normal in color. Most artificial sources generate light that is perceptibly different in color from sunlight. *Incandescent* sources, such as an open fire, a candle, an oil lamp, or a glowing filament in a lightbulb, emit light that is deficient in the shorter wavelengths and thus more reddish than sunlight. *Fluorescent* light is created in a sealed glass tube filled with mercury vapor. An electrical discharge between the ends of the tube excites the mercury vapor into discharging energy to a coating of phosphor on the inner surface of the tube, causing the phosphor to glow. The color of light emitted by a fluorescent tube depends on the chemical composition of the phosphor. Most commonly, the light is somewhat deficient in the longer, "warmer" wavelengths and appears bluish, but fluorescent lamps also are available with phosphors that emit warmer light.

When light falls on an object, the object absorbs a part of the light and reflects the rest back into the environment. Our eyes gather a

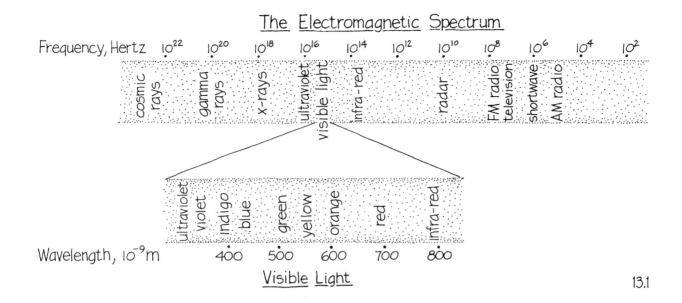

The Electromagnetic Spectrum

Frequency, Hertz 10^{22} 10^{20} 10^{18} 10^{16} 10^{14} 10^{12} 10^{10} 10^{8} 10^{6} 10^{4} 10^{2}

cosmic rays · gamma rays · x-rays · ultraviolet · visible light · infra-red · radar · FM radio · television · shortwave · AM radio

ultraviolet · violet · indigo · blue · green · yellow · orange · red · infra-red

Wavelength, 10^{-9}m   400   500   600   700   800

Visible Light

13.1

small portion of this reflected light, organize it by means of lenses, and convert it at our retinas to nerve impulses that our brains translate into visual images. The color of objects is caused by the selective manner in which they absorb light (13.2). An object that absorbs more of the shorter wavelengths than the longer ones reflects light richer in the longer wavelengths; that is, it has a warm color. Our eyes perceive objects as shaped areas of various colors.

At very low levels of object brightness, the eye can see only large, simple shapes and cannot distinguish colors from one another (13.3). In slightly brighter light, it can see somewhat smaller shapes, but it still cannot distinguish colors. With a bit more light, colors begin to be discernible but are still very muted and grayish. We can read large black print on white paper, but not easily. As the intensity of object brightness is further increased through progressively brighter illumination, we can read finer print, faster and with greater accuracy. Colors appear progressively brighter, and we can distinguish increasingly finer gradations of hue. As intensities become very high, however, visual efficiency increases only marginally. Our eyes begin to be more and more dazzled by intensely bright objects. We begin to feel pain and squint in an attempt to cut down on the amount of light entering our eyes. We can look at brilliant light for only short periods of time before our eyes close from visual fatigue. If we are forced to view objects of painful brightness, our retinas may be damaged.

Our eyes adjust automatically to changes in light intensity. Eyelids, eyelashes, and eyebrows constitute an external system of adjustment. Internally, the pupils change size quite rapidly in response to varying

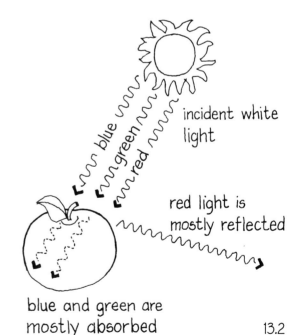

incident white light

red light is mostly reflected

blue and green are mostly absorbed

13.2

129

average illumination on subject of .01 footcandles (0.11 lux)

100 footcandles (1076 lux)

1 footcandle (10.8 lux)

10,000 footcandles (107,600 lux)

13.3

lighting conditions, regulating the amount of light gathered by the eyes. The major internal adjustment mechanism is much slower, however, and occurs in the retina. Eyes adapt quickly to small changes in brightness by changing the pupils but need an adaptation time measured in minutes for large changes. In Nature, where changes of illumination are gradual, this causes few problems. When walking from bright sunlight into a dark theater or basement, however, we experience a condition of "night blindness" for a period of some minutes.

Our eyes can adjust to only a single level of brightness. That is, if a very bright object and a dark object are placed side by side, the bright object will be seen as being very harshly lit and may be too bright to look at for very long. The dark object will be difficult to discern and will at best be seen as a silhouette (13.4, 13.5). Yet when the same dark object is placed against a still darker background in the absence of the very bright object, it appears quite bright and is legible in considerable detail, because the eye has adjusted to its level of brightness. When we look at a person or an object next to a bright object such as the sun, a lightbulb, or a portion of the daytime sky, our eyes adjust to the glare of the bright object insofar as they are able, and we see the remainder of the visual field as a gray blur. We see best when the object we wish to see, termed the *visual task* by lighting designers, is the brightest thing in our field of vision and everything else is less bright, although still within the same general range of brightness.

13.4

13.5

Daylighting

Until quite recently in history, people went to bed when the sun went down. Fires, candles, and oil lamps were very weak sources of illumination and too expensive for most people to afford. Under these conditions, natural light in buildings was a necessity and came to be rather well understood in an intuitive way. Building orientations and configurations, the configuration of window openings, and interior finishes came to be selected in such a way as to ensure sufficient levels of daylighting in interior spaces. Buildings were also developed with architectonic devices such as overhangs, pediments, string courses, quoins, niches, and various moldings to create pleasing, shifting patterns of shade and shadow on their facades as the sun moved across the sky, an art that lies largely forgotten at the present time (13.6).

We are forced to adopt an ambivalent attitude toward the sun in the daylighting of buildings. The sun is, of course, the source of daylight, and a shaft of sunlight entering a window, particularly in winter, exerts a very cheerful influence, brightening interior colors and bringing both psychological and physical warmth. Yet we cannot look directly at the sun itself, and the finer visual tasks such as reading and sewing are almost impossible to carry out in the intense glare of direct sunlight. Even the sky, brilliant with scattered light from the sun, is often bright enough to dazzle the eye. In warm weather, furthermore, we cannot tolerate the heat of direct sunlight in buildings. The bleaching effect of sunlight on carpets, fabrics, and wood can be a problem at any time of year. And finally, we must face the fact that the sun is often obscured partially or entirely by

Rome, Santa Susanna 1597–1603
Carlo Maderno, Architect

13.6

131

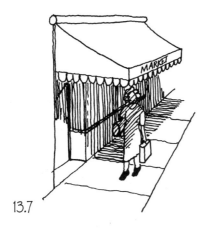

13.7

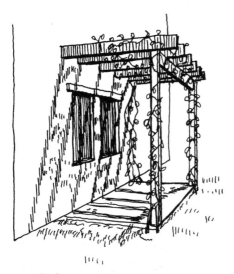

13.8

clouds. For these reasons, we rely largely on diffused sunlight or on reflected, indirect sunlight to illuminate the interiors of buildings. The reflecting surface absorbs much of the heat and scatters the visible light at a much lower intensity than that of direct sunlight.

A large vocabulary of shading and reflecting devices has developed over the millennia. Trees, vines, overhangs, awnings, shutters of every description, louvers, blinds, shades, and curtains are among the more common shading devices (13.7–13.9). Overhead shading devices block or filter direct sunlight, allowing only reflected light from sky and ground to enter the windows. Louvers and blinds can act as shades or can convert direct sunlight to a softer, reflected light. Whitened exterior surfaces and window frames reflect light through windows. Windows and skylights that face north in the northern temperate latitudes receive little or no direct sunlight and so are useful in gathering indirect light from the bright sky without significant heat gain.

When the sun does not penetrate a room directly, the amount of natural light available at a given point in the room is determined by several factors. The most important is the proportion of the total area of the sky that can be "seen" directly by that point through windows and skylights, and the relative brightness of those parts of the sky that are "seen." The sky at the horizon is only about one-third as bright

13.9

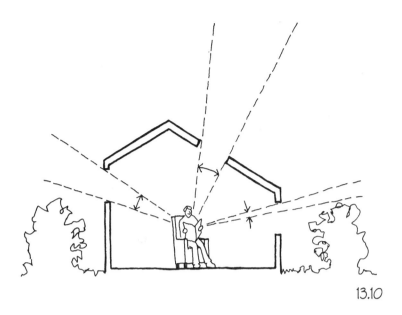

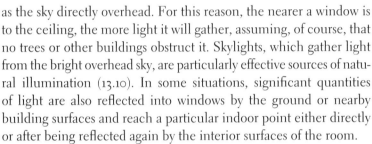

13.10

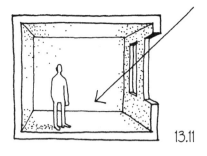

13.11

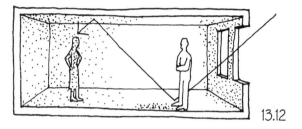

13.12

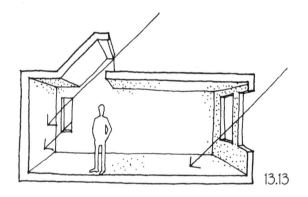

13.13

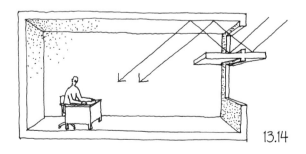

13.14

as the sky directly overhead. For this reason, the nearer a window is to the ceiling, the more light it will gather, assuming, of course, that no trees or other buildings obstruct it. Skylights, which gather light from the bright overhead sky, are particularly effective sources of natural illumination (13.10). In some situations, significant quantities of light are also reflected into windows by the ground or nearby building surfaces and reach a particular indoor point either directly or after being reflected again by the interior surfaces of the room.

The proportions and surface finishes of the room play an important role in daylighting. In general, tallness, shallowness, and high surface reflectances help make rooms brighter (13.11). Low rooms, deep rooms with windows at the narrow end, and rooms with dark-colored surfaces are more difficult to illuminate with daylight (13.12). The farther one moves away from the windows toward the back of the room, the smaller the segment of sky that will be "seen" directly, and the larger the number of successive reflections that will be needed to carry light to the visual task. Highly reflective surfaces—white and light colors, metallic surfaces—absorb less light at each reflection, allowing more to reach the interior of the room. Higher ceilings reduce the number of reflections required to carry light a given distance toward the interior. Windows on a second side of the room, roof monitors, skylights, or clerestories help balance daylighting levels throughout a room (13.13). A *light shelf* is a particularly powerful reflecting device that throws light deep into a room (13.14).

If windows or skylights fall within the normal field of vision of people in a room, they are likely to be distractingly bright compared with other things the occupants want to see. A window next to a

13.15

blackboard in a school, for example, is likely to be many times brighter than the blackboard; its glare renders the blackboard useless. In general, windows should be placed away from interior focal points of rooms. If windows or skylights face large areas of sky, louvers or curtains may have to be installed to reduce their apparent brightness. Light-colored window frames, especially if they are splayed, help reduce uncomfortable contrasts between bright outdoor views and a darker interior (13.15).

Lighting by daylight is an appealing concept for a number of reasons. It provides a pleasant psychological linkage between indoors and outdoors. It is "natural" in color. It varies in interesting ways with the weather and the time of day and year. It usually costs little more money to install windows and surfaces that are appropriate to a good daylighting scheme than to install them at random, and the cost of daylighting energy is forever free. Some maintenance costs are incurred in keeping glass and interior building surfaces clean, but little if any more than the normal costs of building maintenance.

Artificial Lighting

The chief drawback of daylighting is its inconstancy, especially its total unavailability between sundown and sunup. Artificial electric light is instantly and constantly available, is easily manipulated by a designer, and can be controlled by the occupants of the building. This suggests strongly that daylighting and artificial lighting make good partners, with artificial lighting being used mainly for night-time illumination and as a daytime supplement when daylighting alone is insufficient.

The total flow of light produced by three common artificial sources of light (collectively called *lamps*) is approximately as follows:

Wax candle	13 lumens
100-watt incandescent lamp	1,500 lumens
87-watt high-efficiency fluorescent lamp	6,600 lumens

The 100-watt lamp produces about one hundred times as much light as a candle does, at an hourly energy cost that is about a penny at current electrical rates. Its efficiency is 15 lumens per watt. The fluorescent lamp is about five times as efficient at 75 lumens per watt. This means that it can produce the same level of illumination as an incandescent lamp at a much lower energy cost. It also indicates that the fluorescent lamp introduces much less waste heat into the room per lumen output than does an incandescent lamp, a feature that is of considerable importance in a building that must be kept cool in hot weather.

But efficiency is not the only criterion in choosing a light source. Incandescent lamps cast a warm-colored light somewhat similar to firelight or candlelight. A person's skin looks warm and rosy under incandescent illumination; food looks appetizing; and a room takes on a pleasant glow, especially if its walls are made of warm-colored materials such as natural wood or reddish brick. The reflection of the glowing filament sparkles invitingly in glassware, china, silver, or the finish of an automobile. By contrast, people and food look a bit sickly under the bluish light of cool-white fluorescent illumination, and the low-brightness fluorescent source does not create such intense sparkles. Incandescent fixtures also are simple and inexpensive to install and maintain. Thus incandescent lighting still predominates in homes, restaurants, churches, and many retail establishments where warm color and sparkle enhance the appearance of the merchandise. But fluorescent lighting is clearly superior economically in large commercial, industrial, and institutional applications. With the introduction of fluorescent lamps in a wider range of color spectra and shapes, the choice between the two systems is no longer so clear.

In the same range of efficiency as the best fluorescent tubes are *high-intensity-discharge* (HID) *lamps*, including metal halide, high-pressure sodium, low-pressure sodium, and mercury vapor lamps. Despite their high output of light, however, many of these sources give poor color renditions, limiting their use primarily to outdoor lighting. But some high-pressure sodium and metal halide lamps with acceptable color characteristics have been developed specifically as high-efficiency replacements for incandescent lamps in interior applications. Unlike incandescent sources, fluorescent and HID lamps require *ballasts*, which are electromagnetic or electronic components in each fixture that regulate voltage, current, and waveform of the electricity to start and operate the lamps.

Tungsten halogen incandescent lamps are smaller and operate at higher temperatures than standard incandescents. They also are more efficient (though not as much so as fluorescents and HIDs). They provide good color rendition and sparkle, which makes them particularly attractive for homes, restaurants, and retail stores.

Where to place artificial light sources in a building is a question of great importance. Sometimes a poorly placed fixture displays a person or an object "in a bad light," as when a light coming from directly above or below casts underworldly shadows across even the most pleasant of faces. Sometimes a badly located lamp can place an object in shadow, as is the case when a right-handed person tries to write in light coming from a lamp at the right-hand side of the desk. Sometimes a source of light intrudes into the field of vision and causes distracting or damaging glare. Shielding or diffusing

13.16

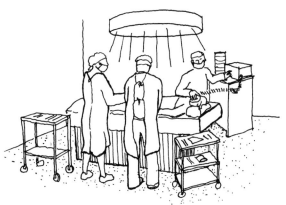

13.17

devices within the light source can do a great deal to counter this glare, but usually it is preferable to locate the source outside the normal fields of vision of persons using a given area.

Lighting Design

An important objective of lighting design is to achieve an appropriate brightness (more properly called *luminance*) of the visual task. The appropriate luminance may be very dim if the visual task is a plate of food on a dining table, very bright if it is someone's appendix on an operating table, or between the two for most other visual tasks (13.16, 13.17). In order to achieve the desired luminance, an appropriate density of light flow to the surface must be provided. This is achieved by selecting and arranging light sources whose pattern and quantity of luminous output work in conjunction with room surfaces of appropriate reflectances. As with daylighting, light-colored, highly reflective room surfaces help provide more illumination from the same amount of energy.

Surface colors play an important role, too, in preventing glare: A white piece of paper on a black desktop causes visual fatigue because of the great contrast in brightness between the two, whereas a white paper on a light gray top may be viewed with comfort for long periods of time. The other essential consideration in preventing glare is to avoid sharp contrasts between the levels of light flow to the task and to the surrounding environment. It is often a good idea to have a small lamp that casts a bright light on an exacting visual task, but unless the rest of the room is illuminated to an intermediate level of brightness, visual fatigue is likely to result.

The correlation between increasing quantities of illumination and increased visual efficiency, which was established in laboratory tests, has led some designers to install systems of extreme brightness and prodigious electrical consumption in offices and factories. Field testing, however, has shown that once an acceptable minimum level of lighting has been established in a room, human satisfaction and performance are more likely to be based on qualitative factors than on the sheer quantity of illumination provided.

When we design a lighting system for a building, we must begin by asking the purpose of the system: Is it to create a certain mood, to enhance the appearance of the building from inside or out, to flatter human faces, to call attention to an object or a person, to make reading or work easier, or some combination of these? How will people enter the building, move through it, and leave it, by night and by day, and how can the lighting design help their eyes and their emotions adjust to these transitions? When a person spends time in an interior space of the building, how can light best contribute to the person's comfort and pleasure? Once these questions have been answered, the design options can be analyzed: What role can daylighting play, and where will artificial light be preferable? What color spectra of artificial light will be most effective? How should the illumination of the building and its tasks change between day and night? Should the light in a particular area of the building be spread evenly throughout the area or largely concentrated on specific places? What types of windows and fixtures will create the appropriate patterns of illumination, and where should they be placed? These decisions are critical, for it is through illumination that the eye perceives a building from inside and outside, and it is through the luminous environment of buildings that the human eye is able to function and to enjoy the unique aesthetic experiences of sight.

Further Reading

M. David Egan. *Concepts in Architectural Lighting*. New York, McGraw-Hill, 1983.

14

Hearing and Being Heard

We take pleasure in the sound of a favorite piece of music, the sound of a friend's voice, the songs of birds on a summer morning, and the spoken words of the actors in a play or on a screen. We derive great satisfaction from creating music with voice or instruments, speaking to a friend, or conveying an important message to an interested audience. Under such circumstances, we want to hear and to be heard. But under other circumstances, we also want the equally important options not to hear and not to be heard, the options of peace and privacy. We wish not to have to listen to continual loud traffic noise or to music that appeals to a neighbor's taste but not to ours, especially if these noises interfere with our sleep, our ability to concentrate, or our ability to hear and to be heard in our immediate surroundings. We wish not to have our secrets known to any but their intended hearers, and we may even wish to make unpleasant sounds—like learning to play the violin or cutting lumber on a power saw—without embarrassing ourselves or disturbing others.

We are sometimes frustrated in our attempts to hear and be heard by the weakness of the sound or by its being obscured and confused by unwanted noise or its own echoes. Often our acoustical privacy is violated by noisy surroundings or by surroundings in which we know that every whisper is audible to a neighbor. Any building, whether or not it was designed with hearing conditions in mind, has numerous important effects on the propagation of sound. If thoroughly understood, these effects can be exploited and manipulated by a designer to create indoor acoustical conditions that are appropriate to the various human functions housed by a building.

Sound

Sound is a sensation induced through the ear by waves of varying air pressure emanating from a vibrating source. Within the ear, the sound waves strike the eardrum (tympanic membrane), setting up vibrations that are transmitted mechanically by tiny levers of bone to an extraordinarily sensitive inner ear mechanism (cochlea), where they are converted to nerve impulses for interpretation by the brain (14.1). The ears of a young listener are capable of detecting frequencies of vibration ranging between about 20 and 20,000 cycles per second (Hz), but with advancing age, we lose our ability to hear the higher frequencies; thus 10,000 to 12,000 cycles per second are typical upper limits of hearing for middle-aged ears.

With respect to the pressure of the sound waves, the average ear can withstand the loudest sounds of Nature and also detect sounds at pressures many millions of times smaller. In order to compress this broad range of sound pressure levels into manageable scale of measurement, a logarithmic scale of *decibels* (db) is used. (A decibel is one-tenth of a bel. The unit is named in honor of Alexander Graham Bell who, in addition to inventing the telephone, did very significant research on hearing and sound.) The accompanying diagram gives a clearer idea of how the human ear is affected by sounds of different pressures (14.2).

The sounds of human speech are produced by vibrations of the vocal cords that are modified by the actions of the throat, nose, and mouth. The various sounds range in duration from about one-fiftieth to one-third second. The fundamental frequencies of the voice lie mostly between 100 and 600 cycles per second, but many of the sounds, consonants in particular, are of much higher frequency and must be heard clearly for maximum intelligibility. Between the most timid whisper and the loudest shout, there is a wide range of sound pressure levels, but the average speaker covers a range of no more than about 30 db. As one would expect, louder speech is generally more intelligible than softer speech.

Musical sounds are usually of longer duration than the sounds of speech and cover much broader ranges of both frequency and sound pressure, especially in the case of instrumental music. Some large pipe organs are capable of producing pitches whose frequencies lie close to the extreme lower end of the hearing spectrum. Very high frequencies occur routinely in the high-pitched overtones of all musical instruments. The softest passages of symphonic music are barely audible, and the loudest rock music exceeds the threshold of pain.

Noise is unwanted sound. It may be speech or music, sounds of natural forces such as wind and rain, or mechanical sounds of

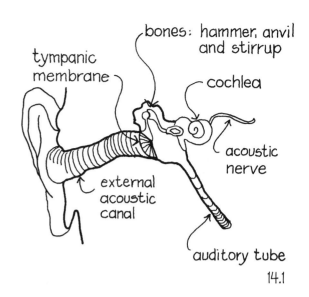

14.1

$\dfrac{watts}{cm^2}$	Decibels	
10^{-2}	140	Jet aircraft at close range
10^{-3}	130	Threshold of pain
10^{-4}	120	Elevated train close by
10^{-5}	110	Symphony orchestra, ff
10^{-6}	100	Power saw
10^{-7}	90	Downtown street
10^{-8}	80	Shouting at close range
10^{-9}	70	Inside automobile, 55 mph
10^{-10}	60	Face-to-face conversation
10^{-11}	50	Average office
10^{-12}	40	Quiet living room
10^{-13}	30	Quiet bedroom
10^{-14}	20	Rural ambient noise
10^{-15}	10	Rustling leaves
10^{-16}	0	Threshold of hearing 14.2

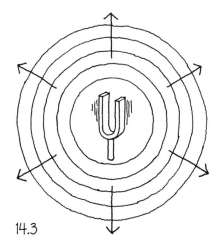

14.3

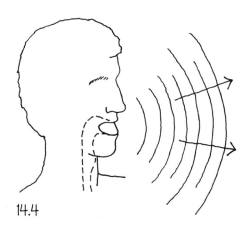

14.4

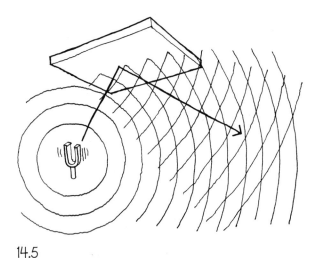

14.5

engines, gears, fans, tires on pavement, squealing brakes, buzzing electrical equipment, or banging pipes. The potential sources of noise in contemporary society are so diverse in their sound characteristics that it is impossible to offer any generalizations about their properties; each noise problem must be analyzed individually to determine its source, its characteristic range of frequencies, and its sound pressure before steps can be taken to rectify it.

In theory, sound waves radiate spherically from a point source (14.3). If the source were suspended in an ideal volume of air, the sound pressure would diminish in proportion to the square of the distance of the listener from the source. In practice, sound waves often originate from sources such as the human voice that radiate more strongly in some directions than in others. Sound waves are invariably acted on in various ways by ground or building surfaces, resulting in the formation of sound fields that cannot be described by means of simple mathematical expressions (14.4, 14.5).

Wavelengths for audible frequencies vary from more than 50 feet (15 m) for very low pitches to less than an inch (a few millimeters) for the very high ones. When sound waves strike an object that is smaller than or similar in dimension to the wavelength of the sound, diffraction occurs, scattering the waves in many directions. When a sound wave strikes a surface that is large compared with its wavelength, a portion of the sound energy is reflected, much as light is reflected from a mirror, and a portion is absorbed by the surface. The harder and more rigid a surface is, the larger the proportion it will reflect. Soft, porous materials absorb a large proportion of the incident sound energy, dissipating it in immeasurably small flows of heat created by friction between the moving molecules of air and the walls of the pores of the materials. For a given frequency, optimum absorption is achieved by pores placed at a distance of one-quarter wavelength from a rigid, hard surface, where the velocity of the air molecules in both incoming and reflected sound waves is at a maximum. This means that greater thicknesses of porous materials are required to absorb lower frequencies. A thin fabric wall covering absorbs only those frequencies near or above the top of the audible range. A padded carpet or thick drapery absorbs the majority of incident sound in the higher portion of the audible range. Deep, porous upholstery absorbs most sound from middle frequencies upward. The lowest musical frequencies cannot be absorbed efficiently by ordinary thicknesses of porous material. A window opened into free air absorbs all sound striking it and is the limiting case of total absorption. A smooth, dense, painted wall of concrete or plaster absorbs less than 5 percent of incident sound; it is an excellent reflector.

Sound is capable of inducing resonant responses in hollow vessels or constructions whose natural frequencies match that of the sound.

The air within the vessel acts as a spring, oscillating at a frequency that is characteristic of the volume and length of the vessel. Because a resonating body absorbs energy from the waves that excite it, resonating devices offer a useful means of absorbing sound energy. In practice, resonators are easiest to construct for the lower frequencies, which makes them a useful adjunct to porous absorbers for the treatment of rooms in which the full range of frequencies needs to be controlled. In new concert halls, resonators are usually constructed as concealed hollows in walls.

Sound is able to travel in media other than air—it can be transmitted through steel, wood, concrete, masonry, or almost any rigid material of construction (14.6). The sound of footsteps (especially of high heels) is readily transmitted through a concrete floor slab into the air of the room below. A metal pipe can carry plumbing noise throughout a building. A beam can carry sound vibrations to an adjacent room or the rumble of an electric motor through a building.

Every building produces sounds of its own, such as the patter of rain and sleet on building surfaces; the whistle of infiltrating wind; the slamming of doors; the creaking of old wood floors underfoot; the mechanical noises of heating systems, plumbing systems, elevator machinery, garbage grinders, and various other machines; and the occasional creaks, cracking noises, and groans of a structure being pushed and pulled by wind, heat, and humidity. We can reduce mechanical noises by selecting quiet devices, installing them as far as possible from the inhabited areas of the building, mounting them with resilient fittings to eliminate structure-borne noise, and housing them in sound-isolating enclosures to cut down on the airborne transmission of their noise. We can usually reduce wind noises with better weatherstripping on windows and doors, which gives the added benefits of lower transmission of outdoor noises to the interior and lower heating and cooling costs. Rain and sleet sounds, if objectionable, can be reduced by using heavier roof and window construction. Structural noises produced by the slippage of building components past one another during sporadic releases of built-up stresses are largely inevitable and difficult to remedy. Sometimes, if the source of the rubbing can be located precisely, a building component can be nailed or bolted tighter, or graphite particles can be blown into the moving joint as a lubricant.

A building conducts sound from room to room in various ways. Sound passes between rooms wherever an opening exists, even a very small one such as a keyhole, the slot at the bottom of a door, or the crack between a partition and the ceiling (14.7). Open or ill-fitting windows and doors transmit sound readily. Ductwork for heating, cooling, or ventilating systems often provides an air path from room to room that, unless lined with sound-absorbing material,

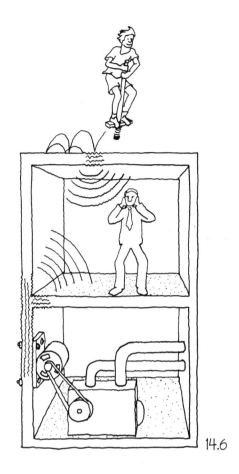

14.6

14.7

14.8

readily transmits conversations and other sounds (14.8). If we want privacy, we should weatherstrip cracks around windows and doors and close all other cracks and openings with airtight sealants. Partitions must go from the top of one floor slab to the underside of the next for maximum sound isolation and should be built in as massive and airtight a manner as possible. A thick brick partition wall makes a good sound barrier between rooms. A partition of concrete blocks is not as good as one of bricks, because the blocks are somewhat porous, and the pores allow some sound to pass through. Plastering one or both surfaces of a block partition to make it airtight resolves this problem.

Most partitions are built of slender, upright framing members to which plaster or gypsum board surfaces are attached on both sides. An ordinary partition of this type is not a very effective barrier to sound. To improve its acoustical performance, layers of gypsum board may be added to one or both sides to increase its mass. If one of these layers is attached with resilient metal clips instead of being screwed tightly to the framing, the structure-borne transmission of sound through the partition will be reduced substantially. Still better acoustic isolation can be achieved by inserting fibrous batts to deaden the transmission of sound across the airspaces inside the partition.

"Acoustic" tiles, which are excellent absorbers of incident sound within a room, help to lower noise levels by absorbing some of the sound energy generated in a room, but because of their extreme porosity and low density, they are of no value in reducing the passage of noise from room to room through a ceiling or wall. The same is true of curtains and carpets, except for the impact-cushioning action of carpets in preventing the generation of noise. An excellent way of reducing the transmission of impact noise through floors is to add a thick carpet and pad to the floor. For more quiet, a resilient layer can be added to the floor construction, such as a layer of compressible plastic matting between the floor slab and the finish flooring material or resilient metal clips to which the plaster ceiling is mounted to the underside of the slab.

Creating Good Hearing Conditions

The acoustical suitability of a room for a concert, dramatic production, lecture, or religious service depends mainly on the shape, size, and proportions of the room and the amounts of sound of various frequencies that are absorbed, reflected, and scattered by its surfaces and contents.

The shape of the room is extremely important because it determines the paths along which sound is reflected. In small rooms with parallel walls, *standing waves* are sometimes evident, in which certain frequencies of voice or music are exaggerated as they repeatedly bounce back and forth between opposite walls. Standing waves can be eliminated by slightly tilting or skewing two adjacent walls of the room or by adding acoustically absorptive material to them. Rooms with concave surfaces tend to focus sound reflections in one or more areas, leaving acoustic "dead spots" elsewhere. A "whispering gallery" is a room in which two participants can stand near a curved surface and hear each other's whispering with startling loudness and clarity (14.9). Or it can be a room with a concave surface at each end, with the participants standing at the foci of the curved surfaces. Concave surfaces are generally to be avoided in performance halls of any kind because they focus sound in some areas and leave other areas with insufficient sound. Convex surfaces, on the other hand, scatter reflected sound widely, helping reinforce sound levels in all parts of a room (14.10). Random, irregular room surfaces can be designed to scatter and reflect sound in patterns that distribute sound more or less evenly to all listeners. Thus an acoustical design for a music performance hall often includes convex and irregular surfaces (14.11).

Sound reinforcement, the amplification of sound by its being heard from various reflections as well as directly from the source, is a very important function of the reflective properties of a room. The ceilings of meeting rooms, classrooms, and auditoriums are often completely covered with sound-absorbing materials by well-intentioned but ill-informed people. This eliminates any sound reinforcement by reflections off the ceiling and results in inadequate sound levels toward the rear of the room. The usual next step, the installation of an electronic sound reinforcement system, often would be unnecessary if much of the center of the ceiling had been

14.9

14.10

143

14.11

left uncovered as a reflecting surface. On the other hand, in some very large halls a reflected sound can take so long a path that it arrives at the ears of a listener significantly later than the direct sound from the stage; it is heard as a distinct echo, which confuses the sound rather than reinforces it. Such long-path reflections must be eliminated through improved room geometry or the selective use of absorptive surfaces. It is important, however, to reinforce sound by creating reflections along short paths, which cannot create echoes.

The period of time during which a sound bounces around a room before dying to an inaudible level is known as the *reverberation time* of the room. In general, reverberation time increases with increasing room volume, because of the longer paths that each sound wave must travel between its successive reflections, and it decreases when we add sound-absorbing materials, which intercept and swallow the waves. Reverberation is important in lecture halls, theaters, houses of worship, and concert halls because it sustains and blends the sounds, an effect that makes them much smoother and richer than the same sounds propagated in the open air. The achievement of an appropriate reverberation time for a given hall is of great importance. For speech, a short reverberation time is best, so that short consonant sounds remain clear. But a certain amount of reverberation helps enrich a speaker's voice and gives a speaker a sense of how well his or her voice is carrying to the audience. For music, longer reverberation times extend and blend the sounds of the instruments or voices in a way that composers, musicians, and audiences have come to expect and demand. Music sounds dead and brittle in a hall with too short a reverberation time but will lose clarity and definition if the reverberation time is too long. A hall of optimum design imparts brilliance and color to the music, without destroying its clear articulation. Houses of worship in which preaching is of prime importance need relatively short reverberation times, whereas those with more ceremonial services need longer ones. It is thought that the practice in the more ceremonial religions of chanting the liturgy grew out of the need to communicate clearly in cavernous buildings with very long reverberation times. Liturgical music, from medieval times to the present, has often depended on large, echoing interiors for much of its emotional effect.

In order to design a hall with good hearing conditions, then, we must develop a room shape that distributes and reinforces sound evenly throughout the audience, and we must determine a room volume that will give a reverberation time that is appropriate for the uses to which the hall will be put. The distribution of sound in the hall is predicted by plotting paths of sound rays and their reflections on plan and section drawings or by using computer graphics. The reverberation time is calculated on the basis of the volume of the hall and the amount of sound that will be absorbed by each of its surfaces. These predictions may be sharpened and elaborated by electronically testing a scale model of the hall, or by a computer simulation.

For good listening conditions in a hall, we also must reduce noise levels to a minimum so as to avoid interference with the sounds of the performance. This is achieved by using heavy, airtight construction in walls, roofs, and floors to keep out external noise and by installing very quiet systems for ventilating, heating, and cooling the hall.

Sophisticated electronic devices have enhanced our ability to design the acoustics of performance halls. When creating a hall out of an existing building that was designed for other purposes, it is sometimes impossible to achieve the optimum configuration and proportions for good hearing conditions. In this situation, a system of speakers and amplifiers often can be designed to remedy the defects in the natural acoustics. Such a system might focus additional sound into "dead" areas of the hall, or it might add a fraction of a second to its reverberation time. It is possible to predict in advance what the acoustical characteristics of any hall will be by modeling them with electronic equipment through which we can hear an accurate simulation of what music will sound like at any designated location in that hall. This allows management, musicians, and designers to "try out" the hall before it is constructed, to propose changes in its acoustical environment, and to hear the results of these changes.

Noise is unwanted sound. Where we need quiet rooms for sleep or study, noise must be kept to a minimum. Noise control begins by planning the building in such a way that the rooms that need to be quiet are as distant as possible from sources of noise such as busy streets, public rooms, kitchens, workshops, gymnasiums, or rooms housing operating machinery. In this way, the intervening rooms shield the quiet rooms from much of the clamor. The walls, floor, and ceiling of the quiet rooms should be heavy and airtight.

If the noise is coming across open land from a factory, airport, or highway, increasing distance helps reduce its intensity. Dense, wide groves of evergreen trees can absorb some of the noise, although individual trees or single lines of trees are of little use. Ordinary wood fences are too lightweight to block noise. A heavy wall of concrete or masonry can be more effective, but it must be high and broad enough to block all direct sight lines between the quiet room and the noise, and it must be close to either the room or the source of noise. The freeway noise barriers that are seen around many large cities are generally close to the roadway, tall enough to cut all direct sight lines, and made of closely fitted pieces of concrete, masonry, or heavy timber. Buildings near airports are exposed to noise that is exceptionally loud and that arrives from planes at many different locations in the sky and on the ground, which makes it particularly difficult to keep the noise out. Some relief can be had by replacing all the windows with sealed units made of two or more layers of laminated glass with air spaces between the layers. Laminated glass is made by sandwiching a layer of very soft plastic between two sheets of glass. The soft inner layer helps to damp the passage of sound vibrations through the glass. When the building is sealed, of course, it must be artificially ventilated and cooled. The low-level noise of the air conditioning system helps to mask the aircraft noise.

Sometimes when noise is particularly persistent and annoying, a building cannot be effectively protected from it, or there may not be enough money for treatment to reduce it. And sometimes a room is so quiet that even a whisper is distracting, and the sounds of one's respiration, heartbeat, and body movements are bothersome. In any of these cases, introducing a low-level *masking noise* can help obscure the unwanted sounds. The best masking noises are the natural ones that almost everyone enjoys: waves lapping against a shore, wind blowing through trees, an open fire crackling, rain drumming on a roof, a brook or fountain splashing. None of these restful sounds has the distractive qualities inherent in music or speech. But if they are not available, a slightly noisy ventilating system may be as effective. In many commercial buildings, masking noise is introduced electronically through a system of speakers distributed throughout. Any masking noise must be strong in the frequencies that predominate in the sound to be masked.

Quieting a Noisy Room

Why are some restaurants so noisy that we have to shout to converse with our tablemates, whereas other restaurants are hushed and relaxed? A noisy restaurant is one with hard surfaces all around: plaster walls and ceiling and a bare floor. The first few diners that arrive for dinner are able to converse normally. When more people arrive and begin speaking, sound levels rise with the considerable assistance of sounds that are reflected from the surfaces of the room. As sound levels rise, everyone must speak more loudly in order to be understood. This creates a still higher level of noise, people have to speak louder still, and a vicious circle is established that reaches climax with everyone shouting amid a level of general noise that approximates that of an airport runway. If the same restaurant were to have acoustic panels on its ceiling, heavy curtains on the windows, deep upholstery on the chairs, and a thick, padded carpet on the floor, it would become a quiet restaurant. If you're seeking a quiet place for a meal, look for the carpet and acoustic panels and avoid restaurants with hard surfaces.

Creating Privacy

If a building must create acoustical privacy—preventing conversations from being overheard—much the same strategies come into play: Construction must be airtight and heavy. Sound levels within the room can be lowered somewhat by the use of sound-absorbing materials. And masking noise can be invaluable. A barroom packed elbow to elbow with chattering people is in fact a very private environment for intimate conversation. There is simply so much noise generated in the frequency range of human speech that only the closest, most attentive listener can understand one's words. This is why, too, master spies and diplomats, whether fictional or real, turn up the radio or television before conducting discussions in a room that is suspected of being "bugged."

Hearing, being heard, not hearing, and not being heard are important factors that we must consider in the design of buildings.

In most circumstances the ordinary materials with which we build are sufficient for the purpose. But they must be correctly and carefully used.

Further Reading

Madan Mehta, Jim Johnson, and Jorge Rocafort. *Architectural Acoustics.* Upper Saddle River, N.J., Prentice-Hall, 1999.

15

Providing Concentrated Energy

Until the late nineteenth century, only two forms of energy were commonly available in ordinary buildings for performing useful work: fire and human muscle power. Today, in most parts of the world, electricity is available in every room of every building as a clean, reliable, exceptionally convenient form of energy for illuminating, heating, operating tools and appliances, and powering electronic communications and entertainment.

Generating and Transmitting Electricity

Electricity is generated in large plants that are powered by either water turbines fed from reservoirs or, more commonly, steam turbines (15.1). The steam is generated by coal, oil, gas, or nuclear fuel. The best steam plants are about 40 percent efficient, which means that one-and-a-half times as much heat is lost up the chimneys of the power plant and into the waterways used to cool the condensers as is put into the transmission lines as potentially useful energy. Further losses are incurred in transmitting the electricity to the user, resulting in an overall efficiency for an electrical generation and distribution system of about one-third. Fortunately, electrical devices in buildings convert the electricity to useful energy at rather high efficiencies, but this does not change the fact that heat-producing appliances that can burn fuels in a building, generally at efficiencies of 80 to 95 percent, are inherently less consumptive of fuel and cheaper to operate than are their electrical counterparts, except in some areas with abundant hydroelectric energy.

The generation of electricity on individual building sites is becoming more common, though it is still relatively rare. Large complexes of buildings sometimes make their own electricity as a part of

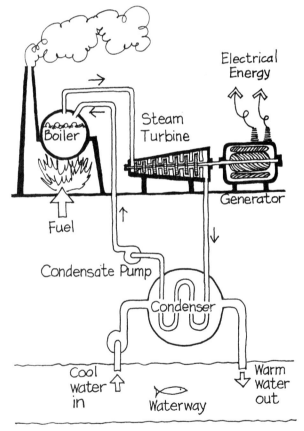

15.1

the output of a *total energy system*. A typical total energy system powers electric generators with internal combustion engines fueled with natural gas. The cooling water from the engines is used to heat domestic hot water or to heat the buildings. The overall efficiency of the system is high because the heat that is incidental to the process is utilized.

On-site generating units, whether powered by internal-combustion engines, water, sun, or wind, are generally expensive to buy and maintain, are of limited capacity when compared with the capacity we have grown to expect of our electrical systems, and are less efficient and reliable than central generating plants. They may also be noisy and smelly; they may be unable to generate steady alternating current; and they may not be able to provide electricity when water levels or wind speeds are low, when clouds are present, or when they break down.

Solid-state *photovoltaic panels* that convert sunlight directly into electricity have come down in price to the point that they are being deployed on the exterior walls or roofs of many new buildings. The popularity of photovoltaics has also benefited from their availability in such forms as photovoltaic roof shingles and transparent photovoltaic glass. The electrical output of a photovoltaic array is usually insufficient to power the building in its entirety, so that supplemental electricity must be purchased from the local utility company. During times when the panels are generating more electricity than the building can use, the surplus is usually sold back to the utility company.

Buildings with critical occupancies such as hospitals, scientific laboratories, and central computer facilities usually contain *standby electric generating units* to maintain uninterrupted power during power failures. Whenever the electric lines stop bringing electricity into the building, the generator starts itself automatically and switches the building from utility power to backup power.

Virtually all electricity is generated as *alternating current* (AC), in which the voltage in the wires oscillates back and forth between maximal values of positive and negative polarity. The frequency of alternation is 60 cycles per second (Hz) in the United States but is lower in some countries. The chief advantage of AC electricity over *direct current* (DC) is that its voltage is easily and efficiently changed by means of simple, efficient *transformers*. Generators put out current at many thousands of volts. This voltage is further increased by transformers at the generating plant before the electricity is passed to the main transmission lines, in order to reduce amperage to a minimum. When amperages are kept low and voltages are high, large amounts of energy can be transmitted for very long distances through relatively small wires with minimal transmission losses.

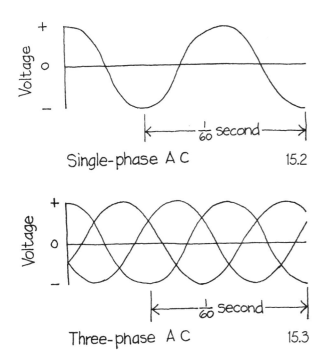

Single-phase A C   15.2

Three-phase A C   15.3

(Amperage is analogous to the volume of water flowing in a pipe. Voltage is analogous to the pressure of the water.)

Most alternating current is utilized as *single-phase* electricity, meaning that the voltage varies as a single sine wave, reaching zero twice in each cycle (15.2). For most purposes this pattern is entirely acceptable, but the more powerful electric motors are relatively large, bulky, and inefficient when designed to run on the intermittent pulses of single-phase electricity. For this reason, *three-phase* AC is distributed in industrial areas, using three sets of generator coils to superimpose three sine waves 120° out of phase. This gives a steadier, smoother flow of energy and enables the use of smaller, more efficient motors (15.3).

Before being passed from long-distance, high-voltage transmission lines to local lines for distribution to buildings, electrical energy is reduced in voltage in local transformer substations (15.4). This results in somewhat higher transmission losses per mile in local lines than in long-distance lines, but the local lines cannot be insulated or protected as heavily as the long-distance lines can. Furthermore, local lines are much shorter, so that higher transmission losses per mile do not add up to high losses overall. The voltage in local lines is still too high for consumer uses, however, so each building or group of buildings is provided with a small transformer to reduce the voltage still further before it enters the building. In individual dwellings and other small buildings, service is usually provided at 230 or 240 volts from transformers that are mounted either

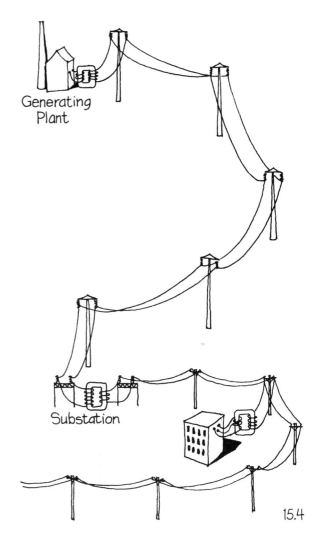

Generating
Plant

Substation

15.4

on power poles, on the surface of the ground, or in underground vaults. Large buildings and building complexes often buy electricity at local line voltage for more efficient internal distribution, reducing its voltage with inside transformers as needed before use.

Electrical Distribution in Small Buildings

Both copper and aluminum are excellent conductors and are commonly used as material for electric wires. Copper is a better conductor than aluminum, but aluminum wire is somewhat cheaper, even taking into account that slightly larger wire sizes must be used than in copper. A disadvantage of aluminum is that its oxide, unlike that of copper, is an electric insulator, and this has caused overheating problems and fires in some buildings where aluminum wire was improperly connected to fixtures, allowing corrosion to interfere with current flow. Copper is generally used for the smaller-diameter wires that are used in local circuits within a building, and aluminum is used for the very large-diameter wires.

The electrical system in a small building is quite simple in concept. Three wires pass overhead or underground from a pole-mounted or ground-level transformer to the building (15.5). One is a neutral wire, which means that no electric potential exists between this wire and the ground. That is, one could stand on wet soil and touch the neutral wire with no danger of electric shock. To ensure that this is so, the neutral wire is connected firmly to one or more long copper-covered steel rods driven into the soil near the point at which the wire enters the building (15.6). The second and third wires are "hot," energized in such a way that they have a potential of 230 volts between them, but only 115 volts between either of them and the neutral wire. Before entering the building, the hot wires pass through an electric meter that measures consumption in units of kilowatt-hours.

Inside the building, the three wires from the transformer enter a main service panel. The neutral wire is connected to the steel box housing the panel and to a copper or aluminum bar to which all building circuits are grounded. Each of the hot wires, color-coded black and red on their insulating layers, is connected to a copper or aluminum bar fitted with connectors by means of which circuit breakers can be attached. These two bars, carefully insulated from the grounded panel box and from each other, are configured in such a way that a single circuit breaker connects a single wire to one or the other of the bars, and a double circuit breaker, occupying two adjacent panel locations, connects one wire to one bar and one to the other. By this means, a single circuit breaker enables the connection of a single 115-volt or 120-volt circuit, consisting of a black-

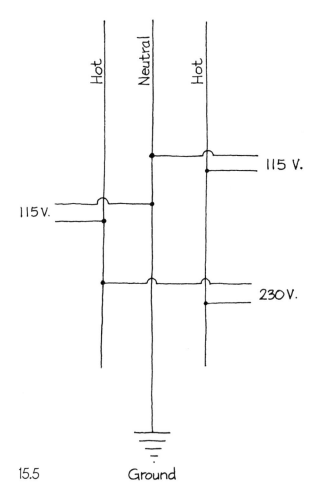

15.5

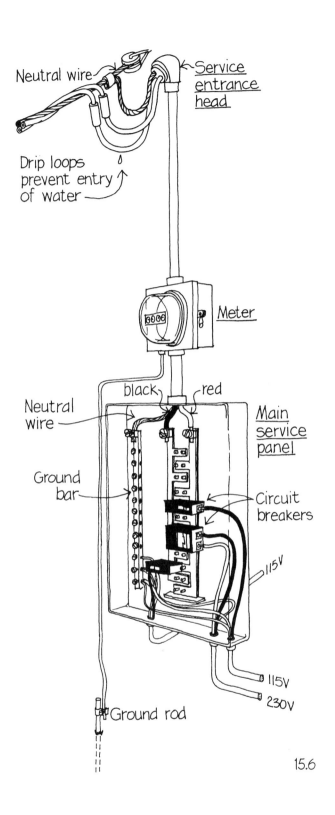

Neutral wire

Service entrance head

Drip loops prevent entry of water

Meter

black   red

Neutral wire

Main service panel

Ground bar

Circuit breakers

115V

115V

230V

Ground rod

15.6

insulated hot wire connected to the breaker and a white-insulated neutral wire connected to the metal grounding bar. Depending on where the breaker is placed in the box, the hot wire for a 115-volt circuit may be connected to either the red or black wire coming from the meter; it is immaterial which. A double breaker connects to both the black and red wires and is used for 230-volt or 240-volt circuits. (Exact voltages are not critical; different power companies supply electricity at slightly differing voltages, and there is always some loss of voltage in the wires that carry the electricity.) Breakers are easily installed as needed to connect the various circuits in a building. Each breaker serves as a convenient on-off switch for maintenance work on its circuit, in addition to performing the important safety function of automatically shutting off current to the circuit if for any reason more current starts flowing than the wire is capable of carrying without overheating and causing a fire. Such a condition can be caused by too many appliances being plugged in at once or by a short circuit created by either faulty wiring or a faulty appliance.

There usually are three wires serving any circuit, whether 115 volt or 230 volt: a black-insulated wire, a white-insulated wire, and an uninsulated wire connected to the grounding bar in the panel. These wires must be protected from damage as they pass through the structure of the building. In wood residential construction, this is usually done by means of a tough protective plastic sheath housing all three wires. In heavier types of construction, the wires are run in steel or plastic pipes called *conduits*. A conduit offers better protection to the wires than does a plastic sheath, and in a building wired through conduits, new wires can be installed by pulling them through existing conduits, something that is not possible with plastic-sheathed cable.

At each electrical receptacle, lighting fixture, or switch, a metal or plastic box must be fastened securely to the structure of the building to support the device and protect its connections (15.7). Each cable or conduit is clamped tightly to the box where the wires enter, thus protecting the wires from being pulled from their connections in case the cable or conduit is disturbed. The bare neutral wire is connected to the box and to the frame of the device to ensure that they will never be able to cause shocks if the device should become faulty. The black and white wires are stripped of insulation at their ends and then are connected to the device by means of screws or clips. After the circuit is tested for safe, satisfactory operation, the device is screwed snugly to the box, and a cover plate of metal or plastic is attached to keep fingers out, to keep the electrical connections free of dust and dirt, and to provide a neat appearance.

Electrical codes specify a maximum horizontal distance between receptacles in a room. This is to ensure that a lamp or appliance with

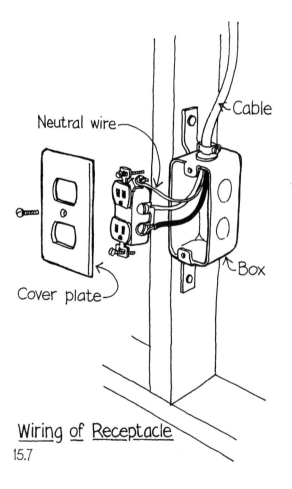

Neutral wire

Cable

Cover plate

Box

Wiring of Receptacle
15.7

a standard-length cord can be located anywhere around the perimeter of the room without requiring an extension cord. Also specified are a minimum number of receptacles per room and a maximum number of receptacles per circuit in order to avoid overloading the wires with excessive flows of current.

The sizes of wires used in an electrical system are determined according to the maximum amount of current to be carried and the length of wire needed, in order to avoid excessive heating of the wire and excessive energy loss. Quite slender wires are used for light-duty circuits at 115 volts, whereas a residential service entrance often uses wires as thick as one's finger.

A safety device called a *ground fault interrupter* (GFI) is required in circuits that serve areas where there is an increased hazard of accidental electric shock, such as bathrooms, kitchens, swimming pools, and outdoor receptacles. If a GFI senses any leakage of current from a circuit, no matter how small, it will disconnect the circuit completely and instantaneously. *Arc fault circuit interrupters* (AFCIs) are required on circuits that run to bedrooms, where an electric arc in a short-circuited electrical device might ignite bed clothing or draperies. AFCIs disconnect the circuit if arcing is detected.

Electrical Systems for Large Buildings

At their extremities, electrical systems in large buildings are much like the small-scale system just described. A large building has many local service panels for its various floors and zones, and each such zone has wiring much like that of a house. When very large quantities of current must be carried at ordinary voltages to serve a number of these zones, large rectangular copper or aluminum *bus bars* are used instead of wires, each enclosed in a protective metal duct. Local panels are then connected to these bars, with wires branching out in conduits from the panels to local fixtures.

As mentioned earlier, large buildings are usually served with electricity at higher voltages than the typical 120/240 volt domestic service. This enables them to buy the electricity at a wholesale rate and to distribute it around the building at higher voltages with correspondingly higher efficiency. In a very large building, one or more large transformers reduce the voltage for distribution to local panels, and additional, small transformers within the building may be used to facilitate interior long-range distribution at voltages that are intermediate between that of the electricity supplied to the building and that of final local distribution. Some commercial and industrial buildings, in addition to 120/240 volt electricity for ordinary purposes, also require electricity at higher voltages such as 277 volts for lighting fixtures and 440 volts for large electric motors.

If the wiring will have to be changed frequently, as it is in some office buildings and most computer facilities, wires may be run through special rectangular underfloor ducts that are supplied with numerous access boxes to which fixtures may be easily attached. Sometimes a *raised access floor* may be provided, made up of small, easily removable panels of flooring supported by pedestals, below which conduits may run at random. Designers of any building much larger than a residence must provide horizontal and vertical spaces for conduits, bus ducts, panels, and communications wiring, and maintenance access for electricians through doors, hatches, or removable panels.

Low-voltage wiring, usually at 12 to 14 volts, is frequently used for doorbell circuits, thermostat circuits, and, through relays, for the switching of lighting circuits, especially where complex switching or remote-control panels are required. The advantage of low-voltage wiring is that it is incapable of giving severe shocks or causing fire, so it may be run through a building in lightly insulated wires without using a cable or conduit. Because the required amperages are also low, the wire itself is small and inexpensive. The current is produced by means of a small transformer connected to a 115-volt circuit. Most telephone and communications wiring is also low voltage, with current provided by the communications company.

Contemporary communications are being carried increasingly by fiber optics rather than copper wires. Fiber optic cables are run through a building just as if they were wires.

Other Energy Systems in Buildings

Forms of concentrated energy other than electricity are often piped into buildings. Fuel gas is the most common of these and is usually piped directly from wellhead to building. Some buildings in remote locations burn compressed gas delivered in a liquid state to pressurized tanks that are connected to the building's gas piping. The liquid boils at ordinary temperatures and gives off propane and other gases in a gaseous state. For any type of gas, the piping system is extremely simple, involving a regulator to step down the high pressure of the main or tank, a meter to measure consumption, and pipes of appropriate sizes to serve the various appliances.

High-pressure steam, usually exhaust steam from the local electric generating plant that is reheated somewhat and distributed through mains and meters to users, is available from underground mains in many urban areas. It is used by many large buildings for heating and absorption cooling, thus avoiding the need to install individual boilers and chimneys. At one time, steam also was used to power elevators, fans, and pumps in buildings, but it has now been replaced by electricity for nearly all these functions.

Compressed air is often provided through pipelines to work stations in shops and factories, where it is used to power portable tools, clamping devices, and paint sprayers. Air-powered tools tend to be cheaper, lighter, and more rugged than their electric equivalents. The air is usually furnished by an electric-powered compressor on the premises. Vacuum piping is common in scientific laboratory buildings. In some urban localities, vacuum lines, compressed-air lines, or high-pressure water mains for use in driving tools were once buried beneath the streets as utility systems. Today, electricity, gas, and steam are the only energy utilities remaining in common use.

Further Reading

Benjamin Stein and John Reynolds. *Mechanical and Electrical Equipment for Buildings* (9th ed.). New York, Wiley, 2000, pp. 853–1045.

16

Fitting Buildings to People

16.1

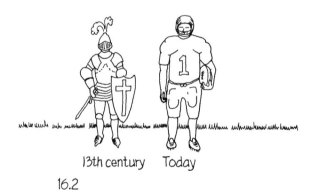

13th century   Today

16.2

People are the true measure of all things in building. Buildings are designed by people and built by people for inhabitation by people. At both ends of the architectural process, the designing and the inhabiting, the dimensions and movements of the human body are the major determinants of the shapes and sizes of things. This presents the problem that people vary a good deal in size, shape, and mobility. On the average, men are larger than women, and children come in all sizes (16.1). The average human today is considerably larger than the average human of a century ago, and we grow measurably with each generation (16.2). There is no such thing as an "average" human figure. Quite average-appearing men vary in height over a range of at least a foot (300 mm), and many exceptionally tall or short ones fall outside this range. The same is true for women. Body builds in both sexes vary in bone structure, musculature, and fat distribution. Young children are much smaller and less physically coordinated than adults but are more active. Adolescent children are nearly as large as adults but more active and in many cases better coordinated. Adults become progressively less agile through middle age until in later years many are quite restricted in their motions. Persons of any age, if on crutches, confined to a wheelchair, or otherwise disabled, are likely to have physical dimensions and requirements very different from those of fully mobile persons. Given this diverse clientele, then, by which of them should we measure our buildings?

The easy answer is, we should custom-design each building for the exact people who will use it. But this is not always possible, because we must often build for unknown tenants. Even when we know intimately the occupants of a building, it is almost certain that someday they will move elsewhere and a new group of persons of unknown sizes and shapes will move in.

16.3

Children present a special problem because they grow. In a school we can resolve this problem to some extent by scaling different classrooms and toilet rooms to different age groups (16.3) while compromising somehow for the comfort of the adult teachers, but in a residence a child often grows up in the same room over a period of many years. A room scaled specifically as a nursery will grow obsolete as the child ages.

There is no fully satisfactory answer to this dilemma. The best we can do in most cases is to size building components to accommodate the preponderance of the adult population while leaving a few people of exceptional size or shape, along with the younger children, in the position of continually having to make accommodations to the building. Much of their strain can be eased through the provision of appropriately scaled furnishings, as seen especially vividly in the case of children. In residences, libraries, lounges, and other buildings in which the inhabitants are free to locate themselves in any of a number of places, spaces of varying scales and degrees of enclosure may furnish important opportunities for persons of different physical and psychic dimensions to find appropriate surroundings.

Building Dimensions

The dimensions of a building grow ultimately from the dimensions of the human figure. At the most basic level, a woman sitting in a soft chair establishes certain important dimensions (16.4). The interior

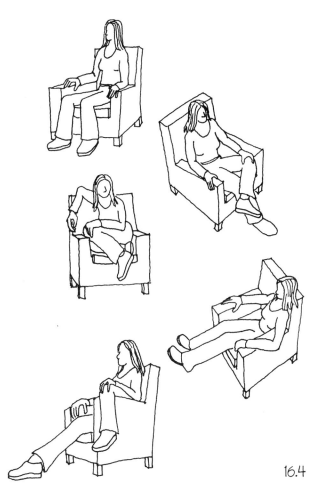

16.4

159

16.5

of the chair must be large enough in all dimensions to support her body comfortably in any of a number of normal sitting postures: feet on the floor, legs crossed, legs tucked under her body, sitting straight up, sitting wedged diagonally into a corner of the chair, even sitting with a leg dangling over one armrest. The distance between the seat cushion and the floor, the angle of the cushion, the angle of the chair back, and the height and angle of the armrests all are based on the size and configuration of the average human body, represented here by a woman. The external dimensions of the chair grow from these dimensions, plus the thickness of structure required to support the weight of her body and the thickness of padding required to distribute her weight comfortably across her flesh. Around the chair, within easy reaching radius of the woman's arms, are other furnishings: a lamp tall enough to cast light over her shoulder and onto her book; a magazine rack large enough to contain ordinary reading matter, which in turn is of a size that comfortably fits her hand and eye; and a side table at a height that puts a cup of tea within easy reach (16.5).

The woman rises and walks to the dining table. As she moves, her body sweeps a volume of space that must be maintained clear of obstructions. There must be space for her to move behind her dining chair, space to pull out the chair, and space to enter between her chair and the next (16.6). The chair must support her comfortably at a height appropriate for eating, and the table must present the tableware and food at a height convenient to her hands and mouth. The plates and cups are of sizes that will serve the quantities of various foods that her stomach is expected to hold. The utensils are fitted dimensionally to her hand and mouth. The dimensions of the tabletop are worked out so as to accommodate a given number of diners,

16.6

160

16.7

together with their tableware, elbows, and knees. It is also worked out to maintain a comfortable distance between people sitting opposite each other (16.7). Even when people are sitting or standing with no table between them, they keep distances that allow sufficiently close visual and aural contact without encroachment on personal spatial territories. A dining table or a living room can be too small for comfort, thrusting people into intolerable proximity. It can also be too large, making communication difficult.

Rooms acquire their dimensions on the basis of such considerations: the dimensions and forms of human bodies, the dimensions and forms of the necessary pieces of furniture, the dimensions and forms of the volumes swept by moving human bodies, and the desired distances between people (16.8). Even a television set has its appropriate distance from its viewer.

In a kitchen, bathroom, or factory, machines acquire at least equal status with people in determining spatial requirements. The machines are arranged in a convenient sequence. Each has its own dimensions: the dimensions swept by its working parts or moving workpieces and the dimensions swept by the moving bodies of its operator and its maintainers. The room must provide amply for all these volumes and furnish other volumes to conduct pipes, hoses, wires, or ducts to and from the machinery as required.

Some very simple sorts of mechanisms that are universal in buildings also demand space for their operation. Sliding drawers and swinging doors are two major examples in which both the operator and the mechanism must have space to move freely.

In general, the larger a building is, the more it will cost to build. Consequently, we usually attempt to make rooms as small as is consistent with comfort. By relegating specific activities and pieces

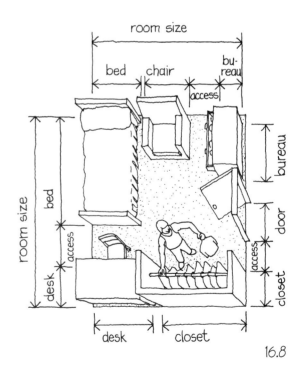

16.8

16.9

of furniture to specific places, we can often create a workable room within remarkably small dimensions. But a compact, carefully worked-out room arrangement has little or no flexibility. Any change in furniture locations would require enlarging the room. This is a choice that designers constantly face: a larger room allows for more subsequent choice and variety in its furnishings, but a smaller room is generally less costly.

The height of an ordinary room is determined, at minimum, by the height of the tallest person normally expected to move through the room, plus a bit to allow for his hat and a small safety factor (16.9). But there is much more to it than this. A ceiling may be high enough to clear the hat but still feel uncomfortably low and oppressive, particularly if the room is large in horizontal extent. In general, the larger the room is, the higher the minimum height of a ceiling must be so as not to appear to bear down on the occupant. Ceiling height has important effects on air convection and the propagation of natural light; these factors also tend to indicate higher ceilings for larger rooms. Primitive houses in subarctic regions are commonly built with very low ceilings, both to minimize heat losses to the outdoors and give a snug, cozy feeling during the cold winters. In warm climates, high ceilings allow warm air to drift to the ceiling and comfortably cooler air to pool closer to the floor, where the occupants are. In churches, concert halls, and sports arenas, high ceilings allow clear lines of sight from all spectators to the performance and achieve a better distribution and reverberation of sound. The heads of ordinary windows are usually placed at least high enough that a standing person can see comfortably to the horizon (16.10). Where natural light is important, windows often are placed as close to the

16.10

ceiling as possible, allowing only for the necessary lintel to support the wall and floor above. Sill heights of windows are much more variable. For ordinary purposes, it may be sufficient that the window reach low enough that one can look out from a sitting position, or perhaps a bit higher so that one can lean out the window while resting one's forearms on the sill. It often is important that a table, chair, or countertop fit against the wall beneath a window. In a room high above the ground, a higher sill may offer a welcome feeling of security against tumbling out. In a private room at ground level, a very high sill keeps out prying eyes. In a window opening onto a garden, a sill set into the floor allows one to walk directly outside in pleasant weather.

In the absence of other factors, the perimeter of a building is shaped by the outermost walls of the most convenient internal aggregation of rooms. When combining rooms, certain proximities are important to maintain. A bedroom should be near a bathroom, without an intervening bedroom or living room. The kitchen should be near the dining room. Such simple relationships are basic to the design of any building.

Doorways are necessary to allow access to and from rooms. They are scaled to accommodate a walking figure, plus a bit more to allow for carrying a bundle of groceries, a suitcase, or a young child (16.11). In public buildings, doorways become exitways whose capacity must be calculated to pass the entire occupant population of the building in a specified minimum time.

Corridors are useful for facilitating complex circulation paths among a number of interrelated rooms. A corridor width of 3 feet (900 mm) is sufficient for a single person, but two people will find it difficult to pass one another. Another foot (300 mm) of width makes passing easy for two individuals but will not permit the comfortable passage of two parallel files of people. Corridors must be sized like water pipes, to accommodate the expected flow. The pipelike character of many unimaginatively designed corridors has led many designers to do away with them, substituting instead a seemingly generous lounge or lobby. Unfortunately, the result is usually little more than a broader corridor, with circulation paths cutting across in all directions, leaving little room free for other activities (16.12). Such situations are easily foreseen by sketching on a floor plan the natural paths along which people will circulate.

Vertical Movement: Stairs, Ramps, Ladders

Designing for vertical movement of people in and around buildings requires extremely careful attention to the dimensions and peculiarities of the human body. The hazard of tripping and the

16.11

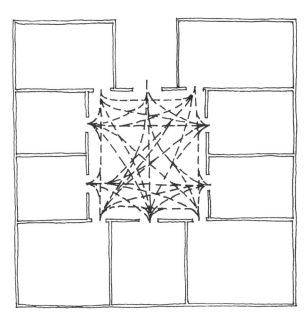

Natural paths through a lobby   16.12

163

16.13

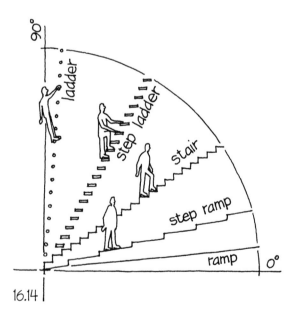

16.14

effort of climbing or descending must be minimized by comfortably accommodating the feet and legs. Handrails must be provided in such a form and location that they can be easily and securely grasped, either to assist in climbing or to prevent a vertical fall over the edge of the stair. And headroom, often a scarce commodity in stairways, must be at a safe height to protect the brittle and vulnerable cranium from damage (16.13).

Architectural devices for reducing an impossible floor-to-floor vertical leap to human-sized steps exist in a range that will let us climb at any angle from the near horizontal to the completely vertical (16.14). *Ramps* provide a smooth, slow ascent or descent that can be traversed at any length of stride, or even by a wheelchair or baby carriage. Ramps are particularly effective in exhibit spaces, theaters, and arenas where large crowds must be accommodated. A ramp cannot be pitched very steeply, however, before our feet feel in danger of slipping, particularly on the descent. As a result, the ratio of run to rise for a ramp is very large—ramps occupy a large amount of space in a building. *Step ramps* can rise somewhat more steeply and economically and are particularly pleasant in a garden. Indoors, we get the unpleasant feeling of possibly slipping on them, as on a ramp, and also of possibly tripping, as on a stair, so they should be avoided. Fixed *ladders* and *step ladders* in buildings are generally restricted to seldom-used access routes to attics, chimneys, boiler rooms, and bookshelves or to playful features of children's rooms and vacation cottages (16.15). Vertical and near-vertical ladders are especially hard to negotiate while carrying anything, which further restricts their usefulness.

Stairs are the most useful vertical movement devices in a designer's repertoire. Risers divide the total vertical climb into small increments that the legs can negotiate comfortably whether ascending or descending. Treads provide reassuringly level, secure footholds. The drawbacks of stairs are that they cannot accommodate people with various sorts of physical disabilities (ramps or elevators must be provided instead); they become fatiguing after only a few stories of going up or down; and a fall on a stairway can be particularly damaging because of the numerous hard edges presented by the stair nosings.

The danger of falling on stairs and the potential for fatigue are minimized if the proportions of the steps are both comfortable and absolutely uniform throughout the stairway. Even a fractional increase in the height of one riser in a stair can lead to more accidents. Uncomfortably proportioned stairs are familiar to everyone: Excessively steep stairs require too much muscular effort at each riser and offer a disturbingly narrow foothold at each tread. Very shallow stairs induce a mincing gait that feels ridiculously

16.15

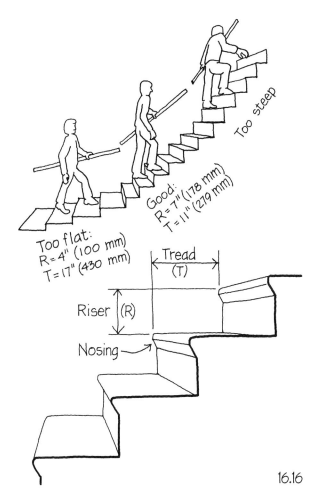

16.16

inefficient (16.16). According to various studies of the proportions of existing stairways, those stairs whose *tread* (T) and *riser* (R) dimensions in inches fit the formula

$$2R + T = 25'' \text{ (or, in SI units, } 2R + T = 635 \text{ mm)}$$

are likely to be both safe and comfortable. Limits must be placed on the application of this equation. For example, it cannot be used for the design of monumental stairs with very small risers and very broad treads; experimentation with full-scale mock-ups is required in such cases. In stairs of more usual proportions, R should not exceed $7\frac{3}{4}$ inches (197 mm) in private residential stairs, or 7 inches (178 mm) in other stairs. T should not be less than 10 inches (254 mm) for residential stairs, or 11 inches (279 mm) for other stairs. Residential stairs can be steeper than stairs in public buildings because they carry less traffic and are used primarily by people who are familiar with them. *Nosings* on stair treads are an important detail; they broaden the foothold significantly without changing

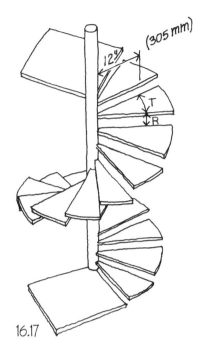

16.17

the fundamental proportions of the stair. Except in single-family residences, stair nosings must be profiled with a sloping underside so that they will not catch the toes of a person who is climbing the stairs on crutches.

Spiral and *winding staircases* present special problems because, even though their riser dimensions remain constant across the width of the stair, the tread dimensions vary considerably. A person walking close to the inside of a tight spiral stair (a misnomer—actually it's a helical stair) is on a near-vertical stair with tiny treads, whereas the outside of the same stair may be excessively broad. For this reason such stairs are illegal in public buildings. In residences, it is customary to proportion the treads and risers of such stairs to legal dimensions at a distance of 12 inches (305 mm) from the inside handrail, which is the line walked by a single person on the stair (16.17).

The number of risers in a flight has an important effect on stair safety and comfort. Flights of fewer than three risers often escape the notice of unfamiliar users, who tend to tumble over them before seeing them. Flights of more than 16 or 18 risers become very tiring (16.18). Long flights must be broken with periodic *landings* whose minimum dimensions are equal to the width of the stair. The maximum vertical distance between landings is 12 feet (3.6 m).

Headroom problems in stairs are vexing because they are so often difficult to avoid—but there is no choice to designers. People often descend stairs with a very rapid up-and-down movement while watching their feet to avoid tripping. Tall people are painfully familiar with the damage that may result.

Too long a flight

Making Buildings Work

When laying out any of the circulation spaces in buildings—doors, corridors, stairways—designers have to keep in mind that furniture and appliances occasionally must pass through the building. That is, doorways cannot be made so narrow as to exclude refrigerators, sofas, desks, or pianos. Tight turns in corridors and stairways may be impassable for such objects unless additional maneuvering space is provided.

Lobbies serve several important functions in the circulation systems of buildings. Entrance lobbies let people entering or leaving a building slow down, button or unbutton outer clothing, think about where to go next, adjust their eyes to the new lighting level, fiddle with umbrellas, comb windblown hair, or wait for taxis or friends. Theater lobbies serve these functions, and they also let members of the audience exercise their legs between parts of a performance. A lobby is really an expansion chamber in an otherwise linear flow

Too short a flight

16.18

166

network, a place at which people can step out of the moving stream and stop for a moment or two.

Outdoors, designers work at a different scale. People are still the measure, but now they are walking more rapidly or riding in vehicles. They need more room to allow for this more rapid movement and for expanded spatial expectations. Space between buildings must let sunlight penetrate. Air must circulate freely. Acoustical and visual privacy must be protected by the distance between buildings and by the buildings' configuration. Comfortable walking distances and times become the yardstick for planning local facilities, and driving times or public transport times measure the convenience of places in an urban region. At this new scale, unfortunately, the small-scale necessities of people's bodies are often overlooked by designers. Who has not yearned for a drinking fountain, a comfortable bench, or a public rest room while in the midst of a shopping or sightseeing expedition? Who has not felt personally betrayed by a nameless designer of a city who forgot that people are human?

Both outside and inside buildings, human safety is an important design consideration. Buildings can cause accidental damage to the body in an alarmingly diverse number of ways, some of which are enumerated in the accompanying chart (16.19). Thousands of Americans are killed in accidents in buildings each year, and tens of thousands are injured, many seriously. Many of these deaths and injuries could be prevented by more careful design and better building maintenance.

Disabled people are entitled by law to access to public buildings that is equal to that provided for able-bodied persons. The disabilities covered by this guarantee include loss of sight, loss of hearing, loss of function in legs or arms, and a host of other physical and emotional incapacities. The rationale behind the law is compelling: about one American in six is disabled in some way, and nearly all of us will experience disability at some time in our lives, perhaps a broken limb as a teenager or failing eyesight or decreasing muscle function as a senior citizen. The consequences for designing circulation spaces in buildings are far reaching, beginning with tactile and audible signals of various types for those with sensory disabilities. Those with physical disabilities need special parking spaces; ramped access through curbs and other minor changes in level; a convenient, linked system of ramps and elevators for moving vertically through a building; wider doors; larger vestibules; special drinking fountains; more ample toilet facilities with grab bars; special telephone facilities; lower counters for banking and shopping—the list goes on and on. An architect must learn to design accessible buildings as a matter of reflex. Circulation paths and facilities for the

Some Accidents Caused by Buildings

Bumping, Catching, Pinching

Low headroom
Uncontrolled door swings
Unprotected door edges
Doors that open into traffic
Blind corners in busy corridors
Projecting doorknobs, railing ends

Cutting, Scratching, Puncturing, Skinning

Sharp edges and corners
Floor-to-ceiling glass
Projecting nails, screws, bolts
Splinters
Rough surfaces

Falls

Tripping: Low obstacles, uneven floors,
edges of rugs, objects left on floors
Poorly proportioned stairs or ramps
Railings too low or nonexistent
Poor illumination
Slippery floors or stairs
Loose rugs

Scalding, Burning

Confusing hot-water taps
Unprotected steam or water pipes
Unprotected heating appliances
Stove too close to circulation path
Building fires

Electrocution

Faulty appliances
Faulty wiring

16.19

disabled must flow from his or her pencil as gracefully and naturally as does any other feature of a building design.

A growing group of architects and designers is promoting *universal design*, which is a step beyond designing for the disabled. In universal design, all parts of a building are designed to be usable by all people, even if on crutches, in a wheelchair, or blind. The key idea of universal design is that separate but equal special facilities for the physically handicapped are not sufficient. Rather, one should eliminate elements of a building that are not usable by every human being and substitute for them elements that are.

People as the Measure

As a coda to this chapter, let us recall how people literally became the measure of buildings through the traditional English system of measurement. In each medieval English village, measurements were standardized to a village pole, the length of the pole being derived from the right feet of 16 randomly selected men placed toe-to-heel after church on a Sunday morning. A common house of that period measured 1 pole by 2. A cord of pole length could be folded and was therefore useful in subdividing the pole into four smaller units called yards; a yard was about 4 feet long (1.2 m) at that time. The same folded cord served to measure a standard pile of firewood that is still known as a cord. The pile is 4 feet wide by 4 feet high by 8 feet long (1.2 m × 1.2 m × 2.4 m), the sum of these three dimensions being equal to the length of the cord.

As textile trade became important in England, the Anglo-Saxon yard of 4 feet had to be abandoned in favor of the continental cloth yard of 3 feet (915 mm), measured along the edge of the cloth between the tip of the nose and the outstretched arm. The pole, by now called a rod, was increased to 16.5 feet (5.03 m), or 5.5 cloth yards. The mile, which originated as 1,000 double steps (*mille passus*) of a Roman soldier, was standardized at 320 rods or 8 furlongs (furrow-lengths) of 40 rods each. Land was measured by the acre (a day's plowing for a yoke of oxen). An acre was later defined legally to be 160 square rods. Later, the mile-square section of 640 acres (259 ha) became the standard of land subdivision in the central and western United States, and a quarter-section farm of 160 acres (65 ha) was the standard homestead grant.

Meanwhile, a curious progression of circumstances grew out of the ancient cord measure of firewood. It became standard practice in England to saw each 4-foot log into three pieces, each 16 inches (400 mm) long, for easy handling. Fireplace and stove dimensions were standardized accordingly. When wooden lath came into use as a base for plaster, it was split from firewood, and so 16 inches

16.20

16.21

became the standard spacing for light framing members in buildings. From this spacing came, in time, the 4-foot-by-8-foot (1,219 mm × 2,438 mm) sheet of plywood or gypsum wallboard, which spans three or six framing modules (depending on which way the sheet is turned), and from these sheets came the standard 8-foot (2.44 m) ceiling of today's tract house.

The common building materials became, in the course of history, rather more directly related to human scale. The brick, despite many small local variations in size, was standardized in medieval times within a range of sizes and weights that could be easily manipulated by the left hand of a mason, leaving the right hand free to operate the trowel (16.20). When wood joinery suddenly became cheap with the introduction of machine-made nails early in the nineteenth century, carpenters quickly adopted the easily handled "2-by-4" as the standard unit of framing (16.21). The heavy timber frame, which required a large crew simply to handle and fit its large components, was soon abandoned, and the standard building crew was reduced to two or three carpenters working only with small, inexpensive hand tools. Hand-size elements are the traditional standard in many areas of small building construction, including shingles, wood siding, wood paneling, window glass, and paving blocks and tiles.

Today we often handle building materials in bulk rather than by hand, using mobile mechanical lifting and transporting devices of impressive capacities. It is often most economical to build using large-scale materials such as factory-built, room-size housing modules. There is nothing inherently wrong with these practices, but designers should be aware that the finished product will not automatically display the human-scale texture that hand-sized components have and that occupants often subconsciously identify with. Designers must also be wary of being forced into unnatural decisions about sizes and proportions of things by the limitations and capabilities of cranes and trucks of superhuman scale.

The metric system of measurement is not directly related to human scale. Its basic unit is the meter, originally defined as one ten-millionth of the distance from the North Pole to the equator. Its unit of volume is the liter, a cube one-tenth meter on a side. Its unit of mass, the kilogram, is the mass of a liter of water. The second is retained as a measure of time, and the Celsius scale, which divides the range between the freezing and boiling points of water into 100 degrees, is the measure of temperature. All other units are derived from this basic group. Because of its logic and simplicity, the metric system has been adopted by almost every country of the world outside the United States. Even in the United States, although most private projects are designed and built in conventional English units, since 1993 all federal government buildings have been built according to metric units of measurement. American-built automobiles have been metric for decades.

A refinement and rationalization of the metric system, the *Système international d'unitès* (abbreviated SI), is widely used and is used in this book as an alternative system of units to the English. The characteristic of SI that is most relevant to architecture is that the centimeter is not used, only the meter and millimeter. This avoids any confusion on technical drawings with how big something is intended to be—a measurement of 9,000 is either 9 kilometers or 9 meters, and one can usually tell from the context of the project which it is.

Careful designers work always from a mental catalog of sizes and proportions of things. Sketches and models from the very earliest stages of building design include representations of people, furnishings, and groupings of furnishings. Room proportions and window and door locations are constantly juggled during the design process to facilitate a variety of appropriate furniture placements in a finished building. Patterns of human circulation are progressively refined into paths that are short, smooth, logical, and pleasant. These paths should pass to one side or the other of the different nodes of human activity within the building instead of cutting through the middle. Through such a design process and the analytical activities that are embedded in it, buildings are fitted to people, and people become the true measure of our buildings.

Further Reading

Julius Panero and Nino Repetto. *Anatomy for Interior Designers.* New York, Whitney Publications, 1962.

Charles G. Ramsey, Harold Sleeper, and John Ray Hoke, editors. *Architectural Graphic Standards* (10th ed.). New York, Wiley, 2002.

17

Providing Structural Support

Loads and Stresses

A building is constantly being pushed and pulled by various forces. The most constant force is gravity exerting its downward pull on the fixed components of the building—roofs, walls, windows, floors, partitions, stairs, fireplaces—a force referred to as the *dead load* of the building. The *live loads* of the building include the less constant forces—the shifting, varying weights of people, furnishings, goods, and vehicles; the weight of snow on the roof; the pressures (predominantly horizontal) of wind on the walls. Earthquakes, which cause rapidly fluctuating horizontal displacements of the ground on which a building stands, also cause horizontal live loads. We must configure every building in such a way that it will support its own dead load plus a live load equal to the worst combined total of people, furnishings, snow, wind, and earthquake that may reasonably be expected.

To do this, we first estimate the magnitude of these loads, which is usually an elementary arithmetical chore. However, buildings of unusual height or in unusually windy locations may require extensive measurements on the site and in a wind tunnel to determine what the actual wind loads will be. Next, we select a combination of related structural devices—a structural system—that is appropriate to the site, the uses to be made of the building, and the expected loads. Finally, we determine the exact configurations and necessary strengths and sizes of the components of the structural system, including all the fastening devices used to hold the larger components together. A glance at any building under construction is likely to lead to the conclusion, largely correct, that the detailed design of a structural system is a rather involved process. At its roots, however, structural design springs from a few very simple concepts. No structure is built that does not stand on these concepts. The depth and complexity of structural design processes lie in the skill with which we select, combine, and proportion structural devices and translate them into buildable form, not in the basic behavior of the devices themselves.

Consider a block of material—limestone, let us say—and what happens to it as a downward load is applied uniformly across its upper surface (17.1). The load pushes down on the block from above, and the surface below the block pushes upward with an equal force. The block is being compressed. The compressive stress at the top face of the stone block is equal to the load divided by the horizontal cross-sectional area of the block:

17.1

$$\text{Compressive stress} = \frac{\text{load}}{\text{area}}$$

If the load is 3,000 pounds and the block is 10 by 15 inches, the compressive stress will be equal to 3,000 pounds divided by 150 square inches, or 20 pounds per square inch. In SI units, this example would translate as a force of 13.3 kilonewtons divided by 0.097 m^2, which equals 137.4 megapascals (MPa). (At the bottom face of the block, the stress is higher than at the top, because the load at the bottom includes the weight of the stone block as well as the applied load.) This concept of stress is useful because it allows us to compare the intensity of structural actions in blocks of differing sizes and shapes under differing loads.

Suppose now that the load on the block is gradually increased by piling more weight on the top. The compressive stress will rise in proportion to the weight. If we have extremely accurate measuring equipment, we can observe that the height of the block is gradually diminished by very small but finite amounts as the load is increased. If we plot a graph of the compressive stress versus this diminution (which is called *strain*), it will be a straight line, telling us that stress is directly proportional to strain (17.2). The slope of the line—the ratio of stress to strain—is known as the *elastic modulus* of the material. Elastic moduli have been determined experimentally for all the common structural materials, giving us a ready means of predicting how much a wall or column will shorten under a given load, or how much a steel rod that is being pulled will lengthen (17.3). The term *elastic* also implies that if the load is removed from the block, wall, column, or rod, it will spring back to its original size, without loss of dimension.

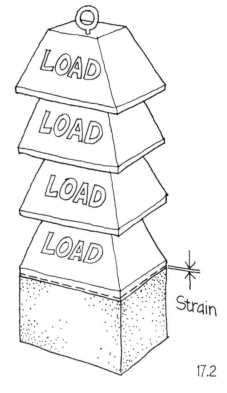

Strain

17.2

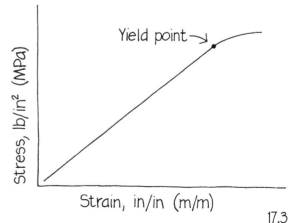

17.3

If we continue to increase the loads on the block, the material within the block will ultimately be squeezed beyond its capacity to resist. The material will crush and will not return to its original size after the load is removed. The stress at which this occurs is known as the *yield point* of the material. In a brittle material such as stone, the yield point is also the point at which the material disintegrates. It is dangerous to design a building structure to be stressed to the yield point, because any tiny additional load, any minute flaw in the material, or any slight miscalculation may make the building collapse. To account for these uncertainties, we normally design structures with a *factor of safety*. A factor of safety of two means that we design to a stress that is just half of the yield point. A factor of three means we use one-third this stress, and so on. We use lower factors of safety for materials that tend to be relatively consistent in quality, such as steel, and higher factors for materials, such as wood, that are naturally inconsistent and flawed. We multiply yield point stresses from laboratory load-test data by factors of safety to calculate standard safe *allowable stresses* for various structural materials.

Suppose that in a laboratory test our stone block has crushed at a stress of 3,600 pounds per square inch (24.82 MPa). For purposes of design, we will apply a factor of safety of three to this stress to allow for possible flaws and inconsistencies in the stone. This results in an allowable stress of 1,200 pounds per square inch (8.27 MPa). If we were asked to design a stone block to support a load of 60 tons (54,480 kg), we could do so as follows:

60 tons × 2000 pounds/ton = 120,000 pounds

$$\textit{Required cross-sectional area of stone} = \frac{120,000 \; lb}{1,200 \; lb/in^2} = 100 \; in^2$$

In SI units:

54,480 kg × 9.8 m/sec² = 0.533 MN

$$\textit{Required cross-sectional area} = \frac{0.533 \; MN}{8.27 \; MP} = 0.064 \; m^2$$

A stone 10 inches square (254 mm × 254 mm) will do the job. This simple procedure is the basis for all structural calculations. The design of even the most complicated structure ultimately comes down to a question of whether a given piece of material can safely carry a given level of stress, either a squeezing stress (*compression*) or a stretching stress (*tension*).

Vertical Support

We can build many kinds of structures with simple blocks of stone, concrete, or brick. A vertical stack of blocks forms a *column* capable of supporting a portion of a floor or roof. A column translated in a horizontal direction becomes a *bearing wall*, which can support the load of an entire edge of a floor or roof (17.4). Provided that such columns or bearing walls are not too *slender* in relationship to their height, their thicknesses can be computed in the same simple manner as in the preceding example (17.5–17.7).

17.4

Columns

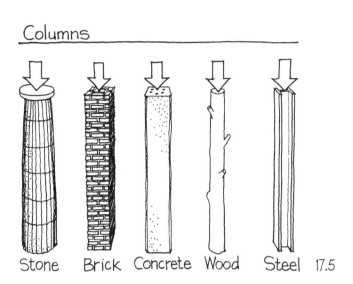

Stone Brick Concrete Wood Steel 17.5

Bearing Walls

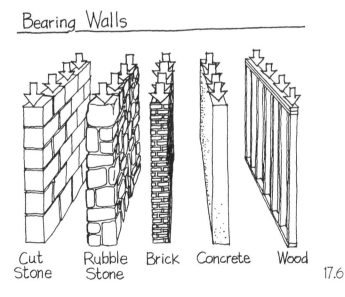

Cut Stone Rubble Stone Brick Concrete Wood 17.6

Tension Members

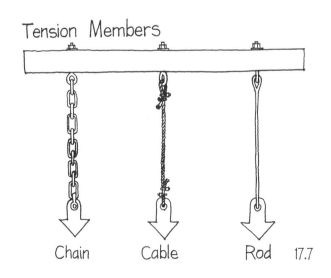

Chain Cable Rod 17.7

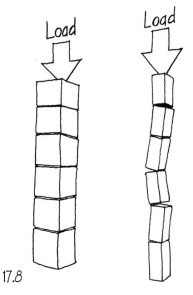

17.8

If a column or wall is very slender, it will *buckle* at a stress that is well below the allowable stress (17.8). Buckling is a lateral displacement whose causes and mathematics are still not completely understood, especially in columns that are neither extremely slender nor extremely thick. Short, squat columns and walls crush before buckling, and very tall, slender ones consistently buckle before crushing, but ones of intermediate length and slenderness may fail in either manner. Consequently, we rely largely on formulas derived from laboratory test data when designing columns of intermediate slenderness.

A column or wall that tends to buckle can be made safe by being thickened sufficiently or by being braced laterally with compressive *struts* or tensile *guys* (17.9). A laterally braced column has the advantage of using considerably less total material to support the same load as a thick, unbraced column. We use braced columns frequently in buildings, radio towers, and many other types of structure.

Buckling is a problem only in structural elements that are under compressive stress. Elements under *tensile stress*, such as ropes, cables, rods, and chains, have no tendency to buckle. Consider a chain hanging vertically with a weight attached to its lower end (17.10). The tensile stress on the chain is equal to the applied weight divided by the cross-sectional area of steel in any single link. The strain, up

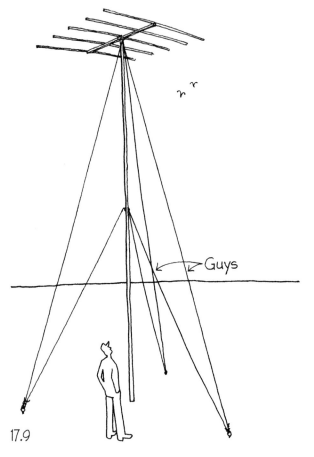

17.9

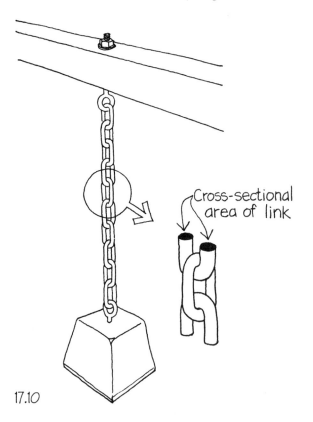

17.10

to the yield point of the steel in the chain, is proportional to the stress. The chain will never buckle as long as it is in tension.

Steel is the strongest structural material in both tension and compression. Wood also has both good tensile and good compressive strength. Though wood is not as strong as steel, its ratio of strength to weight is roughly the same. Concrete and masonry materials are strong in compression, but they are *brittle*, which means that they crack and come apart when subjected to moderate tensile stress. Steel rods are often embedded in the regions of concrete and masonry structures where tensile stresses are anticipated, to produce a strong, economical structure that is a *composite* of the two materials.

Horizontal Spanning: Tension Devices

Vertical loads in buildings can be supported in compression by columns or bearing walls, or in tension by chains, rods, or cables. Except in some cases of column buckling, the behavior of these structural devices is well understood. The greater structural problem in most buildings, however, is to span horizontally over space, to support roofs and floors. How do we do it? There are many ways.

We begin with a simple example: Suppose that we hang a chain across a narrow canyon and suspend a very heavy weight from its center (17.11). The two halves of the chain become very nearly two

17.11

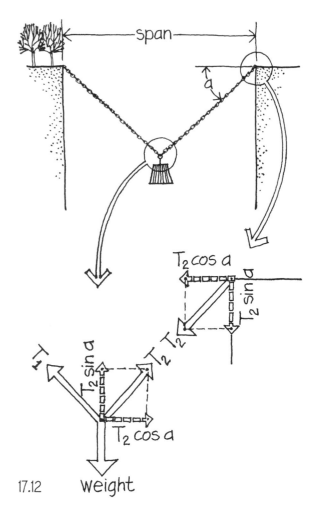

$T_2 \cos a$

$T_2 \sin a$

T_1

$T_2 \sin a$

T_2

T_2

$T_2 \cos a$

17.12 weight

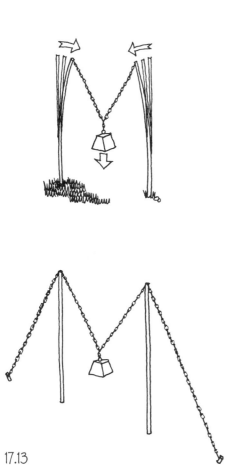

17.13

straight lines, converging at the point where the weight is applied. The ends of the chain will pull on the cliffs at either side at an angle (a), which is determined by the length of chain we have provided (17.12). As we examine what happens at the center of the chain, we note that the two halves of the chain cannot be exerting a direct upward pull against the weight; a chain can pull only along the axis (centerline) of its links. Therefore it must be resisting the downward pull of the weight with two diagonal pulls at angles (a) from the horizontal. The diagonal pulls, T_1 and T_2, each must have a vertical component, Tsina, equal to half the pull of the weight. At each cliff, this vertical component is transferred into the rock. But so is an accompanying horizontal component, Tcosa. The chain cannot support a load across a span without exerting a horizontal as well as a vertical pull on its supports. We can see this more easily if we support the ends of the chain on two slender poles instead of two cliffs (17.13). The poles bend inward under the load. A common way

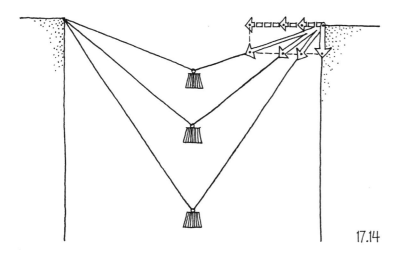

17.14

of dealing with this horizontal pull, in suspension bridges or tents, is to run the chain (or cable or rope) over the poles or columns at each end and down to anchors in the ground some distance outside each column. The chains outside the columns provide a horizontal pull equal to the pull of the chain between the columns. They also, unavoidably, add a substantial vertical load to each of the columns, and so the columns must be strengthened accordingly.

Let us go back again to the problem of spanning the canyon. The chain is attached directly to the rock at each end and exerts its inward pull on the rock rather than the tops of columns. Observe what happens if we use a longer chain. The angle (a) is increased. The vertical component of pull on the cliffs stays the same, but the horizontal component is diminished, and so are the pull and the stress in the chain. Conversely, if the chain is shortened, the horizontal pull on the cliffs will be increased, and the chain will be tensed much more tightly (17.14). An important decision in designing any horizontal spanning device, not just a hanging chain, is *how deep the device should be*. A deep device, such as a deeply sagging chain or a deep truss or beam, has lower internal structural stresses and thus needs less material to carry the same load than does a shallow device, which always has higher internal stresses and needs more material. In practice, however, we often choose the shallower devices because they require less vertical space in a building and thus save money on columns, exterior walls, and other components.

What happens if we add more loads to the chain, spacing them out at various intervals along its length? Each time another load is added, the chain adjusts its shape to maintain a line of pure tension along its axis at every point. The loads may be unequal in weight or unequally distributed along the length of the chain; the chain changes shape automatically to place each of its links in equilibrium

179

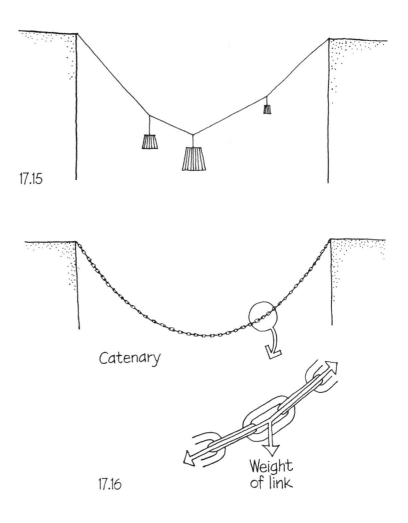

17.15

Catenary

17.16

Weight
of link

under any loading short of its breaking point (17.15). We cannot force a chain to take an arbitrary shape but must work with the shapes a chain takes naturally. The most familiar shape of all is the *catenary*, the graceful curve taken by a chain hanging freely under its own weight (17.16). Each link represents a resolved trio of forces in equilibrium, two exerted at an obtuse angle to each other by the two adjacent links, and the third exerted downward by the weight of the link itself.

The curve of the cable in a suspension bridge differs slightly from a catenary because the weight of the bridge is distributed evenly over the horizontal plane of the roadway that hangs from the cable, not over the curving length of the cable. The resulting curve is a *parabola*.

The shapes taken by a hanging cable or chain are called *funicular* shapes, after the Latin word for "string." For each pattern of loads, there is a *family of funicular shapes*, the shapes that a piece of hanging string would take when subjected to that load pattern. For a cable hanging under its own weight only, the funicular shapes comprise an infinitely large family of catenaries, because the cable can sag a little, a lot, or anything in between. For a suspension bridge, the possible funicular shapes make up a family of parabolas. Over the past several pages and in the accompanying drawing (17.17), we also see shapes that are funicular for a single load and several random loads. Some of these shapes are on level supports, and others are on uneven supports.

Tents represent the principle of the funicular in a three-dimensional form, using cloth on a very small scale, high-tech synthetic fabrics at large scale, or networks of steel cables on a very large scale, to cover space (17.18, 17.19). Extremely long spans between supports are possible if the masts are high enough to accommodate the necessary depth of sag in the fabric and if the fabric is sufficiently tense to prevent billowing or fluttering in the wind. Such tension can be provided by ropes or cables that pull the fabric down at various points, by applying sufficient weight to the fabric, or by giving an *anticlastic curvature* (convex along one axis and concave along the other) to the fabric.

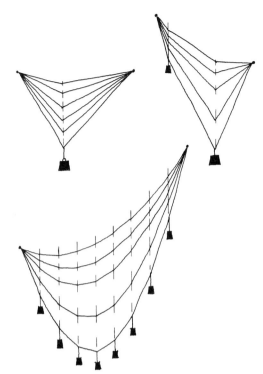

Some families of funicular shapes   17.17

17.18

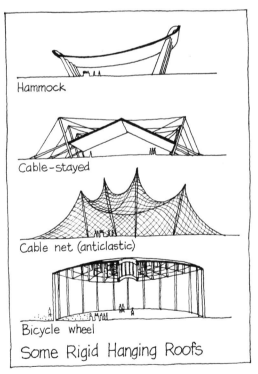

Hammock

Cable-stayed

Cable net (anticlastic)

Bicycle wheel

Some Rigid Hanging Roofs

17.19

17.20

small weights
simulate weight
of stones of
arch

Weight to be
supported

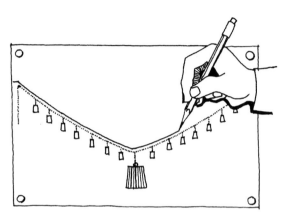

1. Trace curve of chain model

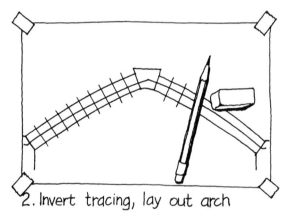

2. Invert tracing, lay out arch

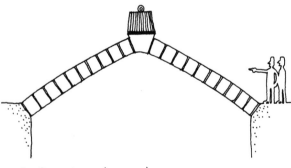

3. Construct arch

17.21

Arches

What happens if we put the chain aside and instead try to support the weight in the middle of the canyon with stone blocks? We could do this by leaning the blocks against each other, upward and across the chasm in just the right configuration so that each block would be in equilibrium with its immediate neighbors. There are various mathematical and geometrical techniques for finding this configuration. There is also an easier way: modeling it to scale with a length of watch chain, key chain, or even cotton string suspended over a piece of paper that is attached to a vertical surface. Remember that in a chain, each link is in equilibrium, its own weight and the vertical components of force from the link on either side just being equal. This is exactly what we want in each block of our stone device, the only difference being that a chain can carry only tension, whereas we want our stones, which are weak in tension, to carry only compression. The solution, then, is to model the situation on a small scale with a weight suspended from a chain. We need to attach a number of small weights to the chain to simulate the weight of the stones (17.20).

The chain and weights in our hanging model quickly reach equilibrium, after which we can trace the form taken by the chain onto a sheet of paper, invert the sheet of paper, and lay out a series of stone blocks whose centerline assumes the same form as the chain (17.21). The result will be a funicular arch perfectly formed to carry the given load by means of pure compression within and between the stones.

If you have never seen an arch of exactly this shape, it is because few arches are built to take a single, concentrated load. Most are built to carry uniformly distributed loads and should, therefore, take the form of a parabola, as we see in many arch bridges (17.22). In buildings, most arches are not parabolic but semicircular, for arches are much easier to lay out as arcs of circles than as parabolas. If the span is not too great, the stones of the arch (the *voussoirs*) are deep

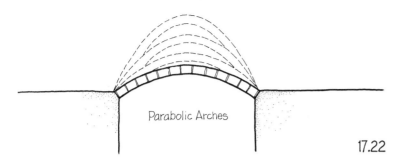

Parabolic Arches

17.22

enough to contain a parabolic curve, and the arch is stiffened by containment within a wall; such simpler arches are quite stable (17.23). Furthermore, because it was not known until Renaissance times that the parabola was the ideal shape for a uniformly loaded arch, all the classical arches of Roman civilization, which we have copied so faithfully through subsequent epochs, are based on circles (17.24). The Romans even used a *flat arch*, a form so apparently wrong that we are tempted to doubt its stability until we see it carrying a load without apparent distress. Then we might visualize a rather flat parabola superimposed on its stones.

It is important to note the mirror-image similarity between the forms developed previously with hanging chains and the funicular arch forms illustrated here. The arch to support each loading condition differs slightly from its chain analogue in that the greater dead weight of the arch itself with respect to the superimposed weight or weights may require a slightly different curvature of form. Notice also that every arch exerts a horizontal force, exactly as a chain does,

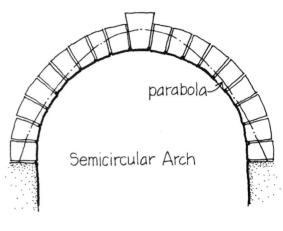

parabola

Semicircular Arch

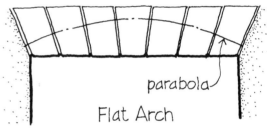

parabola

Flat Arch

17.23

17.24

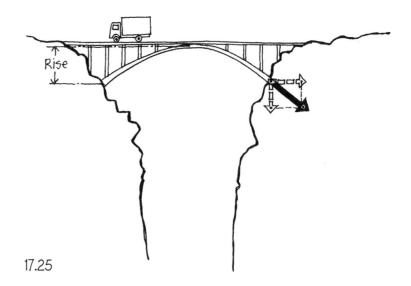

17.25

but in the opposite direction (17.25). The amount of horizontal thrust and the amount of compressive stress within the material of the arch depend on the amount of *rise* given to the arch. The flatter the arch is, the higher the horizontal thrust and the higher the internal forces in the voussoirs will be. Once again we encounter the principle that deeper structural devices have lower forces.

In important respects, the arch is not an exact analogue of the chain. The arch is rigid and cannot self-adjust to changing load patterns as a chain does. Being in compression, an arch can fail by buckling. For both these reasons, an arch cannot be made nearly as slender as a chain or cable. A relatively thick arch is not only more resistant to buckling than a slender one, but also can carry comfortably loads that vary a good deal from the exact loading for which it was shaped. For these two reasons, also, the arch form does not have as great an ultimate spanning capability as does a hanging cable, although it is runner-up to the cable as the longest-span device in the designer's structural vocabulary, especially when it is made of steel.

In both Europe and the Middle East, the arch form underwent enormous development and elaboration over the last two millennia. Today we are able to make many useful forms, both two dimensional and three dimensional, from the arch, some of which are illustrated here (17.26). Most arched forms of construction need some sort of temporary support (called *centering* or *formwork*) during construction. Many materials, including all the masonry materials, concrete, cast iron, steel, and wood, are suitable for arches, vaults, and domes.

The need to resist the horizontal thrust component of arches and vaults has given rise to many ingenious architectural devices. In a

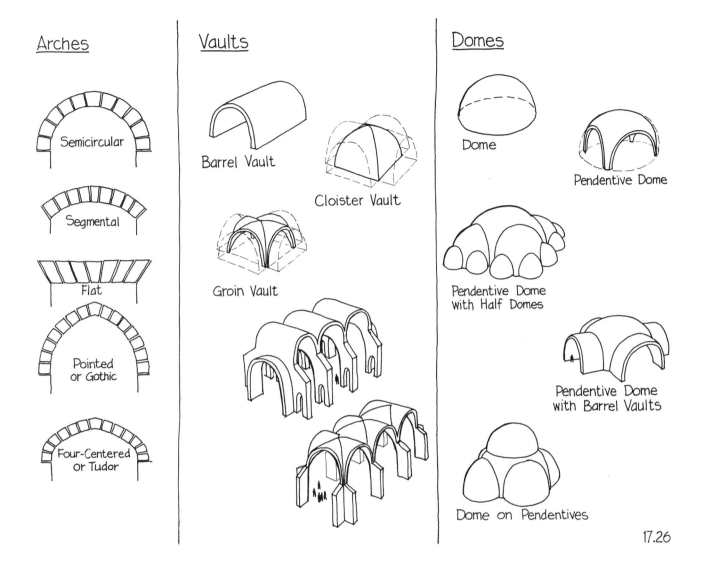

Arches

Semicircular

Segmental

Flat

Pointed or Gothic

Four-Centered or Tudor

Vaults

Barrel Vault

Cloister Vault

Groin Vault

Domes

Dome

Pendentive Dome

Pendentive Dome with Half Domes

Pendentive Dome with Barrel Vaults

Dome on Pendentives

17.26

line of development driven by the desire to open churches to as much natural light as possible, the simple, heavy masonry *engaged buttresses* of early times became the breathtaking *flying buttresses* of the Gothic era, in which the downward gravitational thrust of heavy stone pinnacles inexorably diverts the outward thrust of the vaults until it safely enters the ground through the foundations (17.27, 17.28). In Renaissance times, as wrought iron became available, *tie rods* or chains came into use as an inexpensive (but usually less handsome) alternative to buttresses for all kinds of vaults and domes (17.29).

The availability of new and stronger structural materials in the nineteenth and twentieth centuries brought a new wave of development in vaulting techniques. Vaults and domes of metal trusswork

Engaged Buttresses

17.27

Flying buttresses
17.28

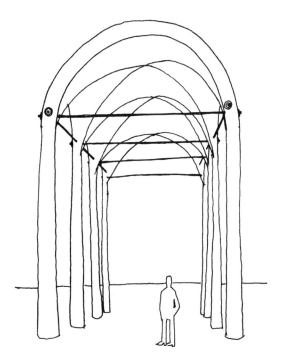

17.29 Tie rods or tie chains

can span vast amounts of space, using little more material than suspension structures of equal expanse (17.30). Vaults of reinforced concrete or clay tiles, often proportionally thinner than the shell of an egg, have become commonplace, and their designers have exploited not only the *synclastic*, spherical geometry of traditional vaulting but the anticlastic curve of the hyperbolic paraboloid as well (17.31).

Thrust-Free Spanning Devices: Trusses

We have developed so far the concepts of the hanging chain, the arch, and the tie chain. Let us now see if we can assemble from these components other ways to span the canyon, trying especially to develop devices that exert no horizontal pull or push on the canyon walls. Such thrust-free devices would be particularly useful in buildings, allowing the columns and bearing walls to support only vertical loads.

We will begin again with the hanging chain that supports a single load at its center, but this time we will connect the ends of the chain to the ends of a very shallow arch whose only function, besides supporting its own weight, is to counteract with its outward push the

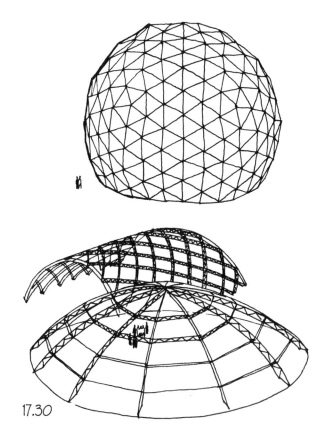

17.30

186

inward pull of the chain (17.32). If this device is properly shaped, we can prove that it exerts no horizontal thrust by mounting one end of it on rollers, so it is free to move back and forth. If the rollers do not move, our design is a good one.

If we wish to support the load at a level that is roughly the same as the rim of the canyon, rather than have it hang down into the canyon below the arch, we can do this by transmitting the load from the weight down to the chain through a column of stone blocks (17.33). The single arch from the previous figure is made into two shorter ones, each shaped for a combination of its own dead weight and the horizontal component of compression that is added by the chain.

Though we could actually make this device of stones and chain, it would be somewhat clumsy, and in practice it would be easier to replace the stones with short *compression struts* of wood, bolted loosely together at their junctions (17.34). It can now be seen more easily that what we have invented is a simple *truss*.

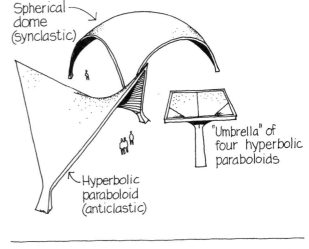

Spherical dome (synclastic)

"Umbrella" of four hyperbolic paraboloids

Hyperbolic paraboloid (anticlastic)

17.31

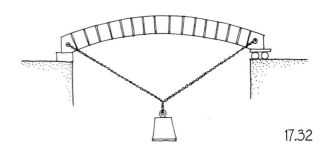

17.32

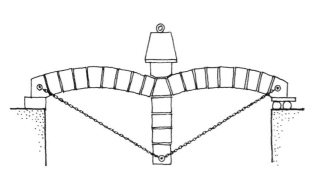

17.33

17.34

187

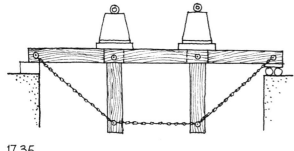

17.35

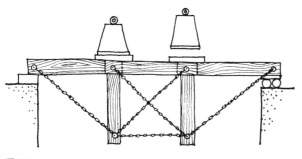

17.36

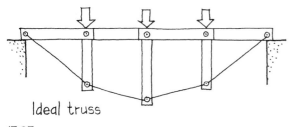

Ideal truss

17.37

We could make a truss to support two concentrated loads, as shown (17.35). Its equilibrium is somewhat precarious, however, because the withdrawal of one of the loads will allow the upper line of struts, called the *upper chord* of the truss, to buckle upward. The addition of two diagonal chains in the center panel eliminates this possibility (17.36).

An ideal truss for three concentrated loads can be developed similarly (17.37). This truss is very efficient mechanically, but it would be easier to build if all the vertical struts were the same length. We can do this by inserting diagonal ties or struts in each panel of the truss to ensure equilibrium (17.38, 17.39). Notice that any diagonal member may be replaced by either a tension tie or a compression strut, depending on the orientation given to the member—one must be placed on the opposite diagonal of each *panel* from the other. By this means we can produce stable trusses of any desired number of panels, although an even number of panels has the advantage of producing a symmetrical truss without the need for two diagonals in a center panel.

We can also invert all these trusses (turn them upside down). When we do this, all tension members become compression members, and vice versa (17.40). This is further evidence of the *invertibility* of any structure that we discovered when we inverted a chain to produce an arch.

Many different types of trusses have been developed (17.41). Trusses are relatively easy to design and to analyze mathematically,

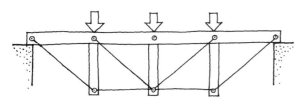

Tension diagonals

17.38

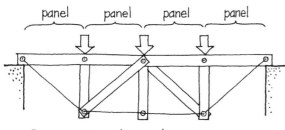

panel   panel   panel   panel

Compression diagonals

17.39

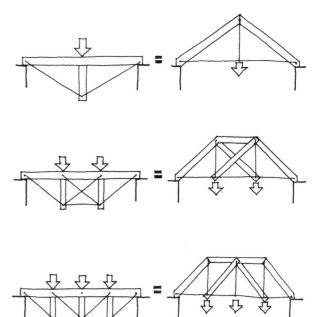

17.40

188

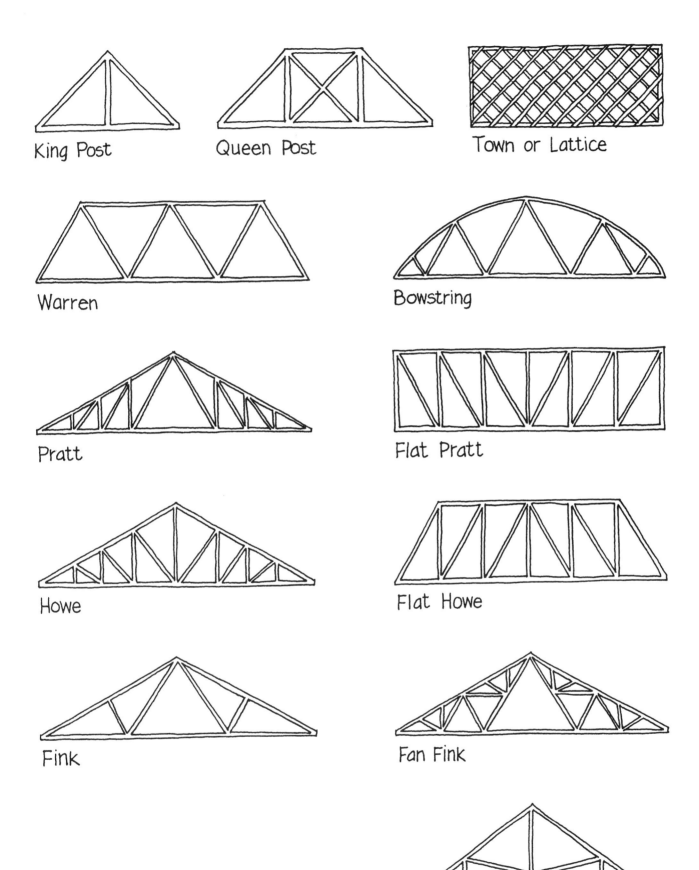

King Post

Queen Post

Town or Lattice

Warren

Bowstring

Pratt

Flat Pratt

Howe

Flat Howe

Fink

Fan Fink

Some Forms of Trusses

Scissors

17.41

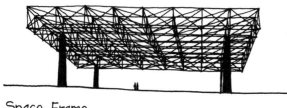

Space Frame
17.42

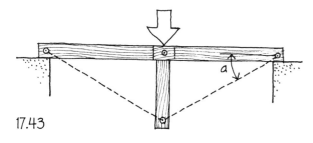

17.43

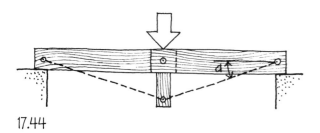

17.44

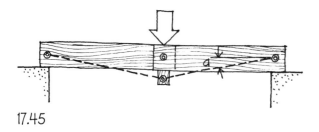

17.45

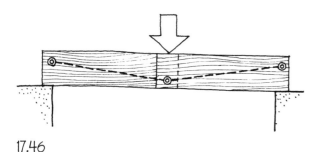

17.46

can be made up of short pieces of material, are relatively light in weight, and can be built of wood, steel, aluminum, or concrete with equal ease. Their three-dimensional counterpart, the *space frame*, has also come into common use in recent decades (17.42). Trusses and space frames are theoretically capable of spans almost as great as those of arches and vaults, though they cannot approach the very long spans that are possible with hanging structures.

With trusses, as with arches and hanging structures, greater depth means lower stresses and, in general, greater economy of construction. But again, we may choose to use shallower trusses to make the building more compact and economize on other costs of building. Let us investigate what happens as the depth of a simple truss is progressively diminished.

In the wooden truss shown in 17.43, we note that the weight of the load is carried through the vertical strut to the chain. The chain carries the load to the end supports, and the horizontal struts serve only to resist in compression the horizontal pull of the chain.

If we shorten the vertical strut (17.44), the angle (a) of the chain will decrease, and both the horizontal pull of the chain and the tension in the chain will increase. We must use a thicker chain and thicker horizontal struts, but the vertical strut in the center of the truss still will carry only a force equal to the superimposed load, so it can stay the same. If we shorten the vertical strut still further (17.45), the chain must become still thicker, as must the top struts. As the truss gets very shallow, forces rise extremely rapidly with each successive reduction in depth. A useful limiting case is reached when the depth of the wooden top struts required to resist the thrust of the chain without buckling is about the same as the overall depth of the truss (17.46). Internal forces in the truss are high, but they are within the capability of ordinary structural materials to resist. The vertical strut can be eliminated entirely, with the center of the chain being bolted directly to the wood of the horizontal struts. What we have arrived at is a truss of minimum practical depth. It is not very efficient structurally because it uses far more steel and wood than a deeper truss would, but it is compact, and in a building it would produce both a flat floor above and a flat ceiling below, resulting in a maximum economy of space. What we have produced is, in fact, a form of beam, one designed specifically for the purpose of carrying only a single, concentrated load at its midpoint.

Beams

In order to arrive at a beam configuration that would be appropriate for a load that is distributed uniformly along the span of the beam, the sort of load for which we normally design the structural members of the floor or roof of a building, we start with a truss that is made up of two ideally shaped members for uniform loadings, a parabolic arch above and a hanging chain below. We make the arch an exact mirror image of the chain. If the two are connected at all points by a very large number of ties, each will carry half the load, and the horizontal pushes and pulls will balance each other exactly at the two ends, so that no horizontal thrust will be imparted to the supports (17.47).

Then we build another, shallower truss (17.48). As expected, both the arch and the chain must thicken as the depth of the truss is reduced and the horizontal forces grow. Ultimately, reaching the useful limiting case, the arch can become flat and still support itself and its half of the load (17.49). The chain, however, must retain some sag if it is to carry directly its portion of the load. The form we have arrived at is exactly the form taken by a post-tensioned concrete beam, in which tightly tensioned steel cables pull against the ends of a concrete beam, following a flat parabolic curve between (17.50).

We know from everyday experience, of course, that a beam can be much simpler than either of the types we have developed here. A length of wood of the appropriate depth and thickness does the trick quite nicely, without the need for fussing with chains or stone blocks (17.51). What is interesting about a plain beam of wood or steel, however, is how the forces of tension and compression operate within it. Analysis of the principal stresses in beams shows that a beam functions by means of both compressive stresses that follow lines similar to arches and tensile stresses that follow lines similar to hanging chains. The two sets of lines are mirror images of each other

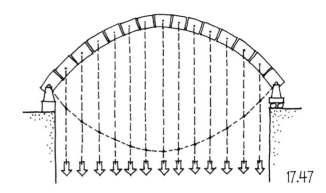

17.47

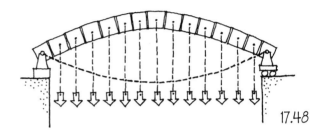

17.48

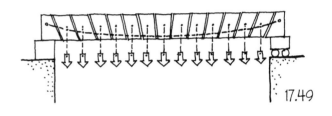

17.49

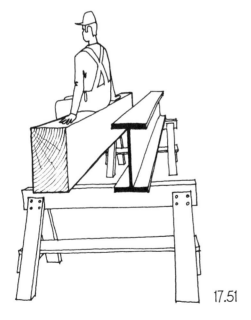

17.51

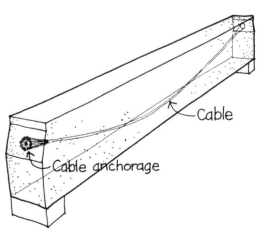

Post-tensioned concrete beam   17.50

Cable

Cable anchorage

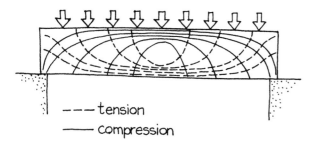

–––– tension
—— compression

17.52

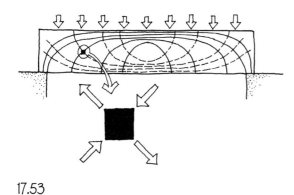

17.53

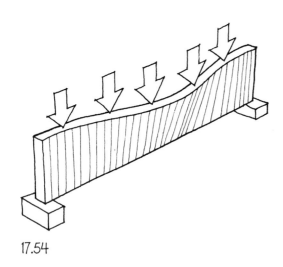

17.54

and are symmetrically arranged so that the horizontal pushes of the "arches" are exactly balanced by the horizontal pulls of the "chains" (17.52). Notice how the lines bunch together at the top and bottom of the beam in the middle of the span—the tension and compression stresses are highest in these areas, and the material in these areas of a well-designed beam is tensioned and compressed to the allowable stress of the material. In the rest of the beam, however, stresses are lower. The material is not working to its full structural capacity and in this sense is being partially wasted. For this reason, a beam is not nearly as efficient a structural form as a hanging cable, an arch, or a truss is, in which most or all of the material is fully stressed. But a beam is compact and convenient to work with, exerts no external horizontal thrust, and easily produces flat ceilings and floors.

The lines of principal stress in a beam indicate another phenomenon that is of interest. Notice that whenever a line of compression and a line of tension cross, they do so at right angles. If we examine a small block of material taken from one of these intersections, we see that it is compressed across one diagonal and pulled across the other (17.53). These diagonal forces become very large near the ends of a beam, and sometimes they are more critical than any other stresses at the ends of the beam, where the lines of principal stress intersect at an angle of 45° to the horizontal, and progressively lower toward the middle of the beam. Thus a beam must be designed to resist not only heavy horizontal tensile and compressive stresses at its upper and lower faces in the middle of the span but also heavy diagonal stresses at the ends. These stresses in the end regions are seldom a problem in steel beams because steel is relatively strong against diagonal stresses, but wood and concrete beams are weaker in this regard. They require special care in design and construction of their end regions.

The part of a beam where compressive stresses are highest is subject to buckling, like any structural device that carries compression. As one would expect, the longer and more slender the beam is, the higher the risk of buckling will be (17.54). Empirical formulas have been developed to predict this risk, and where a risk of buckling is present, either the beam must be made thicker, or lateral bracing must be provided, much as for a column. Such bracing can often be furnished conveniently by the floor or roof deck that is carried by the beam.

In beams, as in all spanning devices, it is important that we be able to predict how much the beam will *deflect* (sag) under its expected loading. Rather exact formulas have been developed for this purpose. By knowing in advance what the deflection will be, we can design beams that are stiff enough to feel solid underfoot and that will not bend so much as to crack plaster ceilings that are affixed

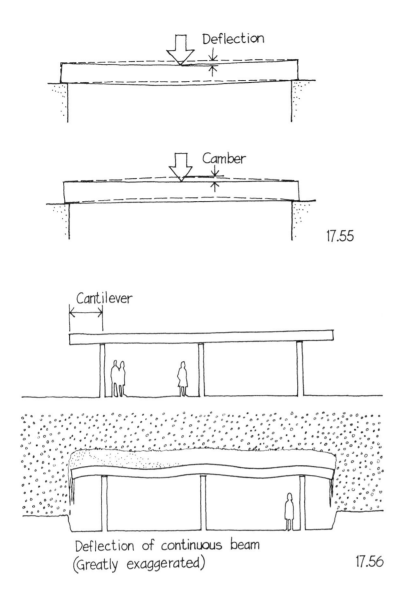

17.55

Cantilever

Deflection of continuous beam
(Greatly exaggerated)   17.56

to them or to apply force to windows, partitions, and other building components beneath them that are not designed to carry major structural loads. We can also *camber* a beam—that is, we can build into it an upward curvature equal to the expected deflection under load, so that it will be flat when in use (17.55).

We use beams in many different ways. To this point, we have been discussing what are called *simply supported beams*, which have a support at each end and deflect downward under a gravity load. Frequently, a single, *continuous beam* is placed across two or more adjacent spans as a single piece or is cantilevered beyond its supports at one or both ends (17.56). Such configurations introduce bending in the opposite direction over the supports. By efficiently stressing more of the beam material to its maximum, continuity

No horizontal thrust in rafters

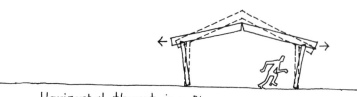

Horizontal thrust in rafters

17.57 Tie resists horizontal thrust

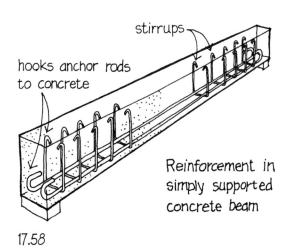

stirrups

hooks anchor rods to concrete

Reinforcement in simply supported concrete beam

17.58

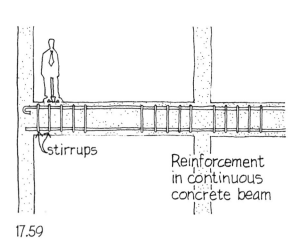

stirrups

Reinforcement in continuous concrete beam

17.59

allows the use of a smaller, less expensive beam than would have to be used if only simply supported spans were employed.

Beams are used in sloping planes as roof *rafters*. If a rafter is supported vertically at both its ends, it does not exert any horizontal thrust (17.57). However, if two rafters are set against each other from opposite walls of the building without a center support, they will act as a simple arch. Each thrusts the other horizontally, and so a tie or buttresses must be provided.

In *reinforced concrete* construction, most or all of the compressive forces are resisted by the concrete, with round steel bars located so that they resist all the tensile forces. Reinforcement against the strong diagonal forces near the ends of the beam is provided by vertical *stirrups* of steel bars (17.58).

For maximum economy, continuous spans are almost always used in concrete building frames. The heaviest concentrations of steel bars alternate between the bottoms and tops of the beams as the direction of bending changes. Wind and earthquake forces can cause the directions of bending in the beams of a building to reverse, so in most cases at least some of the steel reinforcing bars are installed over the full length of the beam at both the top and the bottom (17.59).

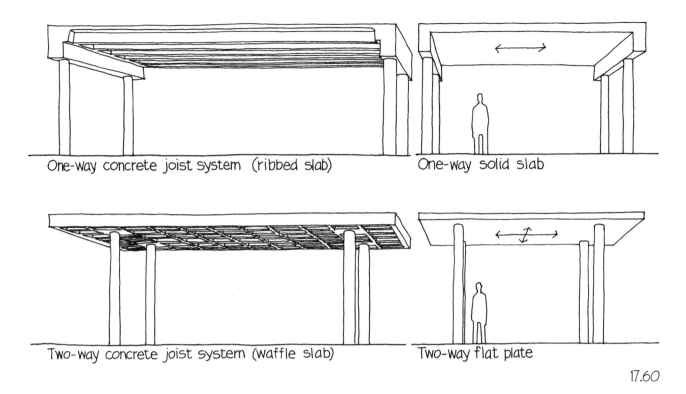

One-way concrete joist system (ribbed slab)

One-way solid slab

Two-way concrete joist system (waffle slab)

Two-way flat plate

17.60

Slabs

A concrete *slab* is a very broad, shallow, reinforced concrete beam (17.60). If a concrete slab spans between two parallel beams or walls, it is reinforced primarily in the direction of spanning and is termed a *one-way slab*. If a concrete slab spans between columns arranged in a more-or-less square pattern, it is reinforced in two directions (both north–south and east–west) and spans in two mutually perpendicular directions at the same time. This *two-way slab* needs less concrete and reinforcing steel to support a given load than a one-way slab and is therefore used whenever possible. For longer spans in either one-way or two-way concrete slabs, further economies can be gained by leaving out much of the concrete between the reinforcing bars in the bottom of the slab, to form a *one-way concrete joist system* (also known as a *ribbed slab*) or a *two-way concrete joist system* (*waffle slab*). In this way, the slab can grow much deeper without becoming much heavier.

For maximum economy of concrete and steel, the reinforcing steel in slabs and beams is often *post-tensioned*. This requires special high-strength steel reinforcing cables that are encased in plastic tubes. The space between the cables and the tubes is filled with an anticorrosive lubricant. The tubes with their cables are placed in the formwork. Heavy wire *chairs* support them along funicular lines of tension. The concrete is poured around them. After the concrete

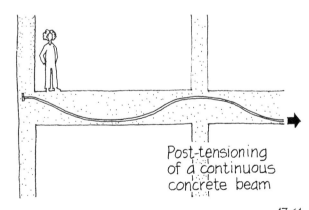

Post-tensioning of a continuous concrete beam

17.61

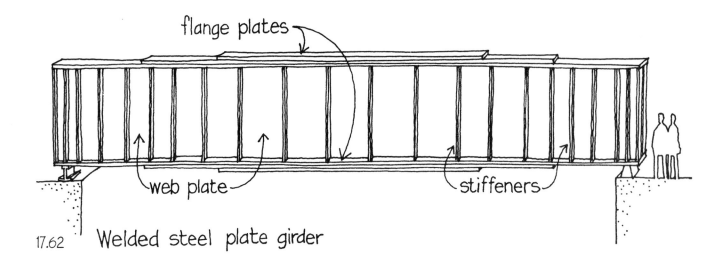

flange plates

web plate

stiffeners

17.62 Welded steel plate girder

hardens, hydraulic jacks are used to tighten all the cables to very high stresses. Because the cables were given funicular curves at the time they were placed, they support the loads on the beams and slabs very efficiently (17.61). The concrete around them acts in horizontal compression to resist the horizontal pull of the cables.

Other Types of Beams

Large beams for heavy loads and long spans are often custom manufactured of concrete, steel, or laminated wood, in such a way that more material is provided where stresses are highest. A welded steel plate girder, for instance, has extra top and bottom plates to resist peak values of tension and compression at midspan, and extra vertical stiffeners to reinforce against shear at the ends (17.62).

A beam is not always straight. For longer spans, it is frequently advantageous to make a bent beam called a *rigid frame*, a combined column and beam with a stiff joint between (17.63). The joint (the point where the frame changes from vertical to sloping) carries very high stresses and is usually thickened accordingly. A rigid frame behaves like both a beam and an arch and must therefore be tied together at the base. This is usually done by means of a steel rod buried in the concrete floor slab.

Rigid frames are capable of maximum spans approaching those of trusses. Beams generally are restricted to shorter spans. The deeper the beam is, the longer the span can be, but beams become cumbersome and uneconomical to build at spans well below those that are easily constructed using lighter, more efficient structural forms such as cables, arches, and trusses.

If a flat plane of structural material, usually reinforced concrete, is folded or scalloped to increase its overall depth, it becomes

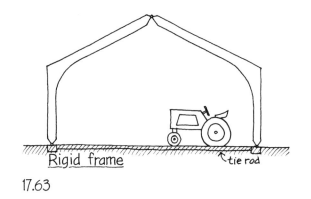

Rigid frame   tie rod

17.63

196

capable of spanning fairly long distances and will act in much the same manner as a deep beam does (17.64). The structural behavior of such forms is easily modeled by folding or scalloping a sheet of paper, supporting it across two books, and loading it with other sheets of paper.

Corbels

A *corbel* is a structural device composed of a number of stones or bricks, each of which acts as a small, stubby cantilever beam (17.65). For its stability, it depends on having the total leverage of the weight that bears on the back end of each block exceed the total leverage of the weight bearing on the projecting portion of the same block. The simple corbel is sometimes used to span window openings in walls or to form projecting brackets on masonry bearing walls to support beams (17.66). It is frequently used in decorative brickwork. Translated into the third dimension as a linear corbeled vault, it was used by the Mayas and other ancient cultures to span narrow rooms (17.67). Its spanning capacity is the most limited of any structural form, however, because the heavy stones or bricks of which it is built are weak in tension and because it uses large quantities of material, compared with other devices that can carry equal loads over equal spans.

Somewhat greater spans are possible, with somewhat more efficient use of material, if a corbel is rotated about its vertical centerline to form a *tholos* (17.68). The tholos employs more than just the corbel principle, however; each of its horizontal rings of stones or bricks acts as a full-circle horizontal arch to resist its own tendency to fall inward under the weight coming from above. Thus the tholos, unlike the other corbeled forms, does exert a thrust that must be resisted in its foundations or supporting walls, but it retains the advantage of all corbeled forms that it can be erected without the

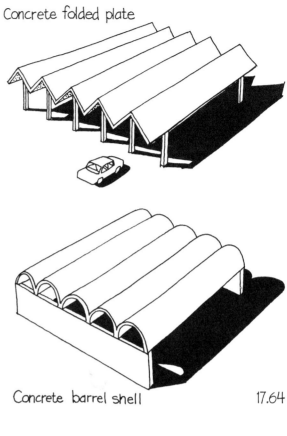

Concrete folded plate

Concrete barrel shell
17.64

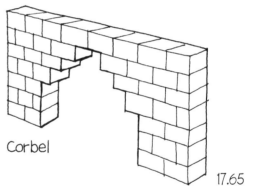

Corbel
17.65

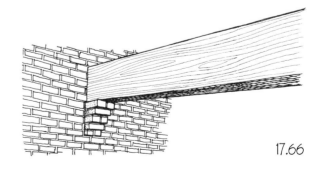

17.66

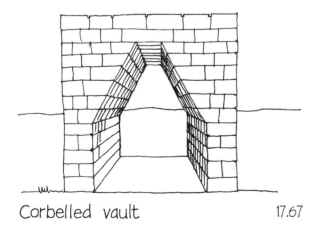

Corbelled vault
17.67

197

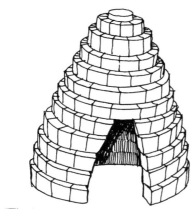

17.68 Tholos

Trullo - Italy
17.69

use of temporary support or formwork. It is superior to its corbeled cousins in its absence of need for a massive counterbalancing weight. It need be only one stone thick. In ancient Mycenaean tombs the tholos spans as much as 47 feet (14.3 m) while supporting a heavy load of earth from above. Spans of 10 to 20 feet (3 m to 6 m) are commonplace in other Mediterranean areas, particularly southern Italy, where the form was used until a few decades ago to construct roofs of farmhouses (17.69).

Pneumatic Structures

A diverse group of spanning devices whose potential has only begun to be tapped are the *fluid-filled* structures. Air is the fluid most widely used. The two categories most often constructed are *air-inflated structures* and *air-supported structures* (17.70), which are

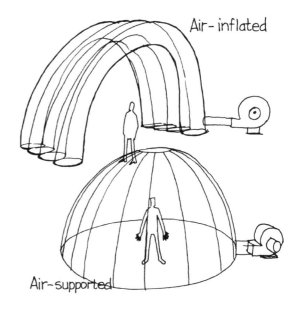

Air-inflated

Air-supported

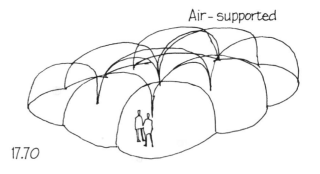

Air-supported

17.70

called collectively *pneumatic structures*. In air-inflated structures, structural members are made of fabric tubes or lenses braced against buckling by internal air pressure. The fabric itself carries the structural load. Only relatively short spans are possible before buckling failure occurs in the thin fabric of air-inflated structures. Air-supported structures, on the other hand, are theoretically capable of unlimited spans because each square foot of fabric is supported directly by air pressure against its under surface. Air-supported structures are often used to cover tennis courts and stadiums. The only stress in the fabric is the tensile stress, usually low, induced by the slight excess of air pressure needed to keep the fabric taut. Air-supported structures pose a unique foundation problem: each must be held down to the ground by a total force equal to the product of its internal air pressure and its ground area.

Lateral Support

So far we have discussed only the basic devices for supporting vertical loads and for supporting loads over horizontal spans. In order to support the loads generated by even a simple building, a number of such structural devices must be combined into a *frame* to support the surfaces of the building, gather these surface loads, conduct them to columns or bearing walls, and then carry these vertical loads to the earth, to which they will be transferred by a system of foundations. In addition, we must provide devices to maintain the entire structure in a vertical position against the *lateral forces* of wind, earthquake, and compressive buckling that would otherwise topple it.

We can provide lateral support in three ways (17.71). One is to make the joints between columns and beams very rigid. This is easily and economically done in concrete building frames. In steel frames it is a little harder, usually requiring that the connections be welded. In wood frames, rigid joints are very hard to make because of the difficulty of making secure fastenings near the ends of pieces of wood.

A second way of providing lateral support is to insert diagonal bracing in various planes in the frame of the building, effectively creating vertical trusses. A third method, akin to diagonal bracing, is to use *shear panels* of steel, plywood, or concrete instead of braces. Both diagonal bracing and shear panels are easily constructed in any common framing material. Masonry walls can also be good shear panels, especially if they are reinforced with steel bars.

With any of the three methods of providing lateral support, the support devices (rigid joints, diagonal bracing, or shear panels) must operate in two mutually perpendicular vertical planes, such as the

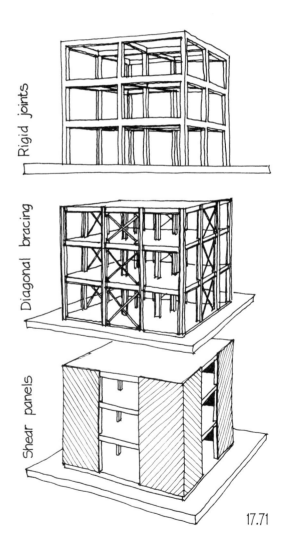

Rigid joints

Diagonal bracing

Shear panels

17.71

Roof and floor transmit load to bracing

Wind load on wall panel

Bracing transmits load to ground

17.72

north–south and east–west directions of the building. They must be arranged, as seen from above, in a more-or-less symmetrical fashion about the centroid of the building.

The floor and roof planes of a building also play a role in its lateral stability. They act as very deep horizontal beams that transmit wind forces from the exterior walls of the building to the vertical planes of lateral support (17.72). Lateral loads on buildings must be carefully computed and devices of sufficient strength provided to resist them, just as vertical loads are computed and resisted with the greatest of care.

Collapse of Building Frames

Recent terrorist attacks have caused the collapse of such major buildings as a federal office building in Oklahoma City and the World Trade Center Towers in Manhattan. In both of these cases, massive explosions blew away considerable portions of the loadbearing structure. In Oklahoma City, numerous adjacent bays of columns and beams were demolished by the blast. In the Trade Center Towers, the airplanes that were purposely flown into the towers cut through perhaps one-third of the vertical supports for the floors above the points of attack. In both cases, collapse of at least a major portion of the building was inevitable. Building frames can be designed to survive an accident or attack that removes a column here or there by strengthening the beams and girders so that they can take over and share the load from the missing member and remain standing. But it is almost impossible to design a building to remain standing when a major portion of its structure is no longer doing its job.

Much has been made of the supposed weakness of the framing system and fireproofing of framing members in the World Trade Center Towers. In fact, the ability of both towers to remain standing with a third of their columns having been cut was a tribute to the work of their structural engineers. What brought the towers down was not the cutting of so many structural members, but the prolonged, very hot fire that was fed by the full fuel tanks of the airplanes. The fireproofing on steel framing members is not designed to protect them against so hot a fire (chapter 19 of this book will be helpful in understanding how heat affects steel framing members). When the floor structure just above the fire in each tower eventually grew hot enough to collapse, the heat-weakened beams and slabs fell to the floor just beneath. This overloaded the already weakened floor so that it collapsed, sending two floors of structure onto the floor below. This process repeated itself floor by floor all the way to the ground, with the load accumulating floor by floor as the collapse approached the ground. The lowest floors were crumpled by the force of a hundred stories of collapsed building that fell on them simultaneously.

Foundations

Where the columns or bearing walls of a building meet the ground, the vertical and horizontal loads of the building must be transmitted safely into the earth. In order to do this, some sort of transitional device usually is required. A steel column carries its load at a stress of some hundreds of tons per square foot (tens of megapascals). No soil or rock is capable of carrying such an intense pressure, and if the column were allowed to rest directly on the ground, it would penetrate into it immediately and uncontrollably, carrying a portion of the building with it. If a steel column carries its load at a stress of 500 tons per square foot (47.88 MPa) and it must rest on soil that can carry safely only 10 tons per square foot (0.958 MPa), we must insert between the column and the soil a block that is

$$\frac{500 \ tons/ft^2}{10 \ tons/ft^2} = 50$$

times as large in the horizontal plane as the cross-section of the column. If the column is one-quarter square foot (0.023 m^2) in cross-sectional area, the block must be 50 times one-quarter, or 12.5 square feet in area (50 × 0.023 m^2 = 1.15 m^2). A block of concrete just over 3.5 feet square (1.07 m × 1.07 m) has an area of 12.5 square feet and will do the job (17.73). This block is called a *spread footing*. Interestingly, this example requires a second sort of spread footing as well, because the concrete, although it is much stronger than the soil, is also incapable of directly sustaining the intense pressure of the steel column. A heavy steel *base plate* must be inserted between the column and the concrete footing to spread the load. The size of the base plate is computed in the same general manner as is the size of the footing itself.

A spread footing can be either an *isolated footing*, as in the preceding example, or a continuous *strip footing*, in which it is used to support a concrete or masonry wall (17.74). A wall can be supported on isolated footings instead of a continuous strip footing if a *grade beam* is provided to conduct the wall load to the footings. In soils of intermediate to low bearing capacity, isolated spread footings may be so large that it is easier and more economical to pour a single continuous reinforced-concrete *mat foundation* under the entire building than to construct the individual footings with only small spaces between them.

Sometimes a firm stratum of soil or rock lies beneath a considerable depth of soft soil that is incapable of supporting a building on

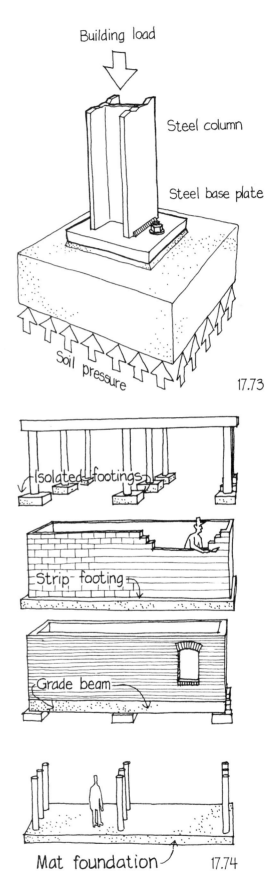

Building load

Steel column

Steel base plate

Soil pressure   17.73

Isolated footings

Strip-footing

Grade beam

Mat foundation   17.74

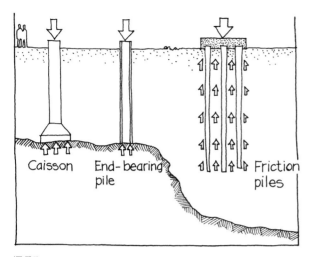

17.75

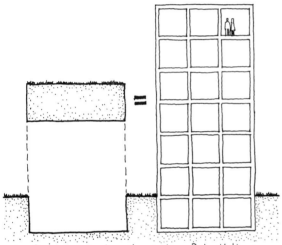

wt. of excavated soil = wt. of building

Floating foundation

17.76

spread footings. In this case, it often is possible to bore a hole down through the soft soil to reach the firm soil, to flare out the hole just above the firm stratum to give a larger bearing area, and to fill the entire hole with concrete. A column or grade beam is then constructed on top of this concrete *caisson*, which transfers its load down past the soft soil and into the firm soil beneath (17.75). An alternative possibility is to use a *pile driver*, which is a very large, heavy hammer powered by steam or diesel, to pound a length of steel or precast concrete vertically through the soft soil until its lower end rests solidly on the hard stratum. This foundation device is known as an *end-bearing pile.*

If firm soil or rock is not within reach of caissons or end-bearing piles, as, for example, in many filled swamplands or waterfront areas, *friction piles* are commonly employed. These are long pieces of wood, steel, or precast concrete that are pounded endwise into the soft soil like giant nails. Pounding continues until the friction of the soil against the sides of the pile creates enough resistance that the pile can sustain a substantial load. Piles are usually driven in *clusters*, with a concrete cap over the top of the cluster to distribute the column load among the individual piles. If a column brings a load of 250 tons (227,000 kg) to earth and each pile can safely support 10 tons (9,070 kg), a cluster of 25 piles will be needed, arranged in five rows of five piles each.

Sometimes a building must be built on soft, weak soil that is likely to compress and settle under the weight of the building. It can be advantageous in this situation to support the building on a *floating foundation*, also called a *compensated foundation*, in which the weight of the building is the same as the weight of soil removed during excavation. One story of excavated soil weighs about the same as five to eight stories of building. Thus, for example, a ten- to sixteen-story building can "float" on a two-story basement. The stress on the soil beneath the building is about the same after the building is built as it was before, which tends to minimize settlement (17.76).

Sometimes a foundation must be designed to resist an upward force rather than a downward one, especially for the anchoring of air-supported or suspension structures. If suitable rock is within reach, holes can be drilled into the rock, and cables or rods cemented into the holes with suitable adhesives. In softer soils, a simple, workable foundation can be created by burying a large piece of concrete. The piece should be large enough that the weight of the concrete plus the weight of the soil above it total more than the expected uplift. For temporary structures, heavy containers of sand or water may be placed on the surface of the ground as anchors, or small metal screw-anchors or stakes can be driven into the soil.

Further Reading

Rowland Mainstone. *Developments in Structural Form*. Cambridge, Mass., M.I.T. Press, 1975.

Fuller Moore. *Understanding Structures*. New York, McGraw-Hill, 1999.

Mario Salvadori. *Why Buildings Stand Up*. New York, Norton, 1980.

Waclaw Zalewski and Edward Allen. *Shaping Structures: Statics*. New York, Wiley, 1998.

18

Providing for Building Movement

A building, even a seemingly solid, massive one, is never at rest. Its motions are usually very small ones that we can't see, but most of them are caused by virtually irresistible forces and would tear the building to pieces if not provided for in some way. The surfaces of the building would crack, twist, and tear; components would pull apart or be crushed together. At best, the building would become merely unsightly. At worst, it would become leaky and structurally unsound.

A building starts to move as soon as the first materials are put in place in the early stages of construction. The soil settles progressively under the foundations as the weight of the building grows. Most materials that are put in place wet—concrete, mortar, terrazzo, stucco—shrink slightly and tend to crack as they harden, whereas gypsum plaster expands slightly and pushes against adjoining materials. Lumber that is not sufficiently dry shrinks after installation. Beams, columns, and other structural elements, regardless of the material of which they are made, sag or shorten gradually as their superimposed loads accumulate during construction. Further sagging, variable in magnitude, occurs throughout the life of the building as live loads on the structure change. In some structural materials, most notably wood and concrete, a long-term, irreversible sagging process known as *creep* takes place over a period of years. Wind and seismic forces cause small lateral shifts in the frame of the building.

Repeated cycles of movements caused by thermal and moisture effects occur constantly. A building grows measurably larger in warm weather and smaller in cold weather. A roof, heated by the sun, grows larger in the middle of the day while the cooler walls below stay the same size. At night, the roof cools and shrinks. In subfreezing temperatures, the formation of ice from water within or beneath a building can crack materials or lift foundations by its expansion. Under humid conditions, wood and wood products expand, often quite noticeably, and when the air dries out, as in a heated building in winter, they contract and sometimes crack. Wood furniture that is inadequately glued occasionally pulls apart at the joints during the peak of the heating season. Wooden doors and windows sometimes stick immovably in their frames in humid weather but fit too loosely under dry conditions. Where building components of different materials are juxtaposed, they are likely to move quite differently from one another. An aluminum window frame grows significantly smaller in cold weather, but the wood building frame in which it is mounted is little affected by temperature differences. A prolonged damp spell, however, expands the wood frame while leaving the aluminum window unchanged.

Certain unwanted chemical reactions can also cause buildings to move. As a metal corrodes, it also expands. Lime mortar or plaster that has not been fully hydrated before application will later expand as it incorporates moisture from the air into its crystalline structure. Portland cement reacts chemically with some minerals that may be inadvertently mixed with it when making concrete, causing destructive expansion. The jamming together of metal components by corrosion is quite common. These conditions can be remedied only by carefully controlling the quality of the materials used during construction and by completely protecting corrosion-prone metals with appropriate coatings.

Control Joints and Expansion Joints

To accommodate the inevitable movements of a building without destructive results, designers take precautionary steps during the design process and throughout construction. The basic principle they follow is to provide the building and its components with the space and the means to move without causing damage. The regularly spaced transverse cracks in an ordinary concrete sidewalk are a good example of this strategy (18.1). They were created at the time the concrete was laid to form intentional lines of structural weakness, in the knowledge that the concrete will shrink as it hardens and that the sidewalk will further shrink and expand as temperatures change and be heaved up here and there by frost or tree roots. If the cracks were not provided, these forces would form their own cracks in the sidewalk in a thousand different directions. The intentionally provided cracks, called *control joints*, absorb these forces in an orderly pattern and allow a certain amount of tilting and heaving to take place without breaking the individual rectangles of concrete. Control joints are also provided at about 20-foot (6-m) intervals in

18.1

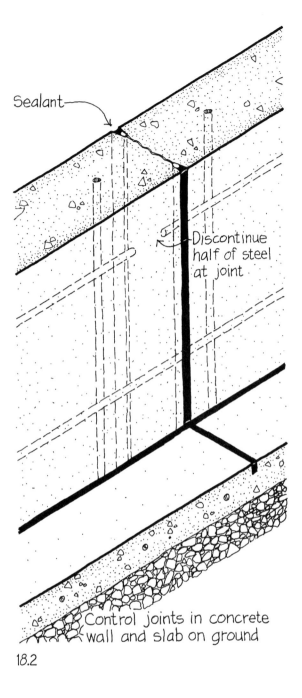

Sealant

Discontinue half of steel at joint

Control joints in concrete wall and slab on ground

18.2

concrete floor slabs that lie on the ground and in most concrete walls within buildings. They may be made with a special grooving trowel while the concrete is still wet, or, for a neater appearance, cut with an abrasive-bladed power saw after the concrete has begun to harden. Half the steel reinforcing bars in the wall or paving are interrupted at each control joint to create a line of weakness that encourages cracks to form there rather than elsewhere (18.2).

Concrete block walls have a tendency to shrink and crack as they cure and give off water. They need control joints at intervals of 20 to 40 feet (6 to 12 m), depending on the moisture content of the blocks at the time they are put in place (18.3). Exterior stucco walls also are prone to shrinkage, and control joints are recommended at spacings of about 10 feet (3 m) to control cracking.

Interior wall and ceiling surfaces usually do not need control joints because they are made of either plaster or wallboard, both of which are made primarily of gypsum. Gypsum expands slightly as it hardens, rather than shrinking. But the expansion of plaster can cause compression cracking, and large plaster surfaces can also crack because of movement in the underlying structure. Thus long

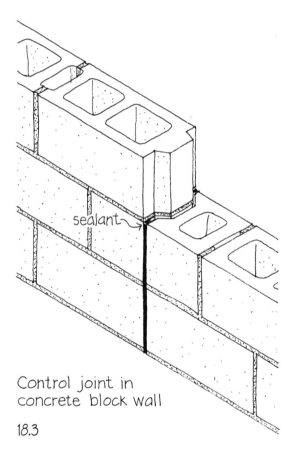

sealant

Control joint in concrete block wall

18.3

plaster walls and large ceilings should be subdivided every 30 feet (9 m) or so with *expansion joints*. In a typical expansion joint detail for plaster, the metal *lath* (rhymes with "math"—the metal mesh to which the plaster is applied) is discontinued at the line of the expansion joint, thereby creating a line of weakness that encourages movement in the wall along that line and not elsewhere. The flexible metal "bellows" strip gives a neat appearance to the joint and keeps the adjoining plaster surfaces aligned despite whatever movement may occur (18.4).

Another material that tends to expand slightly in a building is brickwork. Bricks are completely dry when they leave the kiln in which they are manufactured. In subsequent months and years they absorb small amounts of moisture and expand slightly. Expansion joints are recommended at maximum intervals of 200 feet (60 m) in brick walls (18.5). A hard rubber *spline* in the core of the wall locks the sections of wall together. Exterior aluminum walls of buildings also need to have expansion joints to allow the metal components to expand as they are heated by the sun.

Wherever two materials with different movement characteristics come together in a building or wherever old and new construction come together in a remodeled project, it is wise to provide an *abutment joint*. A wood partition expands and contracts by relatively large amounts with changes in humidity, whereas a brick wall moves very little. Where they adjoin, a broad abutment joint filled with synthetic rubber sealant allows the two to move independently (18.6). Other typical locations for abutment joints are where a plaster wall abuts a stone fireplace, a wooden window frame abuts a concrete column, or the brick wall of a new addition meets the brick wall of the original building.

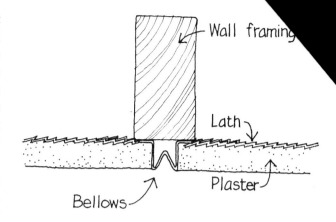

Detail of expansion joint in plaster

18.4

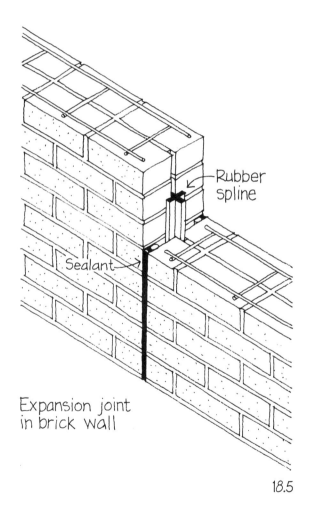

Expansion joint
in brick wall

18.5

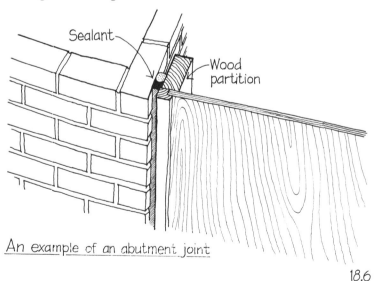

An example of an abutment joint

18.6

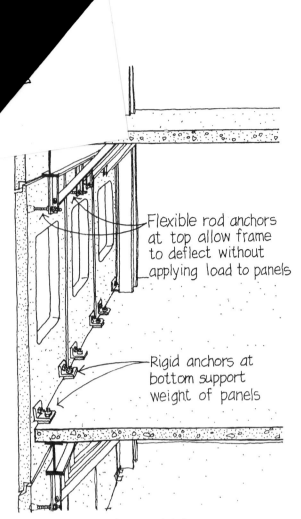

Flexible rod anchors at top allow frame to deflect without applying load to panels

Rigid anchors at bottom support weight of panels

Structure-enclosure joint:
Curtain wall panels
18.7

Structure-Enclosure Joints

Most large buildings today are not supported by their walls; quite the opposite is the case. That is, the interior and exterior walls of a building are supported by its structural frame. A typical large building is enclosed with *curtain wall panels*, and its interior is subdivided with *nonloadbearing partitions*. Neither the curtain wall panels nor the partitions are strong enough to support the load of the building's floors and roof, so it is important to provide *structure-enclosure joints* that ensure that the frame of the building and its walls can move independently of one another. A typical curtain wall panel is rigidly attached to the frame of the building at the bottom but is flexibly attached at the top by means of a flexing or sliding connection (18.7). This allows the floor beams of the building to deflect without applying any force to the panel. Inside the building, the tops of partitions are constructed with a slip joint in the wall framing and flexible sealant joints at the top edges of the wall surfaces (18.8). These allow the floor above to sag under load without applying any force to the top of the partition.

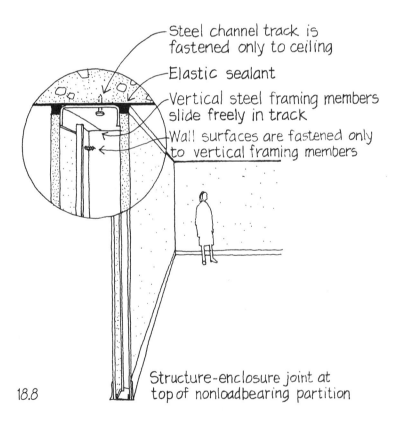

Steel channel track is fastened only to ceiling

Elastic sealant

Vertical steel framing members slide freely in track

Wall surfaces are fastened only to vertical framing members

Structure-enclosure joint at top of nonloadbearing partition

18.8

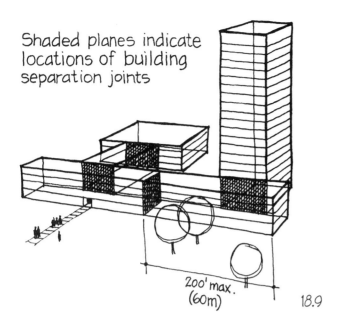

Shaded planes indicate locations of building separation joints

200' max.
(60m)   18.9

Building Separation Joints

A building that is long or broad is not able to respond as a unit to foundation settlement, seismic distress, and thermal expansion and contraction because the accumulation of such forces becomes too great over the long dimensions of the building, resulting in destructive cracking and tearing. Thus a large building needs to be divided into smaller buildings, each of which can act as a compact, rigid unit in response to such movements. These divisions are best made at junctions between low and high portions of a building, junctions between wings, abrupt changes in direction, and other locations that constitute planes of geometric weakness (18.9). At each such plane, the structural frame of the building is interrupted completely so as to create a structurally independent building, with its own columns and foundations, on each side of the plane. The two buildings are separated by a gap of several inches to allow plenty of room for movement. The gap is closed by joint covers that are designed to allow the roof, walls, and floors to function normally despite any movement that may occur (18.10). At the roof, a rubber bellows keeps water out. At the walls and floors, metal plates and rubber gaskets are combined to create smooth, attractive surfaces that can adjust to movement without damage. These joints are commonly but imprecisely referred to as expansion joints. The term *building separation joint* is more descriptive, indicating that the building has been separated into independent parts along the plane of the joint. One part can settle without affecting the other, and roof and wall

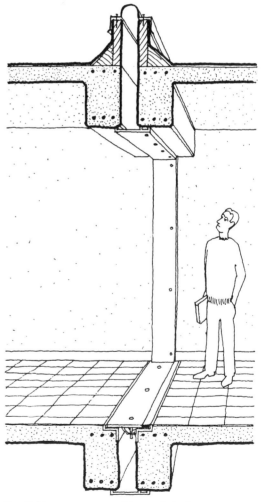

Building separation joint   18.10

209

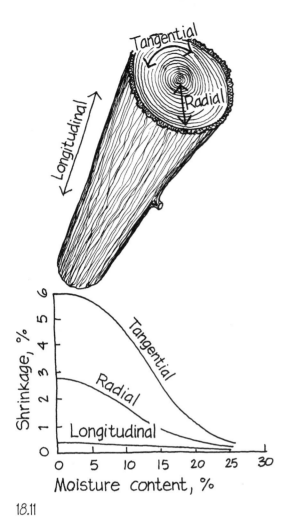

surfaces are free to expand and contract without harm in response to changing weather conditions.

Providing for Movement in Wood

Of those materials that are susceptible to moisture-induced movement, wood is the extreme example. The situation is complicated by the large difference between movement parallel to the grain of the wood, which is slight, and movement perpendicular to the grain, which is quite considerable (18.11). The problem can be reduced by using lumber whose moisture content, through careful seasoning, has been brought to equilibrium with air of average humidity and by protecting the finished construction from extremes of moisture or dry heat. Care must then be taken to minimize the remaining effects of cross-grain movement.

Each horizontal wood siding board is nailed onto a house with a single row of nails located near its lower edge. Its upper edge is held loosely by the lower edge of the board above. This leaves each board free to expand and contract across its width as it gains and loses moisture (18.12).

18.11

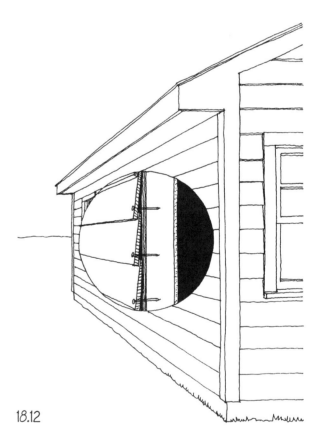

18.12

In primitive circumstances, wooden doors are often made of vertical boards fastened together side by side. The widths of these doors change so much with changes in moisture content that they often jam in their frames during the humid summer months but rattle loosely during the dry winter. The traditional paneled wood door evolved directly in response to this problem. The panels are slip jointed into the stiles and rails to allow for internal movement. Moisture-induced changes in the width of the door are limited to the sum of the changes in the widths of the two outside stiles, which total only about a third as much as the width change in a door made up entirely of vertical boards (18.13).

The floor structure of an ordinary wood-frame house, in which the wood grain runs horizontally, shrinks by a half-inch or so (about 13 mm) in height as the wood framing dries out during the first heating season. However, the walls of the house change height very little between one floor and the next because most of the height of a wall is made up of lumber whose grain runs vertically. Thus it is important when framing a house, especially one that has unusual spaces and forms, to put walls and floors together in a way that maintains the same amount of horizontal-grain wood from one side of the

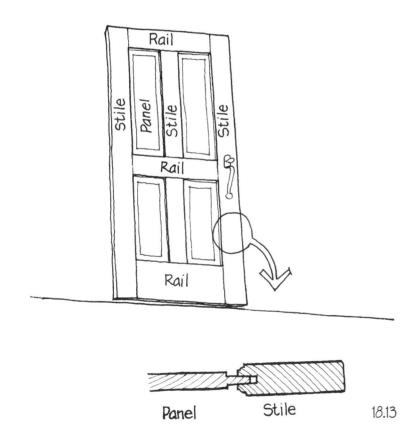

Panel   Stile   18.13

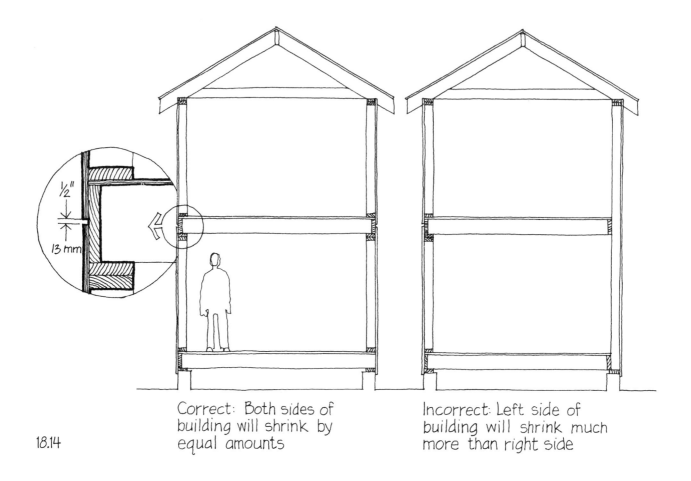

1/2"

13 mm

Correct: Both sides of building will shrink by equal amounts

Incorrect: Left side of building will shrink much more than right side

18.14

house to the other at each story (18.14). If this is not done, floors will slope and plaster will crack because of the different amounts of vertical shrinkage between one area of the house and another. Where plywood exterior wall sheathing passes over the edge of a floor structure, it is wise to leave a horizontal gap of about half an inch (13 mm) in the plywood to allow the floor to shrink. On the interior of a house, plaster does not usually pass vertically over the edge of a floor structure, but if it does, it should be interrupted with a horizontal control joint.

Further Reading

Edward Allen. *Architectural Detailing: Function, Constructibility, Aesthetics.* New York, Wiley, 1993, pp. 75–94.

19
Controlling Fire

Uncontrolled fire in a building is a uniquely deadly and destructive occurrence:

- A building supplies a concentration of fuel for an accidental fire. A wooden building is itself a source of fuel, but even a concrete or steel building usually contains furniture, paper, carpets, and combustible building materials such as wood paneling and plastic insulating materials. Oil, gas, gasoline, paints, rubber, chemicals, and other highly flammable materials are often present in buildings.
- A building supplies many potential sources of ignition for accidental fires. Defective furnaces, spark-throwing fireplaces, leaky chimneys, unattended stoves, loose electrical connections, overloaded electrical wiring, and carelessly handled matches and cigarettes are but a few of the means by which a building or its contents may be set on fire.
- A building, stovelike, contains a fire and encourages its growth by concentrating its heat and flammable combustion gases. Where vertical passages through the building are open to the fire, strong convective drafts fan the flames. Hot gases rise and set new fires in the upper reaches of the structure.
- A building holds dense concentrations of people, subjects them to the heat and gases generated by a fire, and restricts their escape (19.1). If a campfire gets out of control in a wilderness, few people are likely to be present, and there are a multitude of directions in which to escape. But if a fire of similar magnitude starts in a school, a theater, a department store, or an office building, thousands of people are endangered, and only a few escape routes are available.

19.1

- A building serves as a barrier to firefighters. Whereas a wilderness fire can be fought from all sides and even from the air, a fire in a tall building may be 40 stories above the street, accessible only by stairway. Low, very broad buildings can put an interior fire beyond the reach of fire hoses. Building fires expose firefighters to excessive heat, poisonous gases, explosions, dangerous heights, toppling walls, and collapsing floors and roofs.

These diverse interactions of buildings and fire take a terrible toll. Twelve thousand American lives are lost in building fires each year, and 300,000 people are injured, often very seriously and painfully. Property losses due to building fires in the United States are measured in billions of dollars.

Fire begins when a supply of fuel and a supply of oxygen are brought together at a sufficiently high temperature to initiate combustion. As the fire burns, it consumes the fuel and oxygen, and gives off various gases, particulate emissions, and large quantities of heat. Depending on the available fuel, the combustion gases may include carbon dioxide, carbon monoxide, hydrogen cyanide, hydrogen sulfide, and sulfur dioxide. Any of these is toxic if inhaled in sufficient concentrations.

People may be injured by fire in several ways. They may be burned, particularly in the lungs and respiratory passages, by exposure to hot air or on the skin by severe thermal radiation. They may be suffocated by oxygen-depleted air or poisoned by toxic combustion gases. Panic often contributes to loss of life in building fires; people may make irrational decisions with regard to personal safety (such as running back into a burning building to save personal effects), and they may injure one another by pushing, crowding, or trampling as they rush to escape. The most prevalent cause of death in building fires is suffocation or carbon monoxide poisoning that overtakes the victim after he or she has failed to find a means of escape because of a dense accumulation of smoke.

In designing against fire in buildings, our first aim is to reduce the risk of human injury or death to as low a level as possible. Simultaneously, we wish to minimize fire damage to the building and its contents and to prevent the fire from spreading to neighboring buildings. We would like, of course, to eliminate all risk of fire, but contrary to popular myth, there can never be such a thing as a "fireproof" building. Steel obviously does not burn, but it does lose most of its structural strength and sag or collapse at a temperature that is well below its own melting point and the sustained temperatures frequently reached by ordinary building fires (19.2). Concrete is more resistant to fire than steel is, but the crystalline structure of

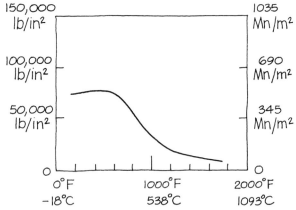

Average tensile strength of structural steel at various temperatures

19.2

214

its cement binder progressively disintegrates when exposed to fire, and if the fire lasts long enough, serious structural damage will result. Brick and tile, which are products of intense heat in the kiln, are not themselves weakened by fire, but their mortar joints are subject to disintegration, thereby weakening the entire masonry construction. For reasons such as these, our buildings cannot be made perfectly resistant to fire. Nevertheless, we have developed a rather effective and rapidly improving arsenal of weapons to protect life and property against building fires.

Keeping Fire from Starting

A natural first step in the fire protection of buildings and their occupants is to prevent fires from starting. Building codes and zoning ordinances regulate the combustibility of the materials with which buildings may be built in different areas of a city, as well as the conditions under which flammable and explosive substances may be stored in or near buildings. Proper building maintenance ensures that rubbish does not pile up anywhere. Firefighters and fire underwriters (insurers) inspect buildings periodically to find whether any unsafe concentrations of combustible materials have accumulated in them. Through these same means—codes, zoning ordinances, maintenance, and inspection—potential sources of accidental ignition are eliminated. Heating devices, chimneys, electrical systems, electrical devices, and hazardous industrial processes are especially stringently controlled. Smoking is prohibited by law in gasoline stations, certain types of industrial plants, auditoriums, and many public buildings.

Lightning can damage and set fire to buildings in exposed locations. A lightning bolt is the instantaneous release of a very high electrical potential between a rain cloud and the earth. Pointed metal rods connected directly to the earth through heavy, highly conductive cables furnish lightning protection for buildings (19.3). By leaking an electric charge from the ground off their points, the rods are often able to neutralize the electrical charges of clouds before lightning bolts form. If lightning strikes the building, the rods and conductors offer a path to the ground of considerably less resistance than the building itself. Thus they attract the lightning away from the fabric of the building and conduct it safely to the ground.

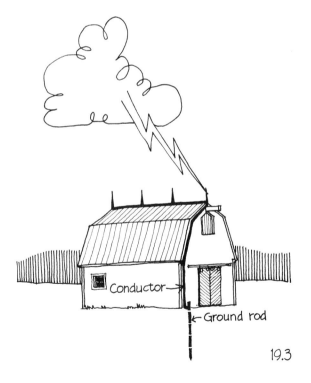

Keeping Fire from Spreading

Compartmentation of a building is designed to prevent the spread of fire, smoke, and heat beyond a restricted area should a fire break out. In a house, a fire-resistant plaster wall and a solid wood door are

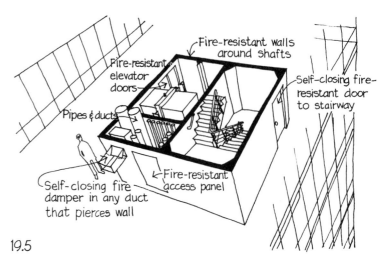

19.5

19.4

required between an attached garage (where gasoline leaks pose a potential fire hazard) and the dwelling. In rowhouses, fire-resistant walls must be provided between dwellings (19.4).

In larger buildings, compartmentation becomes increasingly important, both to protect the larger numbers of people inside and to prevent the unchecked spread of fire by hot combustion gases. Stairways and corridors used as escape routes must be isolated from the rest of the building by fire-resistant walls (usually made of masonry, plaster, or concrete) and self-closing fire-resistant doors (usually composed of steel facings with an incombustible mineral core) (19.5). Fire-resistant walls and doors also are required as separations between different types of functions taking place in the same building. A boiler room, for example, must be separated in this manner from the rest of a building so as to contain any fire that might start there and prevent it from spreading. A woodworking shop or dry cleaning establishment, either of which contains highly flammable substances, must be separated from the remainder of a building that it shares with other functions.

Open vertical shafts of any kind, whether for stairs, elevators, ductwork, electrical wiring, or piping, must be enclosed with fire-resistant walls and self-closing fire-resistant doors at each floor to prevent the convection of fire and combustion products through the building (19.6). The only exceptions to this rule are vertical *atriums*. Building codes define an atrium as a roofed, inhabited, multistory open space contained within a building. Atriums are commonly used in shopping arcades, hotels, and office buildings. To avoid the spread of fire through these vertical spaces, designers must comply with a number of building code provisions: The balconies around an atrium may be open to it, but surrounding rooms must be isolated

216

from the balconies and atrium by fire-resistant walls. An exception is made to this enclosure requirement for any three floors of the building that the designer may choose, allowing lobby spaces on several floors to be continuous with the atrium. The entire building that contains the atrium and the atrium itself must be protected by sprinklers. And the atrium must be provided with a system of fans that will operate automatically in case of fire to bring fresh air into the space at ground level and exhaust smoke at the ceiling level.

Buildings with large floor areas must be subdivided into smaller areas by means of fire-resistant walls and doors. In large, single-story factories or warehouses where this is not practical, incombustible *curtain boards* must be hung from the roof to catch and contain the rising hot gases from a fire. A self-opening roof vent must be provided in each compartment thus formed to allow the hot gases to escape before they can spread the fire (19.7). The roof vent doors are held closed against springs by a *fusible link* of a special low-melting-point metal that releases them to open in case of a buildup of heat.

In theaters, where the backstage area is often filled with combustible scenery and temporary electrical wiring, the audience must be protected by a fire-resistant curtain that is normally rolled up above the proscenium. If a fire breaks out, a fusible link melts and allows the curtain to drop, sealing off the stage from the audience. A large self-opening vent in the roof of the fly loft above the stage relieves the heat and smoke in the backstage area (19.8).

Fire-resistant walls are required on the exteriors of many buildings. The type of materials allowed in these walls and the permissible extent and treatment of windows and doors are governed by the proximity of each wall to the walls of neighboring buildings. If two buildings are within a certain minimum distance, each must have a *parapet*, a fire-resistant wall that projects a distance above the roof in order to prevent fire from leaping from one roof to the next (19.9).

The fire-resistive qualities of roof materials are also regulated by law in urban areas to prevent easy ignition of a roof by burning fragments thrown by a fire in an adjacent building. *Wired glass*,

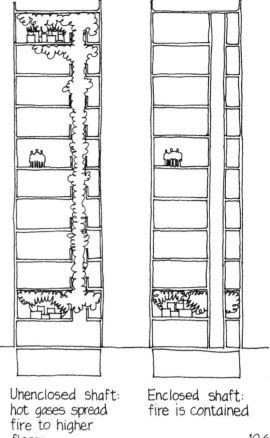

Unenclosed shaft: hot gases spread fire to higher floors

Enclosed shaft: fire is contained

19.6

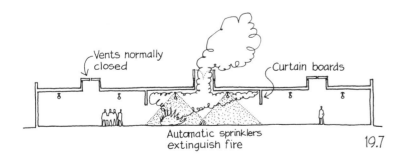

Vents normally closed

Curtain boards

Automatic sprinklers extinguish fire

19.7

217

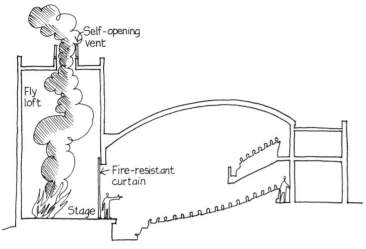

19.8

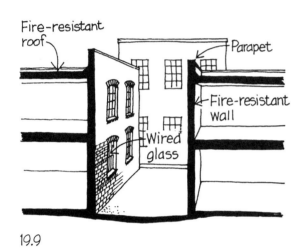

19.9

which holds together against flame for a considerable period of time, is usually required in windows that face a nearby structure. Several substitutes for wired glass have become available in recent years, including a fire-resistant transparent ceramic that stays intact at high temperatures. In multistory buildings, fire on a lower floor can spread to upper floors by crawling up the face of the building floor by floor, breaking windows and igniting combustible materials inside. Two alternatives are open to the designer to solve this problem: a fire-resistant spandrel at least 3 feet (914 mm) high may be provided or else a horizontally projecting flame barrier, also made of fire-resistant materials, at least 30 inches (762 mm) wide (19.10).

Spread of Fire Up the Face of a Building

19.10

Extinguishing Incipient Fires

Rapidly quenching a small fire before it can grow large is an effective way of preventing its spread. Such "first-aid" devices as portable extinguishers and fixed hose reels that can be used by building occupants help put out many small building fires before they can spread. Building codes require that these devices be provided and clearly identified (19.11). More reliable and effective are *automatic sprinkler systems*, in which each sprinkler head is controlled by a plug or link of fusible metal that melts at a temperature of about 150°F (65°C) (19.12, 19.13). So efficient is the resulting spray of water in extinguishing a fire that rarely do more than one or two sprinkler heads open before the fire is put out. Sprinkler systems are costly to install, but the initial expense is often balanced by cost savings that accrue to the building owner because of the presence of sprinklers. Building codes commonly allow several important concessions to a sprinklered building:

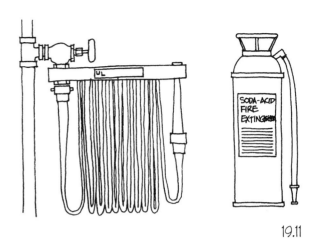

19.11

- Greater distances between exits are permitted in sprinklered buildings, which may have the effect of eliminating one or more exit stairways from a large building.
- Larger floor areas are permitted between fire separations in sprinklered buildings, which may result in the elimination of some fire-resistant walls and doors.
- Larger overall building areas and greater overall heights are permitted for sprinklered buildings.
- A lesser degree of fire protection may be permitted on some structural elements of a sprinklered building.
- Larger amounts of combustible building materials may be incorporated into a sprinklered building.

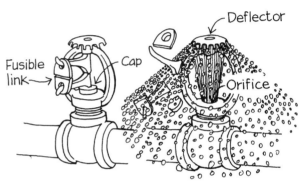

19.12

In addition to these code concessions, fire insurance rates are much lower for sprinklered buildings than for nonsprinklered ones. Most fire underwriters refuse to insure a high-hazard building that has no sprinkler system.

For the occasional building in which sprinkler water would cause irreparable damage to the building contents—a library, a museum, an art gallery—analogous but more expensive systems are available that discharge inert gases or powders onto the flames. Nonwater systems also are useful in areas such as commercial kitchens where grease fires or other types of fires that cannot be extinguished by water may break out.

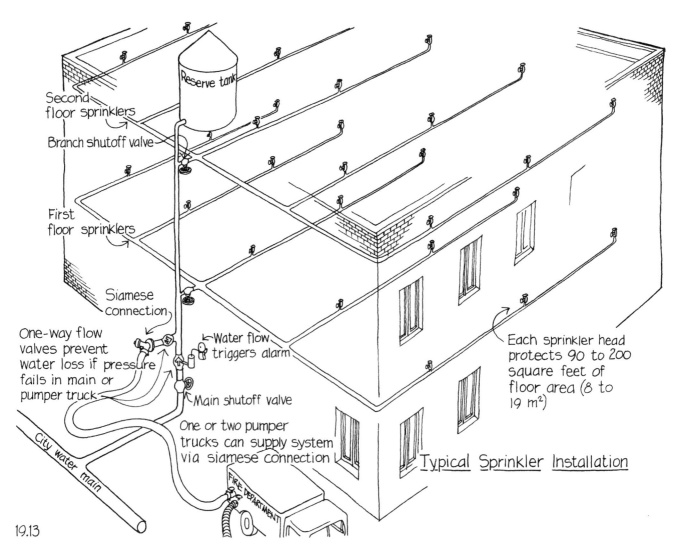

Second floor sprinklers

Branch shutoff valve

Reserve tank

First floor sprinklers

Siamese connection

One-way flow valves prevent water loss if pressure fails in main or pumper truck

Water flow triggers alarm

Main shutoff valve

City water main

One or two pumper trucks can supply system via siamese connection

Each sprinkler head protects 90 to 200 square feet of floor area (8 to 19 m²)

FIRE DEPARTMENT

Typical Sprinkler Installation

19.13

Protecting Human Lives

The most important function that we ask of a building in case of fire is that it let people reach safety quickly. An alarm system must alert them immediately to the presence of fire. Manually operated alarm boxes must be provided and identified by signs at frequent intervals in a building. Automatic alarm systems, which sense smoke, heat, flame, or the ionization products of combustion, are becoming increasingly common. They are required by law in dwellings to combat the high percentage of fire deaths that occur while people are asleep. In some cases, besides setting off warning devices in a building, alarm systems are connected directly to fire department switchboards to avoid delay in summoning help.

When a fire breaks out, rapid, well-protected escape on foot to the outdoors is the best life-saving strategy for able-bodied people. In any

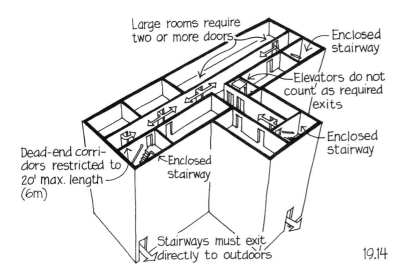

Large rooms require two or more doors

Enclosed stairway

Elevators do not count as required exits

Enclosed stairway

Dead-end corridors restricted to 20' max. length (6m)

Enclosed stairway

Stairways must exit directly to outdoors

19.14

Exit sign and emergency lighting must be on independent, secure power supply

EXIT

Glass in fire-resistant doors must be wired glass, and limited in area

Panic bar

19.15

building, a person emerging from a room must have two escape routes available in two different directions, so that if one route is involved in fire, the other may still be used (19.14). A maximum permissible distance from the door of any room to the farthest protected exit is specified; it is usually 150 to 200 feet (40 m to 60 m). Illuminated exit signs must identify these routes, and these signs, together with sufficient emergency lights to illuminate the corridors and stairs, must be connected to a battery system that will energize them automatically if the building's regular lighting system fails (19.15). The corridors and stairs of each escape route must be protected from fire and smoke by fire-resistant partitions and self-closing doors. (The familiar outdoor iron fire escape that we see in older districts of cities is no longer legal in new buildings.) The doors along an escape route may not lock against persons exiting from the building, and they all must open in the direction of travel from indoors to outdoors, to prevent possible interference with the flow of escapees.

Exit doors in buildings that hold large numbers of people, particularly schools, theaters, and athletic assembly buildings, must be provided with *panic hardware* that opens the door automatically upon pressure from within. Revolving doors must be made so that they fold outward and provide two unrestricted exitways if people try to turn the door in opposite directions at the same time (19.16). Exit stairs must be comfortably and consistently proportioned to prevent stumbling, and they may not have excessive numbers of risers between landings (19.17). Stair landings may not be narrower than the stairs that lead into them. Stair railings may not have projecting ends that might catch clothing. Nothing may be stored in exit corridors or stairs. The widths of exit corridors, doors, and stairs, furthermore, must be determined in accordance with building-code

19.16

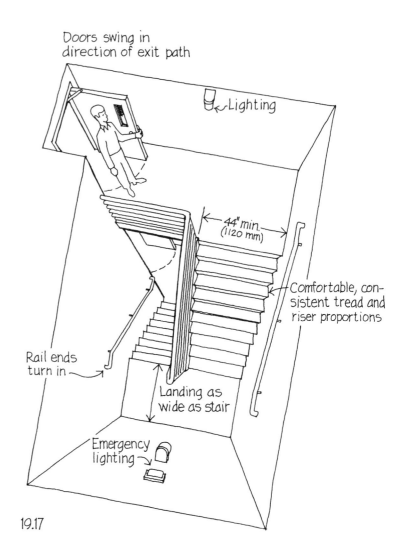

Doors swing in direction of exit path

Lighting

44" min. (1120 mm)

Comfortable, consistent tread and riser proportions

Rail ends turn in

Landing as wide as stair

Emergency lighting

19.17

formulas so that they are adequate to allow the unencumbered escape of the maximum expected population of the building within a short period of time.

Not all occupants of buildings are able to escape by the means just described. Small children often cannot read exit signs or make rational decisions about how to escape. Prisoners are not free to leave their prisons. Bedridden patients in health-care facilities cannot move on their own. Many disabled people cannot negotiate stairs. For these persons, *areas of refuge* must be provided within many types of buildings. An area of refuge must be adjacent to a protected exit stairway, protected from smoke, and provided with communications devices that permit those taking refuge to summon firefighters to rescue them. A *horizontal exit* is often used to provide an area of refuge; it is simply a fire-resistant wall and doors that subdivide a floor of a building into two areas that are, in effect, separate buildings (19.18). Escape from a fire on one side of the wall requires only horizontal movement through self-closing fire doors to the other side of the wall. Horizontal exits can provide refuge for very large building populations in health-care, detention, and educational buildings. Smaller areas of refuge for the small populations of disabled people that are normally present in buildings can be provided by smoke-protected vestibules adjacent to exit stairways (19.19) or by enlarged landings in the stairways themselves.

These design guidelines for exitways are comprehensive. If they seem excessive, one need only remember that each was drawn up to prevent the recurrence of past tragedies.

Protecting the Structure of the Building

Protecting the structural integrity of a building from the effects of fire is crucial to maintaining the value of the building and is even more crucial to protecting its occupants, firefighters, and neighboring buildings. The taller the building is, the more necessary it is that neither the building nor any piece of it be allowed to fall. Even though we do not possess any "fireproof" materials, we do have materials sufficiently resistant to fire to help protect the building structure for substantial periods of time. Among these are fired-clay products—brick and tile—that are chemically unaffected by fire; a variety of mineral fibers that also are unaffected by fire; and concrete and plaster, both of which are composed in large part of hydrated crystals that absorb very large quantities of heat in order to evaporate their water of crystallization during a fire and thus offer a

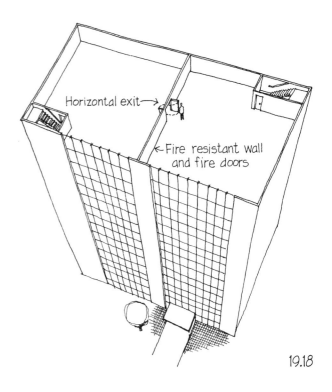

19.18

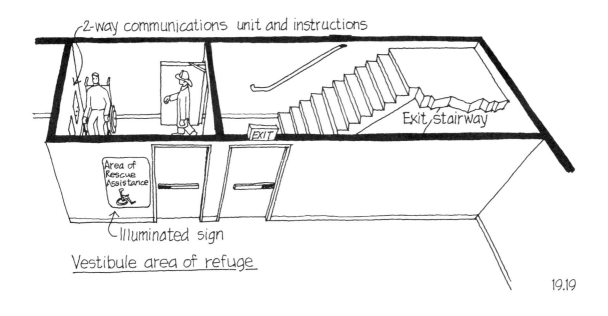

19.19

considerable barrier to fire during their slow disintegration. A more recent development in structural fire protection is the *intumescent coating*, available as either a paint or a thick trowel-on compound. When exposed to heat, the coating softens, releasing bubbles of gas that expand the coating to form an insulating layer over the substrate material.

When using any of these materials, the idea is to prevent the structural collapse of a building within the time that a fire will normally run its course, or at least to delay collapse in low buildings until all occupants have escaped and firefighters have had a reasonable chance to save the building. Plaster or plasterboard walls and ceilings give wooden houses roughly a half hour of protection from collapse. Low industrial and commercial buildings may be built of unprotected steel, in which case they are classified as "noncombustible." In a hot fire their collapse would be relatively rapid but unlikely to happen before the occupants could get out through the easy escape routes. "*Slow-burning*" construction framed with timbers at least eight inches (200 mm) in minimum dimension lasts considerably longer in a fire than does a frame made of unprotected steel. Building codes therefore recognize heavy timber construction as a special category that is safer than framing of unprotected steel. The ends of timber beams and joists must be *fire cut* wherever they enter masonry walls, in order to keep the wall from toppling should the beams eventually burn through (19.20).

Most large buildings are constructed of either reinforced concrete or protected steel. The steel reinforcing bars in concrete beams and columns are buried a specified distance within the mass of concrete so as to be protected by its thermal capacity and natural fire-resistive properties. In the earliest buildings framed with steel, beams and

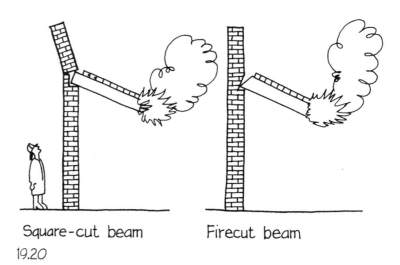

Square-cut beam   Firecut beam

19.20

224

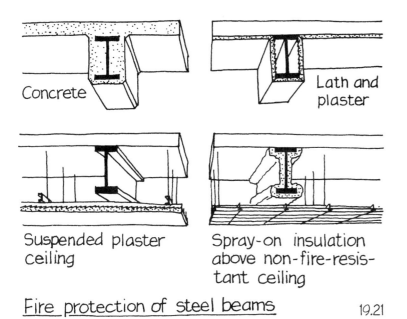

Concrete

Lath and plaster

Suspended plaster ceiling

Spray-on insulation above non-fire-resistant ceiling

Fire protection of steel beams   19.21

columns were protected by embedding them in solid brick masonry or by encasing them entirely in poured concrete. These techniques, though effective, were relatively expensive and added substantially to the weight and structural cost of a building. Present-day techniques include encasing steel members in lath and plaster, surrounding them with multiple layers of gypsum board, spraying lightweight mineral insulations in cementitious binders onto them, and attaching preformed slabs of mineral insulation to them (19.21, 19.22).

Steel beams and columns on the exterior of a building are not usually exposed to such high temperatures during a fire as those inside the building. Designers can determine by mathematical analysis the maximum temperature to which a given exterior steel member will rise in a fire, and if the temperature is sufficiently low, no fire protection need be added.

The collapse of the World Trade Center Towers in Manhattan after a terrorist attack was the result of the inability of fireproofing materials to protect steel framing members from very prolonged exposure to the unusually high temperatures of fires fed by jet airplane fuel. It would be almost impossible to construct a tall building to resist such fires. Even if possible, it would not be economical.

Helping Firefighters

It is vital that a building assist and protect firefighters during a blaze. A building's designers must furnish local fire authorities at the time of construction with information regarding the configuration and

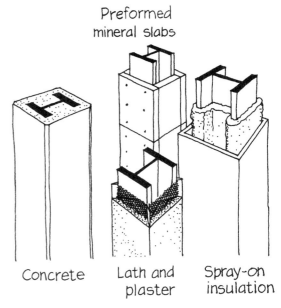

Preformed mineral slabs

Concrete   Lath and plaster   Spray-on insulation

Fire protection of steel columns 19.22

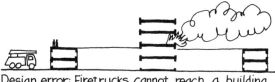

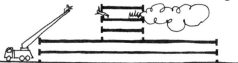

Design error: Firetrucks cannot reach a building isolated in the middle of a complex of buildings.

Design error: Fire ladders cannot extend to windows for access or rescue.

19.23

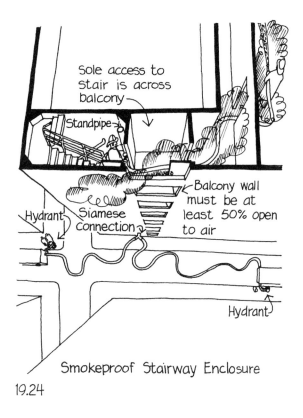

Smokeproof Stairway Enclosure

19.24

construction of a building, its expected contents and use, and its facilities for assisting firefighters. Fire departments keep this information on file so that it can be consulted at the time a fire might break out. Complexes of buildings must be planned so that fire trucks can drive to any building in the complex (19.23). Outdoor hydrants must be located within easy hose reach of the various buildings. Buildings must be designed so that fire-truck ladders can reach lower-floor windows.

One exit stairway in a taller building must be placed in a *smokeproof enclosure* (19.24). This stair either is connected to the main spaces of the building only by open-air balconies or is automatically pressurized with fresh air by a fan in case of fire. Within each exit stairway in multistory buildings, a standpipe must be furnished to which fire hoses may be connected at any floor. To ensure a continuous supply of water through the standpipe, a Y-shaped *Siamese connection* must be connected to the pipe at street level. One or two pumper trucks may couple to this connection to maintain pressure and volume in the standpipe if the city water mains cannot keep up with demand during a fire.

Because of their inherent unreliability, especially during a building fire, elevators and escalators generally may not be used as escape devices in buildings. But specially equipped elevators are required to assist firefighters in gaining quick access to the upper reaches of tall buildings. These must comply with elaborate precautions that ensure reliable smoke control, a secure supply of electricity, and complete isolation from the effects of the fire.

Further Reading

James Patterson. *Simplified Design for Building Fire Safety*. New York, Wiley, 1993.

20
Getting a Building Built

A building begins as a concept of need in someone's mind. If the need is a simple one and the person dexterous and ambitious, the steps needed to realize the concept are simple and direct. In some primitive societies, one or more members of the family or tribe scratch a floor-plan circle or rectangle of suitable size on the bare ground and assemble locally gathered materials—mud, stone, reeds, snow, logs, or poles—into a building on the spot. The design and details of the building require little thought because they are traditional to the society. The suburban American do-it-yourselfer, whether needing a tool shed or an entire house, generally takes somewhat more elaborate steps. He or she spends time developing plans on paper or spends money purchasing ready-made plans in order to resolve as many functional problems as possible before starting construction. The paper plans also allow accurate estimating of the necessary quantities of building materials and labor and facilitate negotiations with the local building inspector for a permit to build. Once everything is in order, materials are bought and delivered, tools are prepared, and construction can begin.

Residential-scale buildings are sometimes built by the owner but usually by a *builder*, a small construction company that often consists of only three or four workers and builds only one project at a time. A *custom* building is one that is planned by an architect or residential designer for a specific owner and built under a simple contract or agreement to build. Some builders specialize in *speculative* building, erecting buildings that will be sold to a buyer who is not known at the time construction commences. Speculative builders may work on a one-at-a-time basis, or they may build dozens or hundreds of houses at a time on large tracts of land.

Builders often work from *stock plans*, ones that are purchased from residential designers for a small fee. The builder, who often works physically on the project, usually builds the frame of the building and applies the exterior finish materials to the walls. The builder hires specialist *subcontractors* to excavate and construct the foundation, apply the roofing material, install plumbing, heating, and electrical services, install thermal insulation, apply interior wall and floor finishes, install cabinetry, and do site and landscaping work. The builder comes back to apply interior baseboards and trim, after which a painting subcontractor finishes the building.

Organizing the Larger Project

For larger building projects, more complex arrangements are necessary. A large number of people and organizations are needed: not just the owner and local building inspector but also an architect;

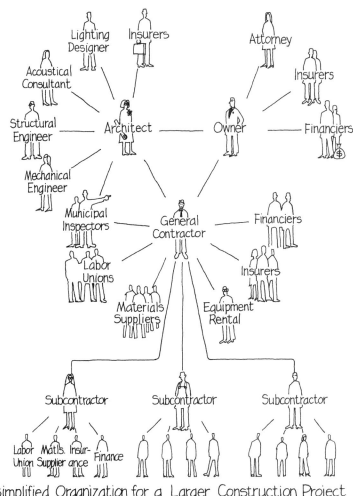

Simplified Organization for a Larger Construction Project

20.1

228

various engineers and specialist design consultants in such fields as structure, foundations, heating, plumbing, electrical work, acoustics; a general contractor; subcontractors and materials suppliers; and a small army of financiers, lawyers, and insurers (20.1). With so many entities involved, with so much money changing hands, and with the ever-present hazards of accident, fire, vandalism, inclement weather, labor disputes, inflation, and materials shortages and delays, firm, written understandings must be established among the various entities regarding who is responsible for what, especially if something should go wrong. As a basis for these understandings, all must agree precisely on what is to be built and how. The "what" and "how" are the purposes of the architect's *specifications* and *working drawings*.

The specifications are a written document that enumerates in detail the type and quality of all the materials to be used in a building, the standards of workmanship to be expected, and which trades will be responsible for which portions of the work (20.2). The working drawings (sometimes called the *blueprints* because long ago they were printed in white on a blue background) show the size, location, and configuration of all parts of the building. These are presented in terms of what each tradesperson needs to know in order to get the building built in its intended form (20.3). The specifications

SPECIFICATION

Chez Rover
R. Dogg, Owner

Foundation:	Concrete, 2500 psi
Floor:	Concrete, steel trowel finish
Structure:	#2 Pine boards, ship-lapped on walls
Roofing:	#1 Red Cedar Perfec-tions, laid 5" to weather
Painting:	One coat oil-base primer, two coats exterior latex paint Furnish color samples to owner for selection

A simple specification   20.2

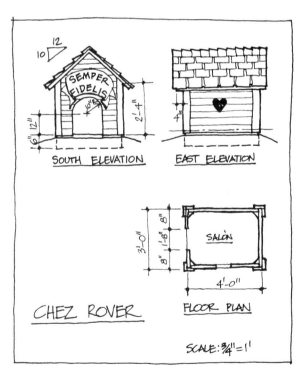

A simple working drawing   20.3

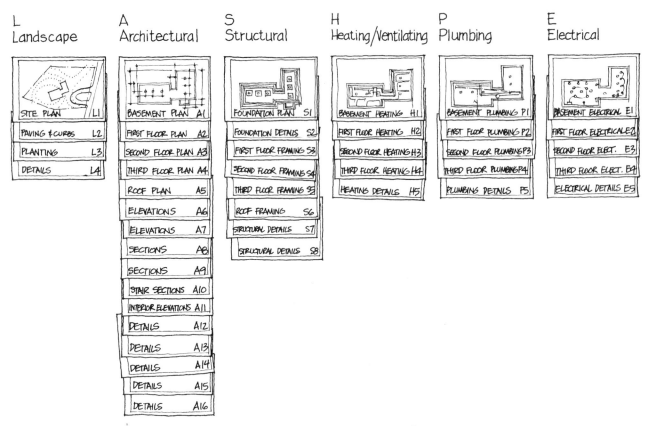

L Landscape	A Architectural	S Structural	H Heating/Ventilating	P Plumbing	E Electrical
SITE PLAN L1	BASEMENT PLAN A1	FOUNDATION PLAN S1	BASEMENT HEATING H1	BASEMENT PLUMBING P1	BASEMENT ELECTRICAL E1
PAVING & CURBS L2	FIRST FLOOR PLAN A2	FOUNDATION DETAILS S2	FIRST FLOOR HEATING H2	FIRST FLOOR PLUMBING P2	FIRST FLOOR ELECTRICAL E2
PLANTING L3	SECOND FLOOR PLAN A3	FIRST FLOOR FRAMING S3	SECOND FLOOR HEATING H3	SECOND FLOOR PLUMBING P3	SECOND FLOOR ELECT. E3
DETAILS L4	THIRD FLOOR PLAN A4	SECOND FLOOR FRAMING S4	THIRD FLOOR HEATING H4	THIRD FLOOR PLUMBING P4	THIRD FLOOR ELECT. E4
	ROOF PLAN A5	THIRD FLOOR FRAMING S5	HEATING DETAILS H5	PLUMBING DETAILS P5	ELECTRICAL DETAILS E5
	ELEVATIONS A6	ROOF FRAMING S6			
	ELEVATIONS A7	STRUCTURAL DETAILS S7			
	SECTIONS A8	STRUCTURAL DETAILS S8			
	SECTIONS A9				
	STAIR SECTIONS A10				
	INTERIOR ELEVATIONS A11				
	DETAILS A12				
	DETAILS A13				
	DETAILS A14				
	DETAILS A15				
	DETAILS A16				

Typical Working Drawing Sheets for a Medium-Sized Building

20.4

and working drawings are, for practical purposes, the sole means of translating the design ideas of the owner and the architect into an actual building. They serve as the basis for just about everything that is involved in getting a building built: construction financing, various insurances, estimating and bidding construction costs, the general construction contract and all subcontracts, material supply contracts, and the legal permit to build the building. As such, they must be complete, clear, unambiguous, and understandable (20.4). They must be written and drawn in a language that is understood by the people who will provide and place the materials. Beauty is of no importance in these drawings, but clarity and precision are essential. Specifications are usually organized according to a standard format developed by the Construction Specifications Institute and Construction Specifications Canada (20.5).

The actual contract for construction is made between the owner of the building and the general contractor. Most contracts are based on standard contracts that take into account all the things that can go wrong with a project. What if the contractor is losing money on a

DIVISION 1	GENERAL REQUIREMENTS
01010	Summary of work
01021	Cash allowances

DIVISION 2	SITEWORK
02150	Shoring and underpinning
02200	Earthwork
02350	Piles and caissons

DIVISION 3	CONCRETE
03100	Concrete formwork
03200	Concrete reinforcement
03300	Cast-in-place concrete

DIVISION 4	MASONRY
04210	Clay unit masonry
04220	Concrete unit masonry

DIVISION 5	METALS
05100	Structural metal framing
05300	Metal decking
05700	Ornamental metal

DIVISION 6	WOOD AND PLASTICS
06100	Rough carpentry
06200	Finish carpentry

DIVISION 7	THERMAL AND MOISTURE PROTECTION
07190	Vapor retarders
07200	Insulation
07250	Fireproofing
07500	Membrane roofing

DIVISION 8	DOORS AND WINDOWS
08100	Metal doors and frames
08500	Metal windows
08700	Hardware

DIVISION 9	FINISHES
09110	Nonloadbearing wall framing
09200	Lath and plaster
09500	Acoustical treatment
09650	Resilient flooring

DIVISION 10	SPECIALTIES
10160	Metal toilet compartments
10500	Lockers

DIVISION 11	EQUIPMENT
11050	Library equipment
11400	Food service equipment

DIVISION 12	FURNISHINGS
12300	Manufactured casework

DIVISION 13	SPECIAL CONSTRUCTION
13034	Sound conditioned rooms

DIVISION 14	CONVEYING SYSTEMS
14210	Electric traction elevators

DIVISION 15	MECHANICAL
15400	Plumbing
15500	Heating, ventilating, and air conditioning

DIVISION 16	ELECTRICAL
16120	Wires and cables
16140	Wiring devices
16500	Lighting
16700	Communications

Typical Specification Sections for a Medium-Sized Building 20.5

construction project and withdraws from it? (The contract provides that the contractor must post a *performance bond* before commencing work. This is a form of insurance that provides cash for the owner to finish the project with another contractor if the original contractor withdraws.) What if the owner does not pay the contractor for work completed, in accordance with a schedule of payments spelled out in the contract? (The contract allows the contractor to stop work if payments are not made in a timely manner.) Who is responsible for insuring the building during construction? (The owner.) Who is responsible for insuring the workers? (The contractor.)

A building under construction creates many temporary disruptions, dislocations, and hazards in its vicinity. The soil and vegetation are torn up. Roads and sidewalks are often obstructed and natural surface drainage patterns interrupted. Heavy construction vehicles often break the pavement accidentally. Construction work generates noise, dust, and fumes. Power tools and construction machinery present hazards to fingers and limbs. Tools and materials may fall or be blown by wind from higher levels of the building. Edges of floors and holes in floors for pipes, wires, ducts, stairs, and elevators create the risk of accidental falls. The chances of accidental fire are higher during construction than in the finished building, with debris accumulating and various fuel-burning torches and heaters in use. The partly finished building is attractive to thieves, vandals, and adventure seekers, making it doubly vulnerable to fire and accident. Therefore the construction process itself needs careful design attention in order to minimize its danger and unpleasantness and to maximize its efficiency and economy.

Temporary utilities are needed during the construction process: water, electricity for power tools and temporary illumination, telephone lines, temporary toilets, and waste removal services. Construction workers need parking or other transportation arrangements. The contractor must provide a system of temporary drainage to keep excavations free of water and to control surface drainage. Precautions must be taken to prevent soil erosion by wind or water. Nearby wetlands, forests, and buildings must be protected from dust and runoff. Trucks bringing materials to the site need delivery routes that will disrupt traffic as little as possible and avoid disturbing residential areas. An area of the site for unloading materials is required, adjacent to dry, safe areas where materials can be stored until needed. There must be lifting and carrying devices to unload trucks, stack and unstack materials, lift materials and workers to the various levels of the building, and transport materials across each level.

On many projects, the contractor must erect temporary fences and barriers of various kinds to protect the public from the hazards of the work and to protect the work from intruders. Trees must be fenced and padded against accidental damage by construction machinery. If excavations are in unstable soil or too close to roads or adjacent buildings, they must be *shored* to prevent collapse of the surrounding soil (20.6, 20.7). If the excavation is to go below the level of the foundations of adjacent buildings, those buildings may have to be supported temporarily against subsidence or sliding. If the level of water in the ground is above the bottom of the excavation, the site must be *dewatered* to make construction possible.

Shoring an Excavation With Sheet Piling

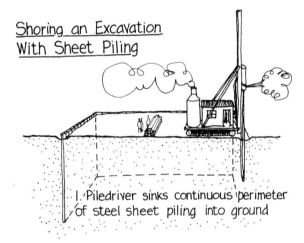

1. Piledriver sinks continuous perimeter of steel sheet piling into ground

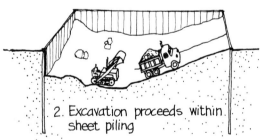

2. Excavation proceeds within sheet piling

As excavation deepens, sheet piling must be braced.

20.6

Dewatering may be as simple as digging a shallow pit in the deepest part of the excavation and pumping out any water that accumulates in it, but often it involves installing *well points* and a system of piping and pumps to draw down the level of ground water around the site (20.8).

As the building rises, workers need scaffolding, ladders, and hydraulic lifts for access to the various surfaces of the building. In taller buildings, one or more temporary elevators may be required.

Man ... rt: knee braces for walls ... sonry arches, and temp ... oughout wood or steel ... structure becomes self-s ... ractors may install temp ... g frames until the perm ... ailings have been insta ...

Te ... equired in several areas ... bcontractors need one ... rs often store tools and ... cific areas of work such ... wood or masonry. Wate ... In severe weather, tarpa ... ding site to shelter work ... ld air. In winter, temporary heating stoves protect concrete or masonry work against freezing and help paint and plaster to dry. In very hot weather, sunshading may have to be provided (20.9).

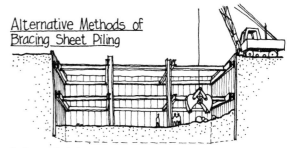

Alternative Methods of Bracing Sheet Piling

1. Cross-lot bracing

2. Rakers

3. Tiebacks (tension ties into firm soil)

20.7

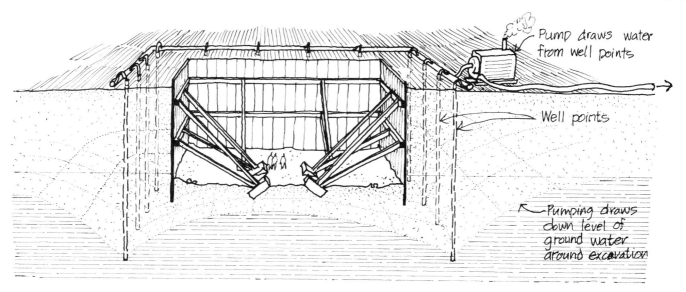

Pump draws water from well points

Well points

Pumping draws down level of ground water around excavation

20.8

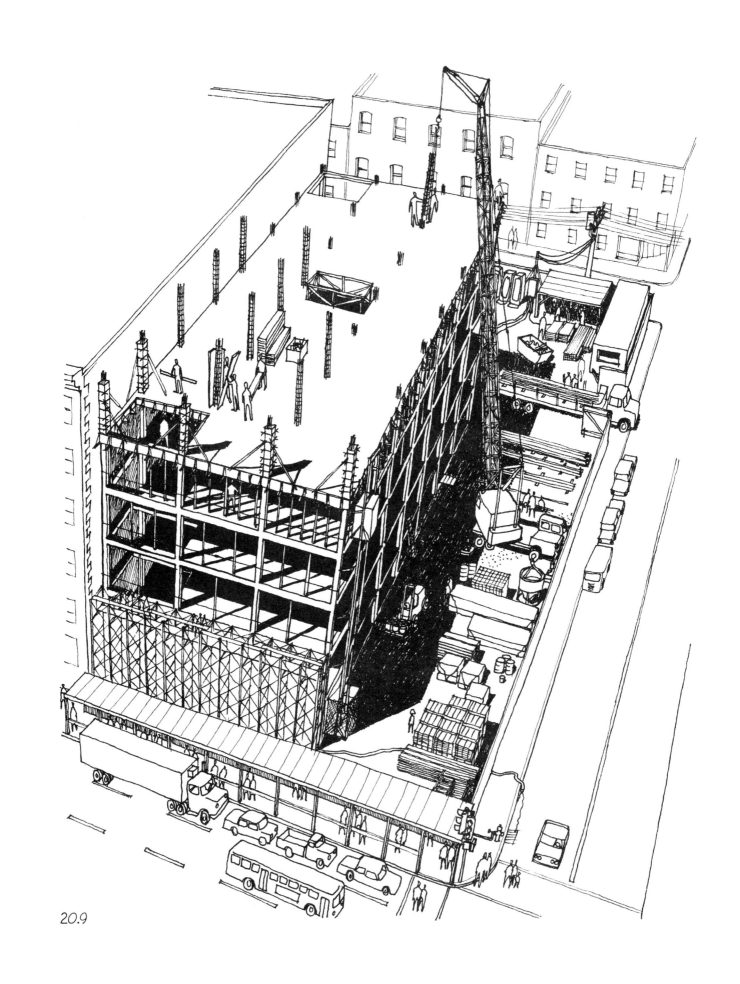

20.9

Workers on a construction job are exposed to many dangers; building contracting has one of the highest rates of on-the-job injury of any industry in the United States. As a result, many protective devices are required for the various trades. The hard safety helmet is universal to protect the head against dropped objects or from bumping against overhead hazards. Hard-toed safety shoes protect feet from dropped tools or materials. Nonslip soles serve an obvious safety function. Goggles of various types protect eyes from the sparks and glare of welding and keep flying chips and dust from power tools out of the eyes. Leather gloves, aprons, dust-filtering respirator masks, and safety belts or safety lines are required for certain trades. Even the ironworkers who erect structural steel frames wear safety harnesses that are clipped securely to safety cables strung tightly between columns, and roofers are secured to roofs with similar devices. Scaffolding must have guard rails to prevent workers from falling off. Most power tools have built-in safety features such as self-returning blade guards, anti-kickback devices, and self-opening switches to shut off the tool if it is accidentally dropped. First-aid kits and fire extinguishers are kept close at hand, and instructions about medical and fire assistance are prominently posted. Medical and hospitalization insurance for injured workers is required by law. A safety officer is appointed by the contractor on each construction site to ensure that all aspects of the work are clean and safe. In the United States, federal government inspectors check construction sites to see that contractors comply with the complex provisions of the Occupational Safety and Health Act (OSHA).

The workers normally own their small construction tools—hammers, handsaws, and so forth. Larger tools belong to the general contractor or subcontractors. But if a contractor does not like to keep a large inventory of construction equipment, he or she may rent or lease very large or highly specialized tools from an equipment-rental firm.

Every shipment of material that goes into a building must be checked upon delivery to ensure that it meets the written specifications. Each piece of lumber or plywood comes from the mill with a printed identification of its species and grade that makes on-site inspection easy. Structural steel is delivered with a certificate from the steel mill of its composition and quality. Most other building materials are similarly marked or certified with indications of their origins and quality.

Materials such as concrete and mortar, which are put in place wet, cannot be thoroughly checked for quality at the time of their placement, because there is no sure way of knowing what their strength will be after they have hardened. The standard procedure is to cast several small samples of material from each batch in special molds. These samples are carefully marked, recorded in a logbook along with the locations in the building where the corresponding batch of material was used, and kept on the site for a standard period of hardening. Then they are transported to a laboratory where their strength is determined by crushing them in a calibrated hydraulic press. If the crushing strength is above the specified minimum value, all is well. If it is not, work done with the batches of material from which the samples were taken may have to be taken out and done over.

With the aid of modern measuring and leveling instruments, buildings are built with a surprising degree of precision, but they are not like watches or cameras. One must assume that even the best-produced building components—because of their large size, shipping damage they may have suffered, water they may have absorbed in transit or on the job site, and variations in temperature—may not be square, flat, true, plumb, perfect, or accurate at the time they are installed in a building. One must also assume that a worker may not always measure or install a piece exactly as it should be, especially in the rougher sorts of work such as concrete work and wood framing. For a few building components, such as structural steel, there is an industry-wide standard specifying the maximum amounts of various sorts of distortions and inaccuracies that can be expected in the product when it arrives at the construction site. For most components, however, we must assume that dimensional accuracy of plus or minus one-quarter inch (6 mm) is reasonable to expect in buildings. Discrepancies of an inch or several inches (25 mm or more) sometimes must be accepted. Under these conditions, joints in which one piece of material simply laps over another are the easiest and safest to make (20.10). Where materials must be butted at two or more sides, it's essential that intentional gaps be provided to allow for inaccurate positioning and fitting. The openings for window and door units in wood-frame walls are always larger than the units themselves. When the units are installed, they are leveled and located accurately by means of small wedges around the perimeter. The siding covers the resulting gap on the outside, and the interior wall finish conceals it on the inside. Concrete or metal exterior wall panels are installed with intentional gaps between them, typically one-quarter-inch to 1-inch wide (6 to 25 mm). These are intended as much for thermal movement and structural deflection as for ease of installation. The metal mounting clips on such panels provide generous adjustments for accurate leveling and locating before a permanent attachment is made.

In planning a construction job, it is important that those materials that must present a good, finished appearance be installed as late in the process as possible and that they be protected from damage until the last worker is out of the building. In many buildings, for example, it would be easiest to install the finish flooring early in construction,

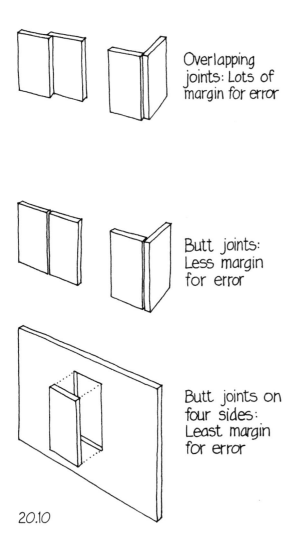

Overlapping joints: Lots of margin for error

Butt joints: Less margin for error

Butt joints on four sides: Least margin for error

20.10

during the framing operation. If this were done, however, the surface would be exposed to the abrasion, chipping, scratching, indentations, dripping, and spotting caused by the feet, tools, materials, spillage, and miscellaneous accidents associated with all the subsequent work in the building. Instead, even at the cost of some inconvenience, installing finish floors is one of the very last jobs to be done in a building.

Designers must consider carefully what is to be left exposed in a building. It might be attractive to expose the wood framing in the wall of a house—but what will the wall really look like, with the irregular member spacings around openings, the natural defects in the lumber, the grade-marking stamps, the dents left by the carpenter's hammer, the leftover pencil marks, and the electrical wiring and plumbing pipes drilled coarsely through? If a wall's framing is to be seen, it demands close attention to appropriate lumber grades and careful routing of pipes and wires. It also demands a higher and more time-consuming quality of workmanship than a framing carpenter is normally asked to do. Usually it is cheaper to follow the standard procedure of bringing in gypsum wallboard workers and painters to cover the wall in several successively better-finished layers of work, letting the carpenter, electrician, and plumber work in their customarily rough and efficient ways.

It is readily apparent when examining any of the traditional ways of putting buildings together in our society that a principle is generally followed of sequencing construction so that each of the trades covers up and smooths over the work of the previous trades. The fourth-from-last trades to do their work in a typical building install large areas of flat material—siding, wall panels, lath, gypsum wallboard—that crudely cover the exposed innards of the building. The third-from-last crews are the smoothers-on of gooey substances—sealants, plaster, wallboard joint compound—that obscure the worst gaps in the flat materials. The next-to-last crews install flooring, cover plates, heating and lighting fixtures, cover strips, and moldings of various sorts. The last crew, the painters, brighten and conceal all these layers with a thin cosmetic and preservative coating, ready for the final cleanup of construction debris, the final inspections of all parties concerned, and the handing of the keys to the owner. The building, after a long and often-troubled period of gestation, is born at last.

The Cost of Building

Buildings are inherently very expensive objects. Expense can be measured ultimately in two quantities, the amount of physical resources consumed and the human time consumed. The physical resources can be assessed only in relative terms, but with human time we can be much more precise. The average house in America requires a total of about one-fifteenth of a human's working lifetime to produce. An average Manhattan skyscraper uses, in total, the equivalent of the entire useful lives of 50 to 100 workers in its construction and the equivalent of several lifetimes per year in its maintenance. Very large buildings often cost several times this amount.

As to why buildings are so expensive, this is best learned by working on the construction of a building. Even a small, utilitarian building uses copious tonnages, volumes, and areas of costly materials, most or all of which must be lifted, positioned, and joined by human labor. The number of nails, bricks, or bolts consumed is often staggering, and each such component involves the expenditure of a finite and nontrivial amount of human time. The number of separate operations required to complete even the simplest building detail is quite surprising. Such necessary activities as managing workers, ordering materials, thinking through problems, planning the next stages of construction, keeping records, and paying bills also take up large amounts of time. The totals rise quickly, and one soon realizes that we have become accustomed to constructing very large and very expensive shelters.

Once the design of a building has been established, economy in building construction is a matter of good management. Good management requires the best and most efficient use of workers, tools, materials, and money. As much work as possible should be done under shelter, preferably in a factory, where working conditions are ideal and there is a high level of mechanization. Workers on the building site need to be choreographed carefully so that they are neither standing idle nor getting in one another's way. Materials need to be obtained at the lowest possible price, but only at the required level of quality, and only from reputable suppliers. They should be delivered as needed. If they arrive on the site too late, they will hold up work. If they arrive too early, they will take up storage space on the site. They are also more likely to be damaged before installation by weather or accident, are more subject to pilferage, and have to be paid for earlier.

A good building contractor treads a tightrope, bidding low enough to win work in competition with other contractors but high enough to realize a fair profit. A contractor that bids consistently low will likely end in bankruptcy through losing money on too many projects. One that bids consistently high will become insolvent by never winning projects to build. When a contractor wins a project at a fair price, he or she must manage the project closely and knowledgeably, both to maintain the expected profit margin and to produce a well-built building. Construction is a risky and highly skilled profession. New contracting companies come and go rapidly. Only responsible, competent contractors survive for very long.

21
Keeping a Building Alive and Growing

Even before a building is completed, Nature begins to destroy it systematically. Gravity, wind, and seismic movements constantly test the stability of the structure. The ultraviolet wavelengths of sunlight fade organic building materials and break down their molecules. Rainwater dissolves carbon dioxide and sulfur dioxide from the atmosphere to form weak carbonic and sulfuric acids that eat away at stone and encourage the oxidation of metals. Where two adjacent metals of dissimilar electrolytic potentials are wetted by rainwater, a galvanic reaction occurs, generating electric currents that cause rapid decomposition of the anodic metal. Water encourages the growth of molds, mildew, and fungi that attack many building materials, particularly wood and wood products. Water also encourages several types of wood-destroying insects, as well as weeds, vines, and trees whose roots burrow into tiny building cracks and wedge them inexorably larger. Falling water spatters soil onto the lower reaches of exterior walls, nourishing insects and fungi. As water freezes in soil, it heaves and cracks foundations and pavings. Freezing water spalls chips from the surfaces of concrete and masonry. Wind transports dust, spores, and seeds and deposits them on buildings. Mice and rats set up residence inside and gnaw passages through a building. Domestic animals rub, chew, and scratch building surfaces and deposit decay-breeding excrement in obscure corners. The human inhabitants of a building do their share to tear it down, too, tracking in moisture and dirt, spilling, spattering, staining, charring, banging, scuffing, scratching, breaking, discarding debris, wearing out doors and drawers, keeping destructive pets, rearing destructive children, and creating smoke, soot, and cooking fumes that stain building surfaces. Nature bears no special grudge against buildings; for the most part these are the same natural forces that level mountains, divert rivers from their beds, change lakes into meadows and meadows into forests, and turn old materials into new ones throughout the natural world. Change is the constant factor in Nature. Birth, growth, maturity, decline, death, decay, and rebirth are the stages in all natural cycles. So too with buildings, but we humans like to keep the cycle under human control, to maintain each building in use until its death suits our purposes.

The forces of deterioration in buildings can be grouped into three categories: Some forces pose such strong or immediate threats to the usefulness of the building that they must be neutralized at all cost. Other forces are inevitable, but we can cope with them satisfactorily on a day-to-day basis. And paradoxically, certain forces of deterioration can contribute to the beauty and utility of the building—if we will let them.

Safeguarding the Building

Among the first category of forces, the most dangerous are those that threaten the stability of a building's foundations. We avoid frost heaving by founding the building below the deepest level at which the soil freezes in winter. We avoid excessive settlement by designing the foundations so that they do not exceed the bearing capacity of the supporting soil. To prevent erosion of the soil from around and under foundations, roof-water drainage systems must be kept in good working order, and any major pipe leaks inside or near the building must be repaired promptly. In dry, windy locations, plantings or other protective devices must be employed to protect the soil against wind erosion. Areas immediately adjacent to basement walls must be kept clear of trees to avoid root damage. Driven piles made of untreated wood should be periodically inspected to ensure that wells or pumps at nearby construction projects have not lowered the water table below the tops of the piles, for unless the piles are totally submerged, decay will set in.

If a building's foundations have settled but the building is not irreparably damaged, *underpinning* is usually an effective remedy, in which new foundations of larger capacity are constructed under or alongside the existing ones, and the building is jacked onto the new ones.

Structural weaknesses also fall into the "dangerous" category. Ordinarily a building's structure is strong enough to begin with, but if faulty design or increased loadings cause structural inadequacies when the building is being used, new beams, columns, or bracing can be added.

Structures require maintenance. Steel structural members must be protected from dampness and rust by either the surrounding layers of a building, or by the maintenance of paint or some other protective coating on all exposed surfaces. Bolted joints in timber frames need to be retightened to compensate for wood shrinkage after the building has been heated for an initial period after construction; access holes or access panels must be provided in any covering materials to allow this. Wood fungi and wood-destroying insects must be kept out of wooden structures. Some wood fungi, such as the blue-gray stain found on recently sawed, unseasoned lumber or the white flecks seen in some woods, are merely unsightly and cause no structural damage. Others, with colloquial names like dry rot and wet rot, are exceptionally destructive. Wood-boring and wood-eating insects, of which there are many species in various parts of the world, can endanger the stability of a structure.

Most wood-destroying organisms consume wood as food, need moisture, and need air. The chief means of controlling the organisms are to poison the wood, to keep the wood completely dry to deprive the organisms of moisture, or to keep the wood completely submerged in water to deprive them of air. Various chemical substances called *preservatives* are used commercially to poison wood against both insects and fungi. They are not very effective if merely applied to the surface and should instead be dispersed throughout the cells of the wood by pressure treatment in a factory. Certain species of wood are naturally resistant to insects and decay by virtue of chemical substances that grow naturally in them. Redwood, cypress, and cedar are the most common American woods with this property.

Keeping wood either dry or wet may seem like contradictory aims, but wood in either condition is safe from attack. Wood that is moist but not submerged or wood that is alternately wetted and dried offers both moisture and air to destructive organisms and is therefore strongly attacked. Wood that is in or very near to the soil is especially vulnerable. Wood laid directly on a brick or stone foundation should be protected from capillary moisture with a damp-proof layer of impervious plastic or asphalt. Wood beams resting in pockets in foundation walls should have similar protection and should be given plenty of space to "breathe" on all sides. It is wise to use preservative-treated wood wherever a wood frame comes in contact with a foundation wall.

Where one piece of wood is connected to another in an exterior location, rainwater is held between them by capillary action, and decay is rapid. The covered bridge illustrates one logical response to this problem: The hundreds of joints in the wood trusses supporting the bridge are kept dry by a waterproof roof and walls (21.1). If the bridge were not covered, it would become structurally unsound within several years because of the decaying of its connections. Where weather protection of wood connections is not possible,

21.1

preservative treatment, or at least a heavy application of paint, stain, or asphalt, can slow deterioration, but exposed wood connections should be avoided except in benches, railings, fences, and other secondary constructions. Even in these, periodic inspection and maintenance are required to replace rotting components before they become dangerous.

Termites are especially liable to attack a building that has untreated wood parts extending into the ground or one with wood scraps or tree stumps buried near the building. Termites are capable of attacking dry wood, however, by carrying water from the ground to the wood. The most common (and most damaging) type of termite found in the United States is the subterranean termite, which nests in the soil but takes its food from the wood of a building above. In order to reach the building, the insects build hollow shelter tubes of mud, wood dust, and excreta over the intervening foundation construction and then tunnel into the wood itself. Where termite infestations are common, the soil in the immediate vicinity of the building should be poisoned, and sheet metal termite shields should be installed between the foundation and the wood structure (21.2). The shields do not prevent the entry of termites, but they do cause the insects to have to build their shelter tubes over the shield, where they can be seen, rather than through cracks in the foundation. If tubes are seen on the shields, an exterminator can be called.

Dry wood termites, which need very little moisture, do not require contact with the soil and are found in wooden buildings in the tropics and subtropics. Infested buildings must be covered with plastic sheets and fumigated with poison gas. Other types of termites and wood-destroying insects are found in various parts of the world, each requiring its own set of preventions and cures.

Closely associated with decay and termite prevention is the prevention of water leaks in buildings. Aside from fire or earthquake, nothing can bring down a building faster than the internal decay caused by a leaky roof. Roofs, rainwater drainage systems, walls, and windows must be maintained diligently. Plumbing leaks and conditions of excessive condensation must be attended to quickly. In the ordinary wood-frame house, water damage and decay from condensation are common in wooden window sashes across the bottom of each pane of glass and in wooden subfloors beneath toilet tanks. Leakage problems and their associated water damage and decay occur frequently next to chimneys and around roof gutters. Through decay of the roof boards around leaks, such problems compound rapidly unless taken care of as quickly as they occur.

Roof maintenance includes keeping drainage systems operational, leakproof, and free of clogging debris, removing soil and growing plants that may settle in crevices, and inspecting for leaks or

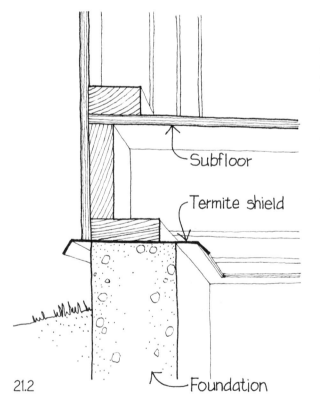

21.2

Subfloor

Termite shield

Foundation

signs of deterioration. Shingles of any sort are gradually eroded by water, ice, and wind; are decomposed by the destructive powers of the sun; and may be split or torn by ice, wind, or tree branches. Membrane roofs erode less rapidly but are susceptible to damage by expansion and contraction of the roof deck, vapor blistering and rupture, and abrasion from excessive foot traffic.

The mortar joints in masonry are vulnerable to damage by the freezing and thawing of absorbed water. Masons can shape and compact mortar joints to make them shed water rather than trap it or absorb it (21.3). Even with such precautions, however, the mortar deteriorates progressively, usually over a period of many decades, and from time to time it is necessary to rake out the damaged mortar near the surface and repoint the masonry with new mortar. Climbing vines accelerate the deterioration of masonry because their roots penetrate the surface and their leaves keep it moist between storms. Building owners must weigh this factor against the undeniable charm of climbing vines, their contribution to summertime cooling through shade and leaf-surface evaporation, and their insulating role in winter.

Continuous inspection is required to maintain a building's fire hazards at an acceptable level. Rubbish must be cleared promptly. Chimneys, appliances, and the loads on electrical circuits must be checked periodically to ensure safe operating conditions. Exits must be kept clear. Fire doors must be kept closed but operable. Misplaced, missing, or deteriorated extinguishers must be replaced, and alarm and emergency lighting systems must be checked regularly. In certain types of buildings, especially schools, occasional fire-exit drills are advisable for the safety of the occupants.

Intolerable health hazards in plumbing systems include blocked or leaking pipes, pipes that are prone to freezing and therefore to bursting, and cracked or defective plumbing fixtures. Inadequate heating and a lack of natural light or ventilation are hazards sufficient to warrant vacating a building until they are corrected, as are accumulations of garbage or infestations of vermin. Window screens to keep out flies and biting insects are a necessity for health in most areas of the world.

Last in our discussion of critical maintenance problems in buildings are the human enemies of buildings, namely vandals and arsonists. When no ulterior motive is apparent, vandalism and arson seem to occur more frequently in buildings that are either in poor repair or abandoned. Inhabited buildings in good repair are likely to suffer damage only if they seem psychologically threatening to the vandals. Schools and low-income housing are frequent targets, especially if they appear authoritarian and depressing. Buildings in which each inhabitant feels a personal involvement would seem to

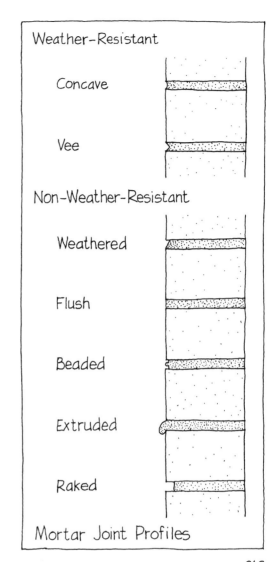

Weather-Resistant

Concave

Vee

Non-Weather-Resistant

Weathered

Flush

Beaded

Extruded

Raked

Mortar Joint Profiles

21.3

be the answer, but we have as yet no sure guidelines for designing and building such structures.

Sick Building Syndrome

Historically, buildings have been quite leaky of air and have more or less ventilated themselves. In recent years, largely in response to calls for increased energy efficiency, we have tended to construct buildings that are virtually airtight. Unless mechanical ventilation is provided in these buildings, moisture levels in the interior air can rise to levels such that various molds and mildews will grow on surfaces and in ductwork. We have begun to use more and more synthetic materials in buildings, some of which emit gases such as formaldehyde. An airtight building can also create problems with fuel-burning appliances that can't get enough air for clean combustion, causing them to give off carbon dioxide and carbon monoxide to the interior air. From problems such as these has arisen the recent phenomenon of *sick building syndrome*, a catch-all term that refers to buildings whose interior air quality is so bad that it makes many of the occupants ill.

Because of its many possible sources, the causes of sick building syndrome in a specific building are often difficult to diagnose. In most cases, a cause can be found, and remedial action can be taken. Sometimes merely cleaning the air-conditioning ductwork will cure the problem. It may be necessary to provide equipment to lower the humidity of the interior air. Moldy or mildewed materials may have to be removed and replaced. Combustion air inlets for furnaces sometimes help by reducing the likelihood that noxious combustion products such as sulfur dioxide and carbon monoxide will be generated by the fire. In the meantime, buildings often must be evacuated until the problem is solved.

Vinyl wall coverings in the interiors of buildings in hot, humid climates have often been problematic. These sheet materials are often impervious to water vapor and air, but when it is hot outdoors and cool indoors, they are on the cool side of the vapor retarder, which is the wrong side. Moisture accumulates on the back side of the wall covering, where it creates ideal conditions for the growth of molds and mildew. Manufacturers of the material have responded by developing pervious versions and by treating the material with long-lasting fungicides at the time of manufacture.

Routine Building Maintenance

Routine building maintenance includes many sorts of repair, renewal, and cleaning operations. On the exterior of a building, impervious wall surfaces such as glazed tile, porcelain enamel on steel, glass, aluminum, and stainless steel have extremely long lifetimes under normal circumstances and need no maintenance other than periodic washing and occasional replacement of the mortar or sealant between units. Exterior paints, stains, and varnishes deteriorate quickly in sunlight and rain and must be renewed every few years. With white paint this rapid degradation has some advantage, because the progressive chalking and washing away of the surface of the paint film keep the coating clean and bright in appearance.

The droppings of pigeons, starlings, sparrows, gulls, and other birds contribute to exterior maintenance problems on some buildings. Eliminating snug crannies from the exteriors of buildings deals with much of the difficulty. Devices that produce unpleasant sounds or electric shocks, or that have rows of spikes to prevent roosting, may be needed in extreme cases.

Window glass quickly accumulates layers of dirt on both sides. In time these will obscure vision and block daylight. Periodic washing is made easier by using window types that allow both sides of the glass to be reached from inside the building. Otherwise, ladders are necessary to reach the windows of low buildings, and movable suspended staging is needed for taller buildings. One glass manufacturer markets a glass with a transparent catalytic coating on the exterior that works with sunlight to convert most dirt to soluble compounds that wash away in the rain. The additional cost of this glass is often justifiable because of the reduction in glass maintenance expense over the life of the building.

Windows must be designed to make occasional replacement of broken panes easy, preferably working from inside the building. Most glazing compounds (the gummy substances in which glass is bedded) harden with age and eventually crack and fall away, needing replacement. Window frames need periodic inspection for corrosion, decay, leakage of air or water, excessive tightness or looseness of operation, and wear or breakage of hardware.

Interior surfaces of buildings are generally safe from the destructive effects of sun, rain, and wind, but they are exposed instead to the wear, tear, and soil of human occupancy. Walls and ceilings collect dust and dirt from the air and from the hands, heads, feet, and furniture placed against them. In areas such as kitchens and bathrooms where walls are especially exposed to soiling, gloss or semi-gloss enamel paints make them easier to wash. Smooth *wainscots* of glazed ceramic tile or plastic laminate are advisable in wet locations (21.4). Doors, windows, and their wooden casings are usually coated with gloss or semi-gloss finishes to make finger marks easy to remove. When interiors are repainted, the first step is to fill any plaster cracks. Serious plaster cracking is often indicative of structural problems or water leakage, however, and should not be smoothed over before a diagnosis can be made and corrective action taken. When choosing

Tile wainscot

21.4

colors of paint, wallpaper, or wood paneling, we should consider what effect the new color will have on lighting levels in the room. Only white and the very lightest tints are highly reflective of light. Other colors absorb much or most of the light that strikes them and may create an effect that is both excessively somber and intolerably dark.

Floors, which undergo the abrasions of grit trodden underfoot, are the most subject to wear of any interior building surfaces. They also are a source of dust that is kicked up by passing feet and deposited on walls and furnishings. Floor maintenance is therefore the largest single component of day-to-day building care. We can keep out much foot-borne dirt by providing a doormat or grille at the entrance door. Vacuuming, dusting, sweeping, and scrubbing remove dirt before it piles up too deeply. Waxing some types of floor surfaces offers some protection against wear and makes washing or dusting the floor considerably easier. Floors of hard stone or hard tile are highly resistant to abrasion and are easily washed. Soft stone, soft tile, and wood floors are abraded much more quickly. In most cases, wood floors can be sanded and revarnished after severe abrasion. Soft tiles and stones occasionally need replacement. On public stairways, where wear is exceptionally severe and eroded stairs present a particular safety problem, hard materials should be used. Stair treads are available with nonslip surfaces made of extremely hard abrasives.

The maintenance of floors, countertops, and wainscots is easier, and their appearance generally improved, if their surface is mottled, streaked, or patterned. Such textures camouflage small splotches and streaks of dirt, making them much less noticeable than they would be on a plain-colored surface. Plain-colored surfacing materials frequently cost more than otherwise identical mottled ones, because even the tiniest manufacturing defect will be cause for rejecting a plain-colored product, whereas it might not be noticed in a mottled one.

Graffiti can be a large problem in public places. The would-be artist usually is discouraged if faced with a surface so rough, irregular, or richly patterned that any superimposed message is likely to be illegible, if it is possible to apply it in the first place. An exceptionally smooth, easily cleaned or easily repapered surface, on the other hand, encourages the addition of ad hoc names, notes, and pictures. As long as the accumulating pattern is pleasing, it can be retained. Obscenity or excessive messiness can be obliterated, and the process can begin anew. Graffiti-resistant surface coatings that repel most types of paints and markers are effective on some types of surfaces.

Except for its mechanical systems, a building has few moving parts that need care. Drawers, doors, and windows require occasional adjustment and lubrication. Hinges, latches, and locks are especially prone to wear and breakage. Doors that accommodate large numbers of people, in markets, schools, and other public buildings, require more frequent maintenance and occasional replacement of worn working parts. Ball-bearing hinges greatly reduce wear and can be helpful in reducing maintenance costs for swinging doors in heavily used buildings.

All the mechanical systems in a building require systematic programs of maintenance. The air filters of heating, ventilating, and cooling equipment must be cleaned or replaced at regular intervals. Burners need at least annual cleaning and adjustment for maximum efficiency of combustion. Motors, fans, pumps, and compressors require lubrication and replacement of rubber belts.

Plumbing fixtures must be cleaned regularly and their drains kept free of obstructions. Faucets and toilet valves need constant repair. Water supply piping may in time fill with mineral scale and have to be replaced. Waste piping is prone to clog now and then with hair, paper, cooking fats, or invading tree roots. Devices ranging from a length of stiff wire to elaborate rotary knives on the end of a long cable can be introduced at cleanout ports in the piping to clear the obstacles. Water heaters are especially susceptible to scaling from mineral-laden water, and their electrical or fuel-burning components need periodic attention.

Incandescent bulbs, fluorescent tubes, and fluorescent ballasts are the items in a building's electrical system requiring the most frequent replacement. Regular cleaning of fixtures and occasional cleaning and painting of ceilings and walls to renew their reflectivity of light are also required for maximum performance of the electrical lighting system. Light switches and electrical appliances wear out relatively quickly. The other components of the electrical system do not usually wear out, but electrical systems as a whole become obsolete fairly rapidly. Older systems are universally too small in capacity, do not furnish enough outlets, and do not meet today's standards of grounding and shock protection. Future developments are certain to eclipse today's most up-to-date wiring installations in a few years. Fortunately, new wiring is fairly easily installed in existing structures, especially where plenty of capacity is available in *conduits*, which are metal or plastic tubes within which wiring is run.

Elevators and escalators are generally serviced at frequent intervals by specialists associated with the manufacturers of the devices, and they are inspected regularly for safety by representatives of the local municipality. Elevators in particular are extremely complex and diverse in their mechanisms and controls and are subjected to heavy wear. Because elevators also present a unique potential for human disaster, their mechanisms are designed with very large factors of safety; numerous safety devices are incorporated into their design; and maintenance must be frequent and thorough.

Among the more subtle skills of an experienced designer is the art of using the natural forces of deterioration to improve the building over time. There are few things more satisfying than seeing a building grow more attractive with age, rather than shabbier. To construct such a building, we must first recognize that the surfaces of the building are both the visible face of the building and the surfaces that must withstand the abuse of sun, rain, wind, soot, dirt, and human wear. Any material that grows steadily worse in appearance when exposed to these forces should be avoided. A new car furnishes numerous examples of such materials: When it emerges from the showroom, it gleams seductively with bright, flawless enamel, polished chromium, and sparkling curves of glass. It cradles the human body in plump, shining tufts of upholstery amid deep-pile carpeting. With each passing day, however, the car becomes less attractive: The paintwork chalks and fades. Any scratch or dent in the sheet metal is immediately visible as a prominent blemish. Rust spots mar the chromium. The glass and paintwork, because of their ultra-smooth surfaces, tend to look even dirtier than they really are. The upholstery sags and the carpets accumulate dirt that refuses to be coaxed out. A motorist who buys a car for its visual appeal is doomed to a life of constant maintenance and ultimate disappointment, because the car will never again look as good as it did on the day it was purchased.

Consider, by contrast, a sloping roof made of cedar shingles. The shingles are somewhat garishly colorful when installed but rather quickly begin to turn gray in the sunlight and rain. For some months they are not very attractive but look a bit dirty and streaky. Then the colors begin to blend and deepen, and the roof takes on a comfortable, silvery gray tone that becomes richer with the passing years. Rain erodes the softer bands of spring growth from the grain of the wood and adds texture to the roof. Lichens or mosses may add color. With no maintenance at all, the roof will not only last for several decades but will actually grow more attractive each year. The automobile starts life with a perfection of finish that can only grow less perfect with age, whereas the cedar roof sidesteps the question of perfection entirely and acquires an ever-richer patina whose beauty has no limit.

There are many building materials that have this same quality. Redwood and cypress are similar to cedar in their weathering properties. Unfinished interior wood in tabletops, doors, and railings that is constantly handled and rubbed looks spotty for a time but then begins to glow with the natural polish given it by human hands. Brass door handles are etched chemically over time by the sweat of hands, to expose the fascinating crystalline pattern of the metal. Copper in the outdoor environment changes slowly from a bright, reflective orange metal to a rich tapestry of blue-green oxide. The oxide clings tightly to the metal to protect it from further deterioration. Lead roofs oxidize to a pleasant white. Aluminum is a metal with similarly self-protective oxides, but the oxides look dirty and streaky and are not especially attractive. Accordingly, most exterior aluminum is chemically oxidized in the factory, often with the addition of a permanent black or brown color, and becomes a material that grows neither better nor worse with age. Most ferrous metals rust destructively, but a steel alloy has been developed that forms a tenacious, self-protecting oxide and assumes a pleasing color and texture after an initial period of splotchiness.

Masonry generally looks progressively better as it accumulates grime and as the mortar weathers to a more subtle color. Climbing vines further enhance its beauty year by year. Unglazed ceramic tile floors or floors of natural stone slabs often wear into pleasing contours underfoot. Glazed ceramic surfaces on masonry change little in appearance over the years and present a bright counterpoint to the softening, deepening colors of the materials about them. Because age so often darkens colors, surfaces that begin life dark in color tend to age more gracefully than light surfaces do. If a surface of white paint or whitewash, however, is frequently renewed, it will in time become pleasantly smooth in texture and will show off to good advantage adjoining areas of darker colors.

Surfaces made up of many small units generally age more attractively and are easier to repair than large, smooth planes. A crack or flaw in a floor-to-ceiling sheet of glass is visually annoying, potentially dangerous, and requires a skilled crew and expensive equipment to replace. But cracks in a small pane or two of a large multipane window are not particularly disturbing to the eye and do not require replacement of the panes unless they leak water or air. If replacement is necessary, a single semiskilled person can do it with a couple of dollars' worth of materials. The large sheet of plate glass must be washed to perfection every few weeks if it is to appear clean, whereas the multipane window can get quite dirty before it becomes disturbingly so. Similarly, a courtyard paved with bricks or small stones has maintenance advantages over one paved in concrete or asphalt. A wall paneled in narrow wood boards is apt to age more gracefully than one made of large sheets of beautifully veneered plywood. A floor of irregular stones or primitive clay tiles shows less evidence of the ravages of time than does one of polished marble slabs.

Secondhand building materials offer many advantages with respect to their visual characteristics: They are already worn, weathered, and hardened by time. In many cases they have already acquired a pleasant patina. They are often richer in design and detail than contemporary materials. They are sometimes cheaper than new materials. And they generally bring a welcome sense of history and continuity with the past into a new building. They blend more and more naturally with the building as it acquires marks of the injuries, repairs, and changes of its own lifetime, to produce a structure that records its own history on its exposed surfaces.

Buildings should be able to absorb life's hard knocks without looking the worse for them. Normal weathering and wear should not diminish the beauty of the finishes. Reasonable amounts of dirt and grime should look quite acceptable on the various surfaces of the building. And the normal, pleasant clutter of the various objects of people's daily lives should not look out of place because the building seems to have been constructed for superfastidious visitors from another planet. Building maintenance is not an end in itself but is intended to make life more livable for the building's inhabitants.

Addition and remodeling are eventually important to the usefulness of most buildings. Through these processes, a building can grow and adapt to changing human requirements, and the useful life of a building can be extended indefinitely. Remodeling usually involves removing at least some of the interior finishes, partitions, and mechanical equipment of a building, reconfiguring the interior and perhaps the facades, and applying new finishes. Remodeling is more difficult if the interior has many load-bearing partitions or if the floor structure is difficult to cut and change, as it is in many concrete buildings. It is easier if partitions, floors, stairs, and mechanical services are relatively simple to demount and relocate.

Adding onto a building is possible in the horizontal direction, the vertical direction, or both. For vertical additions, much expense and disruption can be avoided if the original structure is made to accept additional floors without overstressing the columns and if elevators, stairs, and mechanical systems are planned from the outset to serve the extension. Horizontal additions are bound to look awkward if the original building is a complete, closed form like a dome, a cylinder, a cube, or a hyperbolic paraboloid shell. They are easiest to fit when the original building rambles a bit already and when one or more natural points of connection are provided along the periphery of the existing pedestrian circulation system.

Re-Use of Buildings

Buildings can adapt well to changes in use over time. We continue to live, study, worship, and conduct business in buildings that in many cases are centuries old and that have had to change many times over that period. Re-use is easier if the building has large, unobstructed, rectilinear spaces, movable partitions, and readily accessible mechanical and electrical components. It is more difficult if the building has load-bearing interior partitions, short structural spans, or a form that is very specific to a particular use, such as a chapel or theater.

With periodic remodeling and constant maintenance, a building can live for a very long time. A number of buildings from Roman times are still in use. Even a wooden building, if kept safe from water and fire, can last for centuries. But buildings are abandoned or torn down every day. Sometimes health or safety problems are the reason. Sometimes a building simply cannot be brought up to modern standards of convenience because it is too small or its original configuration is too unyielding to alteration. More commonly, a building becomes uneconomic, through changing needs of its occupants, excessive costs of maintenance and repair, or because it occupies a piece of land so valuable that the owner wishes to build a much larger building in order to maximize the return on investment. In most such circumstances, the building is dismantled and trucked away in pieces by a building demolition contractor. Some of its components may be saved and sold, but usually the entire building ends as broken chunks in a dump.

In rural areas it is not difficult to find a barn or shed dying a natural death after many years of service (21.5). It is sad to know that the optimism, human energy, and skill that originally went into the making of the building are now to be lost forever, but it is a joyous experience to see how Nature takes back the building materials it once yielded, to convert them to other uses. There is dignity in the sagging of decaying wood and reassurance in the slow absorption of the wood by the earth. There is beauty in the gentle, supremely patient attack of Nature on masonry and concrete, as weather softens the surfaces, and tendrils of plants reach into tiny pores and cracks to begin the long process of prying and wedging that will someday, probably lifetimes hence, reduce even these materials to earth. The plants gradually cover the dying building with a shroud of green leaves and bright blossoms, and it becomes a new object in the landscape, a picturesque promise of the new and better order with which Nature will replace it.

21.5

Further Reading

Mohsen Mostafavi and David Leatherbarrow. *On Weathering: The Life of Buildings in Time*. Cambridge, Mass., the M.I.T. Press, 1993.

22

Building Components and Building Function

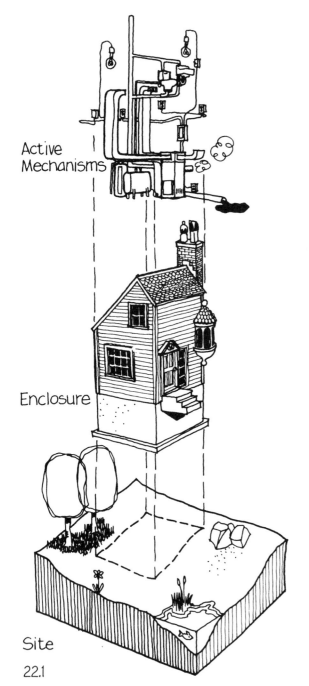

Active Mechanisms

Enclosure

Site

22.1

So far we have examined the characteristics of the outdoor environment, compared them with the environmental requirements of people and society, and noted the range of functions that we expect a building to perform in reconciling the differences between the two. We have discussed at considerable length the various physical mechanisms employed in buildings to perform these functions. It now remains to look briefly at the common components from which we assemble buildings, to see what functions we expect each to perform, and by what combination of mechanisms each works. Simple words such as *wall* or *roof* denote very complicated components that perform a surprising range of functions in a building.

Let us begin with the component we call the *site* (22.1). The site is a building's all-important outer perimeter of devices for modifying the outdoor environment. Trees on the site can block the sun's rays, cool the air, divert the winter wind, and provide visual privacy. The site can keep water away from the foundations. It can protect a building from noise or fire by keeping it sufficiently distant from neighboring buildings. By careful placement and orientation of the building on the site, useful outdoor areas can be created; pockets of warmer or cooler microclimate can be set up; and the penetration of the sun into the building can be controlled for optimum comfort in all the seasons of the year. For many buildings, the site also provides water and disposes of sewage. It may even provide food from a vegetable garden, an orchard, or a chicken coop.

A second perimeter of devices to modify the environment is contained in the enclosure of the building. Here the major work of the building is done: Sunlight is blocked, selectively admitted, or reflected. The passage of air, heat, moisture, sound, and living creatures is closely controlled. Level surfaces are created and stacked for human occupancy, supported on walls or columns. The enclosed volume is divided into a convenient arrangement of rooms, linked by passages both vertical and horizontal.

Within these two concentric perimeters, the site and the enclosure, are the active mechanisms that generate or remove heat, circulate air, provide light, energize tools, distribute water, and collect liquid wastes. It is best to restrict the role of active devices insofar as possible to that of fine tuning the internal environment to optimum conditions, once the heavy work of environmental modification has been performed by the passive devices of the site and the building enclosure. Such a design approach has the advantage, of course, of cutting down on energy consumption in the building. Even more important, it offers maximum comfort and convenience by leveling out temperature flows, reducing noise from mechanical equipment, reducing air pollution, and providing more favorable levels of natural illumination. This approach also helps place people in a more natural relationship with the outdoor environment, one in which they can understand and appreciate more fully the majestic cycles of Nature and the relationship of these cycles to human life. Machines, no matter how powerful, can never substitute fully for the good design judgment of the architect who sites and configures the building, for it is the enclosure of the building, not the mechanical equipment, that must create the basic conditions for human satisfaction, both spiritual and physical.

We are able to make satisfactory buildings, it would seem, from almost anything. Some materials need little processing: mud, broken stone, fieldstone, snow, grasses, reeds, leaves, bamboo, natural asphalt, tree trunks and branches. With a modest expenditure of time and energy, we can make hard-fired bricks, squared lumber, paper, stone blocks, and plaster. With still more processing, cement, glass, metals, rubber, and plastics become available. We build with what we can obtain in a given locale, within a given set of economic restrictions. Through the military, the Peace Corps, or foreign architectural commissions, American architects and engineers have often found themselves building with mud, straw, or bamboo, seeking to cope with unfamiliar climates and patterns of life. Even our own life patterns continue to change, and new materials of construction reach the market every month, each promising certain advantages over the materials it hopes to replace.

In such situations, architects learn to evaluate new or unfamiliar materials with regard to what each can do best and what its disadvantages and weaknesses are. How strong is a material in tension, compression, and shear? How will it be affected by water? Will it allow water vapor to pass? What are its thermal properties? How much will it expand and contract with changes in moisture or tem-

	Site	Foundation	Structure	Floors	Walls	Windows	Doors	Roofs	Ceilings	Partitions	Finishes	Furnishings	Fireplaces	Heat/vent/A.C.	Plumbing	Electrical
Provides clean air	●					●	○							●	○	○
Provides clean water	·							·							●	·
Removes and recycles wastes	·												·	·	●	·
Controls thermal radiation	●		·	·	●	●		●	●		●		●	●		·
Controls air temperature	●		·	·	●	●	○	●	●				○	●		·
Controls thermal qualities of surfaces			·	●	○	○					·	·	●		○	·
Controls humidity	●	·	·	○	●	●	○	●	●		·			●	·	·
Controls flow of air	●		·	○	●	●	○	●	○	○				●		·
Optimum seeing and visual privacy	●		·	○	●	●	●	●	●	●	●	·		·		●
Optimum hearing and acoustic privacy	●	·	○	●	●	●	●	●	○	●	●	●		○	·	·
Controls entry of living creatures	●	○	·	○	●	●	●	●	○		●					·
Provides concentrated energy	·							·								●
Provides channels of communication					·	·	·				·	·				●
Provides useful surfaces	●	·	·	●	○	·	·	·			●	●	●			
Provides structural support	●	●	●	●	●	●		●	·	○						
Keeps out water	●	●	·	·	●	●	●	●			·				·	·
Adjusts to movement		●	●	○	○	○	○	○	○	○	○		○	○	○	
Controls fire	●		●	●	●	●	●	●	●	●	●	●	●	●	●	●

Key: ● Major function ○ Minor function · Sometimes plays a role

22.2

perature? Can its surface be left exposed in a floor or wall? How will the material be affected by fire? What are its acoustical properties? How can the material best be put in place? How will it cope with normal wear and weathering? If laboratory test figures are unavailable, we can still judge these qualities rather well by hefting, pulling, poking, bending, scratching, wetting, and holding a match to the sample or by seeing how the material is used and has endured in existing buildings. Having learned what the material can and cannot do, we must then determine where it can be of use in a building and with what other materials it should be teamed to make building components that perform all the functions required of them.

The accompanying table (22.2) shows the major functions performed by various building components. An exterior wall probably serves more important functions than does any other part of a building. No single material can do all these jobs well. As a result, even the wall of an ordinary wood-frame residence is extraordinarily sophisticated in its combination of materials. Reading from exterior to interior, such a wall might include several coats of exterior paint, wood siding, an airspace that acts as a pressure equalization chamber, a spun-bonded polypropylene air barrier paper, plywood sheathing, wood two-by-six framing, mineral-fiber insulation, electrical wiring, heating ducts, a plastic sheet vapor retarder, gypsum wallboard, and several coats of interior paint. About fifteen separate construction operations, carried out by six different construction trades, are required to make this wall. But its efficiency in performing its appointed functions is unsurpassed.

Windows and doors are special cases of "wall"; they are designed to allow controlled penetration of the wall's environmental defenses. A door primarily controls the passage of people but often acts as a valve or filter for the selective passage of air, heat, animals, insects, and light. A window is one of the most fascinating of the building's components. A standard residential window of the most common type allows for the simultaneous and independent control of

- natural illumination;
- natural ventilation;
- view out;
- view in;
- passage of insects;
- passage of water; and
- passage of heat—radiant, conducted, convected.

Considering this multiplicity of functions, a window is a surprisingly simple mechanism. To architects, the possibilities of a window are limitless. To design a single window for a building involves consideration of

- orientation of window;
- location of window in the wall;
- size of window;
- proportions of window;
- external shading devices;
- mode of window operation (fixed, sliding, etc.);
- material and color of frame;
- type of glass;
- type of shade or shutter;
- type of curtain, material, color; and
- type of insect screen.

Windows are important not only as functional elements of the building enclosure but also as major elements of the visual patterns of both interior and exterior, as revealers of particular views, as illuminators of interior space, as gatherers of solar heat, and sometimes as the means of passage between interior and exterior. To achieve our design goals in these many respects, we must learn to manipulate the technical choices at our disposal. The results can approach the sublime: A sunny, plant-filled bay window. A cathedral rose window of richly colored stained glass. A large sheet of glass that hovers invisibly before a panoramic view of a wooded valley below. A snug window seat for reading on a rainy Saturday afternoon. A skylight that illuminates a bright tapestry. But the results can also be mundane, even depressing: A "picture window" that pictures only a street full of parked cars and simultaneously destroys interior privacy. A tenement window that faces on a bleak air shaft. A too-small window that leaves an interior space too dark.

The story is much the same for each of the other components of a building: Each must serve a multiplicity of functions. Each must be made of a combination of materials of complementary capabilities. Each offers to us its unique set of aesthetic possibilities to be exploited or, at our peril, to be ignored. These components are the building blocks of architecture, the only stuff with which we can work the unique magic that results in a satisfying building. The most solid basis for architectural creativity is an ordered and accessible knowledge of how buildings work. There is a natural order to architecture, and true design freedom springs from an everyday, easy familiarity with this order.

This book has outlined the natural order of physical function in buildings. Architecture has other important functions, too—each building serves an economic function, justifying its existence in dollars and cents, and a symbolic function, evoking emotions in those who experience it. But these are the provinces of other books. Here the message is simply that the scientific fundamentals of building are always the same. A house of snow in the Arctic obeys the same physical laws as does one of bamboo in the tropics, and a steel-framed skyscraper is not so far removed from a tree house as we would sometimes believe. If we understand from first principles how to moderate the forces of Nature for human occupancy, we are prepared to build well under any circumstances.

256

Glossary

Absorbtance: The proportion of incident heat radiation that enters a body and raises its temperature, expressed as a decimal fraction of one.

Absorption cycle: A heat pump process in which the hygroscopic property of a concentrated salt solution is used to evaporate liquid from a vessel and thereby to cool the liquid.

Abutment joint: A joint that allows for relative movement between dissimilar materials that meet at the joint.

AC: *See* Alternating current.

Acoustical privacy: A state in which intelligible sound is not transmitted between users of a building.

Acoustic tiles: Small units of ceiling finish material that absorb a major percentage of incident sound.

Activated charcoal filtration: The cleansing of air or water by passing it through a volume of charcoal that is specially produced to have a large ratio of surface area to volume.

Active: Adjective for any system that requires the application of energy from an external source for its function, as contrasted with a passive system, which uses only ambient flows of energy.

Adiabatic: Changing volume without the loss or gain of heat.

Aerobic: Taking place in the presence of oxygen.

Air barrier: A sheet material or coating that is designed to prevent the passage of air through the enclosure of a building.

Air chamber: A short, capped extension of a plumbing supply line that contains air that acts as a cushion to absorb the shocks that would otherwise cause water hammer.

Air, combustion: Air whose oxygen content is used to sustain a flame.

Air-inflated structure: A structure made up of one or more tubes of thin, airtight material which are stiffened against buckling by being inflated with air.

Air-supported structure: A structure made up of a thin, airtight material that is supported by a slight air pressure in the inhabited space that it shelters.

Allowable stress: *See* Stress, allowable.

Alternating current (AC): Electricity delivered in the form of current that reverses polarity at rapid, regular intervals, usually 50 or 60 times per second.

Ambient: Occurring naturally in the environment.

Anaerobic: Taking place without the presence of oxygen.

Anticlastic: Saddle-shaped, curved positively along one principle axis and negatively along the other.

Aqueduct: A large pipe or channel that transports water from a distant source to a city.

Arc fault circuit interrupter: A device that shuts off electricity to any circuit on which a spark or arc is being generated.

Arch: A structural device, usually concave on its underside, that translates applied loads, usually vertical, into inclined forces that flow along the axis of the device.

Area of refuge: An area within a building that is securely protected against heat, smoke, and flames in case of fire.

Artesian well: A vertical hole in the ground, dug or drilled, that fills with water because of subterranean pressure.

Artificial lighting: Lighting other than daylighting, usually electric lighting.

Atmospheric inversion: A stagnant layer of cold air near the ground.

Atrium: An interior courtyard in a building, often covered with a skylight.

Automatic sprinkler system: *See* Sprinkler system, automatic.

Autumnal equinox: The day in late September when the north-south axis of the earth lies perpendicular to the sun's rays. Day and night have the same length on the autumnal and vernal equinoxes.

Awning: A sloping, rooflike cover projecting outward over a window or door.

Awning window: An operating window whose sash is hinged along a horizontal axis on or near its top edge.

Backer rod: A ropelike cylinder of soft plastic foam that is pressed into a joint to limit the depth to which a mastic sealant material will penetrate.

Ballast, fluorescent: An electrical assembly in a fluorescent light fixture that serves both to provide the high voltage necessary to start the lamp and to limit the current to the lamp once it is started.

Base plate: A steel slab that serves to spread the heavy load from a steel column over an area of concrete large enough that the allowable stress of the concrete is not exceeded.

Beam: A solid structural member that resists transverse bending forces by means of a latticelike pattern of internal forces of tension and compression.

Bearing wall: A vertical, planar building element that supports superimposed gravity loads.

Bioremediation: Using life processes in plants to purify sewage and other toxic wastes.

Brittle: Having little tensile strength and a tendency to break without warning.

Builder, custom: A person or company that builds buildings to order.

Builder, speculative: A person or company that builds buildings before their buyers are known.

Bus bar: A rectangular strip of highly conductive metal, usually copper or aluminum, used to carry large quantities of electricity to points of distribution in a building.

Buttress: A structural device made of concrete, brickwork, or stonework in which the dead weight of the material combines with the angular thrusts of vaults or arches to produce a resultant force whose line of action falls safely within the foundations of a building.

Buttress, engaged: A buttress that is integral with the walls of the building.

Buttress, flying: A buttress that uses inclined arches to reach across an intervening space such as a church aisle to brace the central portion of the building.

Building separation joint: A planar discontinuity through a building to divide the building into smaller buildings that are able to move without distress.

Caisson: A vertical, columnar foundation element made of concrete cast into a hole drilled in the ground so that it rests on a firm layer of soil or rock at some distance below the surface. Also the cylindrical steel shell used to prevent the drilled hole from collapsing.

Camber: An upward curvature built into a beam so that the beam will be flat when it is fully loaded.

Cant strip: A beveled piece of material that prevents a sharp, 90-degree crease in a roofing membrane where it goes from a horizontal roof deck to a vertical parapet wall or perimeter curb.

Cantilever: The portion of a beam or truss that projects beyond its nearest point of support.

Capillary action: The drawing of water through a fine crack or small hole by the combined forces of cohesion in water and adhesion between water and the material through which it is drawn.

Capillary break: An intentional widening of a crack or hole so that a drop of water cannot bridge across it and pass through by capillary action.

Casement window: An opening window that is hinged on a vertical axis at or near a side jamb.

Catchment area: An area of ground or roof used to collect rainwater.

Catenary: The curve of a cable or chain that hangs freely under its own weight.

CAV: See Constant air volume system.

Cavity wall: A masonry wall that contains a vertical, planar airspace that is intended to eliminate water leakage through the wall and, incidentally, to reduce heat flow through the wall.

Cement, portland: A dry, gray powder that is mixed with water to form a binder for concrete. Not to be confused with concrete — there is no such thing as a cement sidewalk or a cement slab.

Centering: A structure used temporarily to support an arch, dome, or vault during its construction.

Cesspool: A pit in the ground used to disperse sewage into the ground without first digesting it; generally illegal.

Chair: A device used to support steel reinforcing bars until concrete has been poured around them and cured.

Chase: A hollow space provided in a building to house a run of pipes, wires, and/or ducts.

Chiller: A machine that produces cold water for cooling a building.

Chimney: A vertical tube to conduct smoke out of a building.

Chord: The top or bottom elements in a truss.

Circuit: A single run of electrical wiring that serves a limited number of fixtures and/or receptacles.

Circuit breaker: A device that shuts off electrical flow automatically if the capacity of an electrical circuit is exceeded, thus preventing damage to the circuit and building.

Cistern: A vessel for the storage of water.

Clerestory: A vertical window placed at the junction of two roof planes that meet at different levels.

Cloud gel: An extremely low-density, transparent solid that can be used as an insulating material between panes of glass in a multiple glazing assembly.

Column: A vertical, linear element of structure that supports primarily vertical loads.

Combustion air: See Air, combustion.

Compartmentation: The partitioning of a building into smaller units by means of fire-resistant walls and floors to restrict the spread of fire.

Compensated foundation: See Foundation, floating.

Composite: Made of two or more materials that work together.

Compost: The product of fermentation of organic waste materials, used to modify soil to increase its agricultural productivity.

Compression: A squeezing together.

Compression cycle: A heat pump process in which a working fluid is compressed and cooled, then allowed to expand and absorb heat.

Compressive stress: The intensity of a squeezing action, expressed in units of force per unit area.

Concrete: A rocklike material made by mixing together gravel or crushed stone, sand, and a binder of portland cement and water.

Concrete, air-entrained: Concrete that contains microscopic air bubbles. Air-entrained concrete flows more freely when freshly mixed and is much more resistant to freeze-thaw damage than ordinary concrete.

Condensate: A liquid created by condensing a gas, such as the liquid water produced when moist air contacts a cold surface.

Condensation: The changing of a material from a gaseous state to a liquid state.

Condenser: A component of a steam-driven power plant in which spent steam is cooled to return it to a liquid state.

Conduction: The passage of heat or electricity through a solid material.

Conduit: A plastic or metal tube through which electric wires pass.

Constant air volume system (CAV): A heating and/or cooling system in which the rate of air circulation is constant, but the temperature of the air varies.

Continuity: In a structure, the property of having structural elements joined rigidly together so that they act as a single unit.

Control joint: An intentional, usually straight-line crack in a surface of material that tends to shrink, used to avoid random cracking in the material.

Convection: Circulation that is powered by the difference in density between warm and cool air or water.

Convective: Using convection as a mode of heat transfer.

Convector: A device for heating air by means of steam or hot water that circulates through metal tubing that is exposed to the air. A convector usually has many metallic fins attached to the tubing to increase its surface area. The fin-tube assembly is usually housed in a sheet-metal enclosure with openings for the circulation of air.

Cooling, radiational: The cooling of the earth at night by direct radiation of terrestrial heat into the blackness of space.

Corbel: A masonry structural device in which each brick or stone projects slightly over the one below it.

Crawl space: A continuous access area, not tall enough to stand in, beneath the ground floor of a building.

Creep: The long-term shortening of concrete under compressive stress.

Cross connection: A faulty plumbing installation that allows sewage or contaminated water to be drawn into water supply pipes if water pressure in the pipes should fail.

Crown: A slight upward curvature in the paving of a road; a curvature in a piece of lumber.

Curtain board: A noncombustible sheet material that hangs from the ceiling of an industrial building to help restrict the spread of fire through the building.

Damper: A metal flap that acts as a valve for air flow in a duct, a fuel-burning appliance, or a fireplace.

Damp-proof coating: A thin asphaltic coating applied to the outside of a building foundation wall in order to limit the penetration of moisture through the wall.

Daylighting: Lighting the interior of a building with direct or indirect light from the sun.

DC: *See* Direct current.

Dead load: The weight of building components and other loads that do not change over time.

Decibel: A measure of the intensity of sound.

Deciduous tree: A tree that drops all its leaves in winter.

Deflection: The amount by which a given point on a structural member moves when the member is placed under load.

Dehumidifier: A machine that removes moisture from the air, usually by condensing it on metal coils that are cooled by a compression cycle.

Dewatering: Lowering the level of water in the soil of a building site in order to keep the excavation dry during foundation work.

Dew point: The temperature at which water will begin to condense from a given mass of air.

Diffraction: The bending of light or sound waves by their being passed over sharp edges, especially a series of edges whose spacing is similar to the wavelength of the light or sound.

Direct current: A flow of electricity that is constant in polarity and intensity.

Direct gain system: Heating a building by admitting sunlight into the inhabited space.

Dome: A structural form consisting of an arch rotated about its vertical axis. A dome is often a hemisphere or some other portion of a sphere.

Double-envelope building: A building with two independent, complete enclosures, one inside the other, with an air space between.

Double-hung window: A window with two sashes, both of which slide on vertical tracks.

Double-skin facade: A building wall with two layers separated by an air space.

Downspout: A vertical pipe that conducts water runoff from a roof to the ground.

Drainage composite: A thick, highly porous material placed against the outside of a foundation wall so that ground water approaching the wall falls down through the material to drainage pipes at the base of the wall instead of reaching the outside surface of the wall.

Drip: Any building feature that causes water to fall clear of the building at that point rather than run along the surface.

Dual duct system: An air conditioning system in which parallel ducts carry warm air and cool air. In each room of the building, thermostatically controlled dampers regulate the relative amounts of air from each of the two ducts that are mixed to achieve the desired temperature.

Duct: A round or rectangular tube through which air is circulated.

Eave: The lowest edge of a sloping roof.

Echo: A reflection of sound that occurs long enough after the original sound to sound like a separate sound.

Effluent: The supernatant of decomposed sewage.

Elastic modulus: The ratio of stress to deformation in a given material; a measure of the stiffness of a material.

Emittance: A measure of the ability of a material to radiate heat to another body.

Equinox: A position in the earth's orbit where the north and south poles are equidistant from the sun. There are two equinoxes each year, occurring on or about March 21 and September 21. Day and night are of equal length at all latitudes on these days.

Evaporative cooler: A device in which air is cooled by passing it through a wetted pad.

Evaporative cooling: Cooling air by causing it to absorb moisture. The latent heat of vaporization of the water is furnished by the air, which reduces the temperature of the air.

Exit, horizontal: A passage through a self-closing, fire-resistant door to an area of refuge on the same level of a building.

Expansion joint: A linear device that allows a material to expand without damaging itself.

Facade: The principle face of a building.

Factor of safety: The ratio of the stress for which a structure is designed to the ultimate stress of the material of the structure.

Fan room: A space in a building in which fans and other air-conditioning equipment are located.

Fire cut: A beveled cut on the end of a heavy timber beam or girder that allows the member to fall harmlessly out of the wall if the member should burn through during a fire, rather than topple the wall.

Flashing: A continuous strip of metal, plastic, or composite that acts as a barrier to the passage of water.

Flat arch: A masonry arch whose top and bottom edges are straight and level.

Flat-plate collector: A device for gathering heat from the sun by allowing sunlight to impinge directly upon a flat surface from which the heat is removed by circulating air or liquid.

Floating foundation: See Foundation, floating.

Fluid-filled structure: A surface that is supported by internal pressure of air or water.

Fluorescent: A device in which an electrical discharge activates a phosphor to generate light.

Flue: A tube for evacuating combustion gases.

Flux: A flow of energy.

Flying buttress: See Buttress, flying.

Formwork: A temporary structure of wood, metal, and/or plastic that gives shape and support to a structure of masonry or concrete until that structure becomes self-supporting.

Foundation, floating: A foundation in which the weight of the soil excavated for the building's basement(s) is equal to the weight of the building.

Foundation, mat: A single spread footing that is as large in horizontal extent as the building that it supports.

Funicular: Having the shape that would be taken by a flexible rope or chain that supports a given set of weights, or having the inversion of that shape.

Fusible link: A connector made of a special alloy with a very low melting point, used for the automatic control of fire safety devices.

Gable: A roof consisting of two sloping surfaces that intersect at a level ridge; the triangular end wall of such a roof.

Gasket: An elastic strip used to seal a joint between two adjacent components.

Glare: Excessive contrast in brightness between a visual task and its surroundings.

Glass, heat-absorbing: Glass that is tinted so that it absorbs heat from light that passes through it.

Glass, heat-reflecting: Glass that is coated with a reflecting layer that bounces back a portion of incident light and heat.

Glass, laminated: Two surface layers of glass bonded to a viscous plastic core.

Glazed: Having a glassy surface.

Glazing: The installation of glass in a building. A transparent material, usually glass, in a window. The application of a glassy finish layer to a ceramic material.

Glazing compound: A mastic in which glass is bedded in a window sash.

Glazing, double or triple: Two or three sheets of glass with air spaces between.

Grade beam: A concrete beam that spans across isolated foundation elements to provide continuous support for a wall.

Greenhouse effect: The trapping of solar heat behind a barrier such as glass in a building or a layer of selectively transparent gases in the earth's atmosphere.

Ground fault interrupter: A device that shuts off the flow of electricity in a circuit if current leaks from the circuit to the ground.

Gutter: A sloping channel that gathers water from the low edge of a roof surface and conducts it to a downspout.

Guy: A sloping cable that stabilizes a vertical structural element.

Gypsum: A naturally occurring mineral, calcium sulfate hemihydrate, used to make plaster, wallboard, fireproofing, and other building materials.

Hard water: See Water, hard.

Heat exchanger: A device for transferring heat from one medium to another, such as water to air or air to air.

Heat pump: A device that utilizes either a compression cycle or an absorption cycle to move heat from a cooler medium to a warmer one.

Heat sink: A mass or substance with a very large thermal capacity compared to the amounts of heat flowing through a system.

HID, High-intensity discharge lamp: A type of high-efficiency device for artificial lighting.

Hopper window: A sash that is hinged along the bottom edge and tilts inward to open.

Horizontal exit: See Exit, horizontal.

Hot wire: A current-carrying electric wire that is not connected to the ground.

Humidity, relative: The ratio of the amount of water vapor contained by a given mass of air to the maximum amount of water vapor it could contain at the given temperature.

Hydronic: A system that uses hot water to distribute heat within a building.

Hyperbolic paraboloid shell: A thin, saddle-shaped concrete slab used as a self-supporting structure.

Hypothermia: A condition in which the human body is unable to maintain its normal core temperature.

Ice dam: A barrier of frozen water across the eave of a roof behind which liquid water accumulates.

Incandescent: Emitting light as a result of being at a very high temperature.

Infiltration: The movement of air in or out through cracks and defects in the enclosure of the building.

Infrared: Electromagnetic wavelengths longer than those of red light.

Intumescent coating: A layer of paint or mastic that expands to form a stable, insulating char when exposed to the heat of a fire.

Inverse square law: Radiational intensity from a point source is inversely proportional to the square of distance from the source.

Inversion: *See* Atmospheric inversion.

Inverted roof: A low-slope roof construction in which polystyrene foam insulation is placed above the waterproof membrane.

Invertibility: When any structure is turned upside down with its external loads remaining in their original positions and directions, the force in each member of the structure changes from tension to compression or vice versa.

Isolated footing: A concrete foundation element that supports a single column by spreading its load over a large area of soil.

Joist: A slender beam used repetitively at narrow spacings to support a ceiling surface or the decking of a floor or roof.

Knee brace: A temporary diagonal member used to support a wall or column during construction; a permanent diagonal member that joins a column above its midpoint.

Labyrinth joint: An open joint between wall panels that is configured so that there is no straight-line path through the joint.

Lamp: A light bulb or light-emitting tube.

Landing: A broad platform on a stair.

Latent heat: The heat required to change the phase of a material without changing its temperature.

Lateral force: A force that is considered to act in a horizontal direction, usually caused by wind, earthquake, soil pressure, or water pressure.

Lateral support: Structural elements that resist lateral forces in a building frame.

Lath: Any mesh, strip, or sheet material used as a base to which to apply plaster or stucco.

LEED System: Acronym for "Leadership in Energy and Environmental Design," a proprietary initiative to evaluate the sustainability of designs for buildings.

Leaching field: A level bed of crushed stone just below the surface of the ground into which effluent from a septic tank is distributed through perforated pipes or open chambers in order that the effluent will be absorbed by the soil below.

Light shelf: A light-colored horizontal surface, usually located above head level, that serves to reflect daylight into the part of a room that is more distant from the windows.

Lime: Calcium hydroxide, produced by burning limestone or sea shells and adding water. Used in construction as an ingredient of mortar and plaster.

Lintel: A beam that supports a wall above a window or door opening.

Live load: The weight exerted on a structure by people, goods, furniture, machinery, vehicles, snow, and other things that change over time.

Louvers: Closely spaced, parallel strips of material used to obstruct the passage of light or rain while allowing the passage of air.

Low-emissivity (Low-e) coating: A thin layer deposited on glass to make the glass selectively reflective of long-wave infrared radiation.

Lumen: A unit used to measure the rate at which light is produced by a lamp.

Luminance: The brightness of a visual task.

Masking noise: Noise intentionally introduced into an environment in order to make certain noises less obtrusive, or to make conversations more private.

Masonry: Brickwork, stonework, or concrete blockwork.

Mastic: A substance that is semiliquid, viscous, and sticky.

Mat foundation: *See* Foundation, mat.

Mean radiant temperature (MRT): The weighted average of the temperatures of all the objects that exchange thermal radiation with a given point.

Membrane roof: A low-slope roof that is made waterproof by a single sheet of impervious material.

Monitor: A boxlike protrusion above a roof that contains windows and/or ventilating louvers.

Mortar: The substance used between masonry units as a cushion, spacer, shim, adhesive, and sealant.

MRT: *See* Mean radiant temperature.

Neutral wire: A wire that is connected to ground.

Night blindness: An inability to see in darkness immediately after leaving a much brighter environment, due to the time that it takes the eye to adjust from one level of illumination to another.

Night-sky radiation: Long-wave infrared radiation from terrestrial objects into space.

Night soil: Human excrement.

Noise: Unwanted sound.

Nosing: The projecting front edge of a stair tread.

One-way: Structural action in a slab or plate that takes place only in one principal direction.

Panel, truss: A portion of a truss bounded by a top chord, a bottom chord, and two adjacent vertical members.

Panic hardware: A door latch release mechanism that works automatically if pressed against.

Parapet wall: A wall that projects above surrounding roof areas.

Passive: Working by ambient energy flows rather than by the introduction of energy from outside sources that are under human control.

Pattern staining: Discoloration of a wall or ceiling caused by the variable adhesion of dust to surfaces at different temperatures.

Pediment: The ornamented gable end of a roof in classical architecture.

Performance bond: An insurance policy that guarantees money to finish a construction project if the original contractor should fail to do so.

Photovoltaic panel: A group of photocells mounted on a roof and wired together to produce electricity from sunlight.

Pile: A foundation element consisting of a long, slender piece of wood, steel, or reinforced concrete driven vertically into the ground.

Pile, end-bearing: A pile that is driven until its lower end rests on firm soil or rock.

Pile, friction: A pile that develops its load-bearing capacity by means of friction between the sides of the pile and the soil.

Pile driver: A heavy, mechanical hammer used to drive piles into the ground.

Portland cement: *See* Cement, portland.

Post-tensioning: The application of compressive stress to a concrete structural member by means of internal strands of high-strength steel that are stretched to a high tension after the concrete has hardened.

Precast concrete: Concrete that is cast and hardened away from the building site, then put in place in the building as rigid elements.

Precipitation, chemical: Causing constituents of a solution or suspension to fall to the bottom of a container by combining them chemically with compounds that convert them to dense solids.

Principal stress, lines of: Lines drawn to trace the directions of maximum tensile and compressive stresses in a structural member.

Pressure equalization chamber (PEC): An airspace in an external building component that is pressurized by the wind in such a way as to prevent strong air currents from passing through the wall.

Primary treatment of sewage: Anaerobic fermentation of sewage.

Pyrolysis: The heating of materials to reduce them to their constituent inorganic components.

Quoins: Square blocks of masonry built into the exterior corners of a building, originally as a means of stabilizing a wall made of weak materials, but now as ornament.

Radiation: The passage of electromagnetic waves through space or air.

Radiational cooling: The cooling of terrestrial objects by radiating heat from the objects to the night sky.

Radiator: A heating device in which heat from steam or hot water is transferred to the air in a room. The transfer is achieved mainly by convection, not radiation, but the name persists.

Rafter: A slender, sloping beam used repetitively at narrow spacings to support a roof plane.

Rainscreen: The outer layer of a wall that has a pressure equalization chamber and air barrier.

Raised access floor: A floor made up of rigid, square, removable tiles supported a short distance above a structural floor on pedestals, so that pipes, wires, and ducts may run freely beneath to any point in a building.

Recycling: Sending used materials back to factories for reprocessing and reuse rather than discarding them.

Reflectance: The proportion of incident radiation that is turned away by a surface, expressed as a decimal fraction of one.

Regenerative wheel: A rotating mass of metal mesh through which air is blown to transfer heat from the air in one duct to the air in another.

Reglet: A slot into which a flashing or the edge of a roof membrane may be tucked.

Regulator, gas: A device for reducing and controlling the pressure of gas at the point of use.

Reinforced concrete: Concrete into which steel bars have been cast to resist tensile stresses.

Reinforcement, sound: Strengthening sound in a performance hall by means of reflections from surfaces in the hall.

Relative humidity: *See* Humidity, relative.

Relay: An electrical switch that is activated by another electric current.

Reservoir: A large container or pond for the storage of water.

Resonator: A hollow chamber that vibrates sympathetically and thereby absorbs sound energy at a given frequency.

Reverberation time: The time it takes for a loud sound to diminish to inaudibility in a performance hall.

Ribbed slab: A concrete spanning element consisting of a thin slab supported by closely spaced, parallel joists.

Ridge: The intersection of two roof slopes in a gable roof.

Rigid frame: A structure in which rigid joints provide lateral stability.

Rise of an arch: The vertical distance from the lowest part of the center line of an arch to the highest.

Rise of a stair: The total vertical dimension between the bottom and top of a stair.

Riser: A vertical planar element between two treads in a stair.

Roof, low-slope: A roof that has too shallow a slope for shingles and must be made waterproof by a continuous membrane.

Roof monitor: *See* Monitor.

Roof, steep: A roof that can be made waterproof with shingles.

Roof, thatched: A roof that is covered with bundles of reeds, grasses, or leaves.

Run of stair: The total horizontal dimension of a stair, measured from the lowest riser to the highest.

Sash: The portion of a window frame, often movable, that holds the glass.

Scaffolding: Temporary platforms for the convenience of construction workers.

Scupper: An opening through a parapet or curb for draining water from a roof.

Sealant: An elastic substance used to close a seam or opening in the enclosure of a building. Most sealants are injectable mastics, but some are tapes, gaskets, or expanding foams.

Self-opening roof vent: A roof hatch that opens automatically during a building fire so as to allow smoke and heat to escape.

Sensible heat: Heat that raises or lowers the temperature of a substance without changing its phase.

Septic tank: A watertight underground vessel designed to foster the anaerobic decomposition of sewage and to separate the decomposed sewage into a precipitate (sludge) and a supernatant (effluent).

Service panel: A metal box that contains the circuit breakers for a number of electrical circuits and from which the wiring for these circuits radiates.

Sewage: Wastewater from a building.

Sewerage: A network of underground pipes that collect sewage and conduct it to a treatment plant.

Shaft: A vertical opening through multiple floors of a building to house elevators, pipes, ducts, or wires.

Shear: A relative motion, force, or stress of two masses of material that are pushed or pulled in opposite directions along a common plane.

Shear panel: A planar element of structure that resists lateral loads by means of forces within its plane.

Shelter: Any natural or constructed object that offers protection from wind, precipitation, sun, and/or extremes of temperature.

Shelter belt: A swath of trees planted to obstruct the wind.

Shingle: A small, flat piece of material overlapped with similar pieces on a wall or steep roof in such a way that water will drain off by gravity before it can penetrate.

Shoring: A temporary compression member erected to support a wall of an excavation or a newly poured concrete structure against collapse.

Short circuit: An accidental or inadvertent interconnection of a hot wire with a neutral wire.

SI units: *Système internationale d'unités,* a rationalized system of measurement based on the meter. In order to avoid confusion in linear measurements, the centimeter is not used in SI.

Siamese connection: A Y-shaped pipe connection at the base of a building that allows one or two pumper trucks to connect to a building's standpipe or sprinkler system.

Sick building syndrome: A condition of being uninhabitable because of poor interior air quality due to molds, mildew, spores, organic chemicals, sewer gases, combustion products, or other causes.

Sill: The horizontal lower edge of a window or door. The portion of a building frame that rests on the top of the foundation.

Simply supported beam: A beam that is supported by hinges and/or rollers at its ends.

Single-phase electricity: Alternating current that varies in voltage as a single sine wave.

Skylight: A window in a roof.

Slab: A horizontal, planar element of concrete, usually reinforced or post-tensioned, used most commonly as a floor, roof, walkway, or roadway.

Slab-on-grade: A concrete slab that rests directly on the ground.

Slow-burning construction: A heavy timber frame that meets certain code requirements for minimum sizes of members.

Sludge: The precipitate of decomposed sewage.

Smokeproof enclosure: An exit stairway that is protected from smoke by being accessible only by means of a balcony ventilated to the outdoors or by mechanically forced introduction of fresh air.

Snow fencing: A slatted fencing used to induce drifting of snow at a distance from a roadway so as to keep it from drifting onto the roadway.

Solar flux: The flow of radiant energy from the sun.

Solar heating: Using sunlight as a heat source for a building comfort system.

Solstice, summer or winter: A date when one pole of the earth is closest to the sun.

Space frame: A three-dimensional truss that spans with two-way action.

Spalling: The flaking off of chips of material from a surface.

Spandrel: The zone of a wall between the heads of windows on one floor and the sills of windows on the floor above. Also, the area of wall between a masonry arch and an imaginary rectangle that would contain the arch.

Specific heat: The ratio of the unit heat storage capacity of a material to that of water.

Specifications: Written documents that specify standards of quality and workmanship for a construction project.

Splay: A divergence in the interior surfaces of the jambs of a window.

Spline: A strip of material used to keep two adjacent building components in alignment.

Spread footing: A block of concrete that distributes the force from a column or loadbearing wall over an area of soil in a foundation.

Spring: A naturally occurring flow of water from the earth.

Sprinkler system, automatic: A system of water pipes and sprinkler heads in which a fusible link opens a head to extinguish an incipient fire if the temperature at the head rises substantially above normal levels.

Standing waves: Single-frequency sound that is reinforced by repeated reflections back and forth between parallel walls whose distance from one another is a multiple of the wavelength of the sound.

Standpipe, fire: A vertical pipe that serves fire hose outlets at each level of a building.

Step ramp: A stair with very broad, sloping treads.

Stiffener: A ridge of material added to a structural element to increase its resistance to buckling.

Stirrups: Loops of reinforcing steel used to resist diagonal tension near the ends of concrete beams.

Stock plan: A generic design for a building that is sold in the form of construction drawings, ready to build.

Stove, heating: A self-contained heating device, located within the occupied space of a building, that burns fuel within a metal enclosure that transfers heat to the surrounding air.

Strain: Change of dimension in a structural material caused by structural stress.

Stress: Force divided by the cross-sectional area of material over which it is distributed.

Stress, allowable: A stress at which a structural material may safely function. Allowable stress is the product of yield stress and factor of safety.

Stress, yield: The stress at which a material begins to deform irreversibly.

String course: A projecting horizontal molding on the face of a building.

Strip footing: A linear spread footing that supports a wall.

Structureborne sound: Sound transmitted through the solid material of a building rather than through the air.

Structure-enclosure joint: A joint that allows differential movement between the frame of a building and the enclosure of the building.

Strut: A linear compression element in a structure.

Subcontractor: A specialty contractor who works under an agreement with the general contractor on a building project; for example, a plumbing contractor.

Sump: A pit in a basement floor used to accumulate any water that may leak into the basement.

Superinsulated, sun-tempered: An approach to energy efficiency in a building that emphasizes high levels of thermal insulation and airtight construction, coupled with a limited amount of south-facing glass for direct solar gain.

Surface film: A thin layer of air held by friction on the surface of a building.

Sustainable building: Building in such a way as to satisfy the needs of the current generation without compromising the ability of future generations to satisfy their needs.

Synclastic: The property of a surface of having the same sense of curvature, either concave or convex, along both its principal axes.

Système internationale d'unités: See SI units.

Tensile: Having to do with stretching of material.

Tensile stress: The intensity of tension in a material, measured in units of force per unit of cross-sectional area.

Tension: A stretching or pulling apart.

Terminal reheat system: An air conditioning system in which chilled air is circulated through ducts to points of use, where it is heated with a thermostatically controlled hot water coil to adjust its temperature.

Termite shield: A sheet metal flange that projects from the junction between a foundation wall and the sill of a building, over which termites must build their tubes if they are to infest a building. The flange makes it easy to detect the presence of termite tubes.

Terrazzo: A decorative concrete flooring produced by grinding and polishing a slab made of colored marble chips and selected colors of fine aggregate and cement.

Terrestrial: Having to do with the earth.

Terrestrial radiation: Thermal radiation from the earth or among objects on earth.

Thatch: *See* Roof, thatched.

Thermal break: A layer of low-conductivity material placed between parts of a metal frame to reduce its conduction of heat.

Thermal bridge: A highly conductive path that transmits comparatively large amounts of heat through an otherwise well-insulated building assembly, such as a metal framing member in an insulated wall.

Thermal capacity: The ability of a material to store heat.

Thermal "feel": Whether a material seems warm or cold when contacted by the human body.

Thermal resistance: The ability of a material to retard the flow of heat.

Thermostat: A device that turns another device off and on depending on whether the ambient temperature is above or below a preset temperature.

Tholos: A corbeled dome.

Three-phase electricity: Electric current that is made up of three overlapping sine waves of alternating current so as to furnish more constant energy for large electric motors.

Tie: A tensile structural member. A tensile connecting device.

Total energy system: A system in which an on-site generator driven by an internal combustion engine creates electricity for a building or complex of buildings, and the cooling water from the engine is used to heat water or air.

Transformer: A device for reducing or increasing the voltage of electric current by means of two coils of a differing number of turns of wire wrapped around a single magnetic core.

Trap, plumbing: A U-shaped piece of waste pipe that holds a small quantity of waste water that acts as a seal to prevent sewer gases from entering the building.

Trap siphoning: The evacuation of the water seal from an unvented plumbing trap.

Tread: A horizontal plane in a stair.

Trombe wall: An east-west wall of concrete, masonry, or containers of water, placed near a south-facing wall of glass to absorb and later re-radiate solar heat.

Truss: A structural spanning device in which loads are translated into axial forces in a triangulated system of slender members.

Two-way structural action: Resisting bending in two mutually perpendicular directions, as occurs in a concrete two-way flat plate or two-way flat slab.

Ultraviolet light (UV): Electromagnetic radiation of shorter wavelengths than violet light.

Underpinning: Strengthening the foundations of an existing building by temporarily supporting the building on jacks while adding or enlarging foundation components.

Unit air conditioner: A small, self-contained electric-powered device that utilizes a compression cycle to cool and dehumidify room air, usually mounted in a window opening or in an opening in an exterior wall.

Unit ventilator: A device in an exterior wall that recirculates room air, exhausting a fraction of it to the outdoors and taking in a similar fraction of outdoor air, while passing the air over coils that heat or cool it as needed.

Universal design: An approach to building design that gives equal access and convenience to all people regardless of physical handicaps, avoiding separate, special provisions for the handicapped.

Vacuum breaker: A device in a water supply line that introduces air into the line if water pressure is lost, so as to prevent contaminated water from being drawn into the line.

Vapor barrier: *See* Vapor retarder.

Vapor pressure: The partial pressure exerted by water vapor in the air.

Vapor retarder: A sheet material or coating that is highly resistant to the passage of water vapor, used to prevent water from condensing inside a wall or ceiling. Often called, incorrectly, a vapor barrier.

Variable air volume system (VAV): A heating and cooling system for a building that regulates temperature by varying the amount of conditioned air that is delivered to each space or zone.

Vasomotor regulation: The human body's expansion or contraction of blood vessels as a means to regulate body temperature.

Vault: A structural device consisting of an arch translated along an axis perpendicular to its plane, or a combination of such forms.

VAV: *See* Variable air volume system.

Vent, plumbing: A pipe that opens a system of waste piping to the air so that it remains always at atmospheric pressure and avoids trap siphoning.

Ventilation, infiltration: Renewing the air in a building by means of air passing through cracks and holes in the building enclosure.

Ventilation, mechanical: Renewing the air in a building with electrically powered fans that introduce a percentage of outdoor air as they recirculate indoor air.

Ventilation, natural: Renewing the air in a building using only the forces of wind and/or convection.

Vernal equinox: The day in late March when the north-south axis of the earth lies perpendicular to the sun's rays. Day and night have the same length on the vernal and autumnal equinoxes.

Visual task: The focus of one's attention in a luminous environment.

Voussoir: A wedge-shaped component of an arch.

Waffle slab: A two-way concrete joist system, which resembles a waffle when viewed from beneath.

Wainscot: An interior wall facing that starts from the floor or baseboard but does not extend to the ceiling.

Warm-air heating system: A system that uses air as a medium to transport heat to the interior of a building.

Wash: A slope on a top surface that causes it to shed water.

Water hammer: A loud knocking sound in water supply pipes caused by the instantaneous deceleration to zero of water in the pipes.

Water, hard: Water that is rich in calcium ions.

Water softener: A device that replaces calcium ions in water with sodium ions.

Weatherstripping: Linear gaskets, pads, metal strips, brushes, or other devices designed to reduce air leakage through cracks around doors and windows.

Weep hole: An opening in the exterior of a wall or window frame that drains to the exterior any water that may accumulate within.

Well: A hole drilled or dug into the ground for the purpose of obtaining water.

Whispering gallery: A concave surface or surfaces that focus sound in such a way that faint sounds can be heard over comparatively long distances.

Wind tunnel: A laboratory device that houses a scale model and simulates the flow of wind around buildings or other objects with a small-scale flow of air around the model.

Wired glass: Glass sheet material formed around a wire mesh that serves to hold the glass together if it should break during a fire.

Working drawings: The technical drawings from which a building is built.

Wythe: A vertical layer of a masonry wall that is one brick, one block, or one stone thick.

Yield point: The stress at which a material begins to distort permanently.

Index